Balmy Ne
The best of Boa

By Jessica Boak & Ray Bailey

Copyright © 2019 by Boak & Bailey

All rights reserved. This book or any portion thereof may not be reproduced or used in any manner whatsoever without the express written permission of the publisher except for the use of quotations of 100 words or less in reviews and articles.

boakandbailey.com

Foreword... 4
Introduction... 6
The eternal beer geek... 8
Brew Britannia: the women... 11
A pint of Old & Filthy... 18
Only a northern brewer... 21
Nineteen-seventy-four: birth of the beer guide... 24
The pub crawlers... 31
Nineteen-seventy-five: birth of the beer festival... 35
The Campaign for Unreal Ale... 43
Craft before it was 'a thing'... 47
The beer hunter was human... 54
Belgophilia... 61
Panic on the streets of Woking... 65
Swanky beer: a lost Cornish style? ... 77
The quiet one... 81
Newquay Steam: Cornwall's own beer... 88
Mellow Brown vs. the Amarillo Kid... 96
Ordinary, Best, Extra Special... 101
Watney's bleedin' Red Barrel... 105
Where the Boddies is buried... 113
The secret of Doom Bar's success... 118
Guinness jumps the shark... 126
Pale and hoppy... 132
The mystery of Old Chimneys... 136
Mixmaster, mix faster... 140
The pubs of Boggleton... 144
The German Invasion... 153
Welcome to Adnamsland... 156
The Good, the Bad and the Murky... 161
Don't worry, be (mostly) happy... 191
Pub Life... 208
Acknowledgements... 219

Foreword

By Tim Webb

The problem with reading about beer and pubs is that so many of the people who write about them are paid to say nice things that are not strictly true, while a large proportion of the rest say straightforward things, usually without payment, that are not strictly true either.

To find writers whose knowledge and attention to detail is matched by both integrity and a natural sense of knowing what matters is rare indeed. This is what makes Boak & Bailey's stuff worth reading, despite the absence of words like 'awesome', 'iconic', 'essential' and so on. They are people who realise understanding history matters, while claiming to understand the present is not mandatory.

I first met Jess and Ray in their granite outcrop years, soon after their first big writing award had underpinned a growing reputation as purveyors of relevant truths and clever observations about beer and pubs. It was already clear that even among established authors who normally turned their noses up at those who 'only' blog, these guys were special.

In my case it was a bit of business that took me to Penzance, not a life choice. To someone from my scientific background, managing to impact on any mainstream opinion from a town that is so far from London that the night sleeper cannot reach it till eight in the morning deserves its own accolade. I like to think that surviving the near rainy mist of several Cornish winters somehow helped to sharpen their abilities to mine for details in the strangest places, and hone views that are less touristic.

Beer drinking has always suffered from the perception that because it is part of a communal leisure pursuit, it is trivial. That is how we used to think about sport until the Olympic movement taught us otherwise, or cooking and dancing until TV schedulers recognised that the familiar fascinates more readily than the exceptional.

In reality, beer and pubs have, in their different ways, limitless lessons to teach us about how agriculture and industry, government and institutions, should interact with the concerns of ordinary consumers, and how we balance our human desire to socialise with that of others to control how we behave. Each should be the subject of thought, opinion and exposition beyond those who seek simply to sell or restrict.

Beer and pubs are each worth at times lionising, at other times taking down peg or two. The informed and concerned consumer needs reliable talkers and writers to provide solid information and interpretations that balance out the fake news and fake views bought by marketers. Each is worth over-thinking in case in doing so we unearth something of greater importance.

This is what Boak & Bailey do rather well, as you may discover.

Tim Webb is the author of the World Atlas of Beer *among many other books.*

Introduction

> 'I must here mention that during the terribly hot weather beer was my great stand-by. In fact, I scarcely think I could have existed without this balmy nectar — it put such vigour and strength into my sadly exhausted frame.'
>
> General Sir James Hope recalling the 1857 siege of Delhi

Beer should bring you joy. All kinds of beer can do this — bog standard lager, straightforward bitter, flowery IPAs, imperial stout, anything.

And all kinds of beer can do just the opposite.

It all depends on you, your taste, and the moment.

It's the difference between a great pint of cask ale and one that, though you'd struggle to pin down the difference in concrete terms, is an utter chore.

A joyful beer hits the spot. Either it doesn't touch the sides, or it makes you linger for an hour, savouring every sip. Even if only for half a second before you get back to the conversation, it demands your attention.

It ought to be between you and the beer, this moment of joy, but you might say to your drinking companions that it's bob on, cock on, bang on, or perhaps if you're feeling especially expressive not too bad at all actually. Or you might just sigh, "Aah."

A beer that is a joy will make you want the same again. The problem is, it's elusive, that first-drink-of-the-session jolt. Returns diminish.

The most reliable route to joyful beer is to stick to beers, breweries and pubs you trust. But there's a joy in exploring, too, and the joy you feel on finding a good beer after three duds is among the most potent strains.

Joy needn't mean fireworks. There's joy in a nice mug of tea or clean bedsheets and beer ought to be the same kind of everyday, attainable pleasure.

We don't know if beer writing ever brings the joy that beer itself does. Well, perhaps not to the reader, but writing these blog posts and articles has certainly made us happy over the past decade and a bit.

We're better writers now than we were at the beginning, or at least more confident, purely through persistence. Writing about 200 posts each year, a few articles, and the odd book, has helped us find our shared voice, and become quicker at drawing it in anger.

Sometimes, we feel ignorant – we once mistook a field of wheat for a field of barley; we don't always use technical brewing terms correctly – and then there are other times when it dawns on us just how much we've learned. Hurling ourselves in at the deep end, letting others savage us over our mistakes, and submitting to education by those more inclined to mentor, we've found ourselves oddly knowledgeable in all sorts of esoterica.

Would we have enjoyed beer as much, or perhaps more, without writing about it? As there's no way to know, there's no point in speculating. All we can say is that, contrary to the impression our public earnestness might suggest, we've had what can only be described as a right laugh along the way.

Please take this book to the pub and dip into it between and alongside pints and bites of pickled egg.

That, after all, is how we wrote most of it.

Ray & Jess

The eternal beer geek

First published at allaboutbeer.com in 2016.

People these days take beer too seriously, right? Caring about what you drink, talking about it, and especially recording *tasting notes* seem to be regarded by some as a sign of the end times. But being a beer geek is not something that emerged alongside the books of Michael Jackson and the craft beer movement: people have been obsessing over beer for much longer.

One very early example can be found in the letters of James Howell (1594-1666). In a 1634 epistle to Lord Cliff he gave a long, detailed account of drinks popular around the world, including beer and this passage amounts to an early example of a Jacksonian beer style guide:

> In the Seventeen Provinces hard by, and all by low Germany, Beer is the common natural Drink, and nothing else, so it is in Westfalia, and all the lower Circuit of Saxony, in Denmark, Swethland and Norway; The Prusse has a Beer as yellow as Gold made of wheat, and it inebriates as soon as Sack. In some parts of Germany they use to spice their Beer, which will keep many years; so that at some Weddings there will be a But of Beer drunk out, as old as the Bride.

In the 19th century lager beer emerged from Munich, Vienna and Pilsen. As it made its way around the world it appealed to a certain type of drinker – the craft beer enthusiasts of their day, such as the anonymous, presumably British author of an 1871 article published in a London magazine: 'With my true Vaterland taste, I am glad the various conduits of beer are set flowing in the metropolis.' Presaging the rhetoric of craft beer, Victorian fans of lager spoke of drinking for flavour rather than intoxication, of the delicacy of its flavour, and the importance of dainty glassware. They also argued that mainstream beer was full of additives while lager was pure, just as modern drinkers decry adjuncts and praise all-malt brews. On that basis, they defended the high price of lager: quality beer, enjoyed in moderation, was worth paying for.

Leaping forward to the 1930s, there are a few more tantalising hints that, even if they didn't have Untappd and RateBeer accounts for broadcasting their interest to the world, there were people whose interest in beer was positively cerebral. *A Book About Beer*, published in 1934 under the pseudonym 'A Drinker', is evidence enough – it is perhaps the earliest example of what we would now recognise as (just about) book-length beer writing aimed at consumers rather than industry insiders. It also contains, however, a specific significant line: 'In the view of the violent purist... bottled beer is a barbarism; one of the barbarisms of civilization, like bottled mayonnaise sauce.' The author tends to the flippant but, still, that suggests that not only were there enough people interested in beer to warrant the writing of a book but that some of them were the kind of swivel-eyed beervangelicals we've all encountered from time to time.

The same decade gave us the Mass Observation sociology project whose study of Bolton in the north of England involved teams of mostly young students descending on the town and writing down *everything* they saw. They focused on pubs in particular resulting in the 1942 book *The Pub and the People* – a remarkable volume which is as close to experiencing time travel as any of us are likely to get. Among details of how many people used spittoons and the male-female mix in different pubs at different times there is a description of a particular subset of beer drinkers: 'Most pub-goers simply drink the cheapest available beer, while a minority exist for whom quality is most important.' One pub landlord whose words were recorded by the Observers told a story about a particularly well-matured cask of bitter which, when tapped after six months, particularly impressed one drinker:

> The stranger said that it was wonderful – 'like wine'. This man took to calling in regularly for it, until the barrel was finished. It went soon because he told his friends, and they came in for it too.

The survey team also interviewed another drinker who sounds a lot like a modern day completist 'ticker':

> There is, I think, many different brands of beer which so far I have not had the Pleasure of Tasting. Those I have, such as: Magee's, Walker's, Hamer's, Cunningham's, and

one or two others, all have a nice Flavour... The Price question I will not Dispute, because I do not Drink Excessively, so I don't favour any particular Beer.

There it is again: that suggestion that price is less important to those who are drinking for some reason other than the quickest or cheapest route to intoxication.
Maurice Gorham wrote a book about London pubs, *The Local*, published in 1939. It contains a brief hint of a modest, dowdily British period version of the novelty-seeking urge:

> ...you have heard that an out-of-town brewery has a London pub where the bitter is unusually brilliant, and you decide to go and find it. You make many discoveries and draw many blanks... Between Halkin Street and Wilton Street there are no fewer than five pubs, all small, local, pleasant, giving you a choice of four different brews.

When he rewrote and expanded that book in 1949, publishing it under the title *Back to the Local*, he gave a lengthy description of how a connoisseur went about choosing his beer. The variety of draught beers, he argued, was complex and variable and they 'take a bit of knowing, and repay study'.

The first half of the 20th century also saw a flurry of societies dedicated to beer in one way or another. The National Society for the Promotion of Pure Beer was founded in the county of Sussex in 1923; The Ancient Order of Froth Blowers was founded in London in 1924; the Pub Users' Protection Society, also in London, in 1946; and in Derbyshire in 1959 the Black Pig Society was founded by a group of twenty-somethings outraged at the spread of bland pasteurised beers. The Society for the Preservation of Beers from the Wood, with similar aims but more ambitious, held its first meeting in a pub on the outskirts of London in December 1963.

Our book, *Brew Britannia*, took 1963 as the starting point for the 'alternative' strand in beer which, we argue, led to what we now know as craft beer, but perhaps we could have begun the tale earlier. Who knows how much more evidence lurks in out-of-print magazines, or in diaries and letters as yet unearthed?

Brew Britannia: the women

First published on our blog in 2013.

As we worked on *Brew Britannia*, our book about British beer between 1963 and the present, we felt uneasy at the overwhelming maleness of the story – men in pubs, men in societies, men writing angry books, men brewing beer, and so on. Though women have been less visible they have certainly played their part in shaping today's lively alternative beer culture, often in the face of considerable difficulty. So, we went back over the ground a second time, looking for women in the story. This is what we found.

Women weren't made to feel all that welcome in the early days of the struggle against the Big Six brewers. The essentially backward-looking and conservative Society for the Preservation of Beers from the Wood (SPBW), founded in 1963, received its first application for membership from a woman in 1965 – an eventuality which had not been taken into account when the constitution was drawn up. After much debate, founder member John Gore proposed a compromise: women should be permitted to join, but only as associate members.

When the Campaign for Real Ale came along in 1971, it borrowed much of its style and rhetoric from socially liberal protest groups, and its senior ranks were filled with young, open-minded people who had grown up during the sexual revolution of the 1960s. Though a streak of 'robust' (i.e. sexist) humour was, according to Roger Protz in a 2004 article, a core part of CAMRA's identity in those early days, the Campaign not only *allowed*, but positively *encouraged* women to join. In April 1973, Valerie Mason was elected to its ten-strong National Executive... as secretary, of course. Margaret Clark-Monks joined the NE in 1977 and served for seven years, though Chairman Tony Millns' comment when she stood down is telling: 'She was much more than the statutory woman...'

In an email, Christine Cryne, now a director at CAMRA, recalled the experience of being a female member in the Campaign's first decade:

> My grandmother used to drink beer including the bottled Worthington White Shield... [so] I had no preconceptions

that women didn't drink beer… I joined CAMRA in 1977 to attend AGM in Blackpool that year but I had been involved with the local branch (Reading) for about a year before then, helping out at the local beer festival… It was a much smaller organisation in those days and there was a good cross section of people of all ages and a real commitment to making a difference… My second branch was Bedford and, like Reading, there were a few women involved so that helped but I studied a science course and I was the only female on it so I suppose I was used to being in an environment that was male dominated (and having two brothers, both of whom I signed up to CAMRA).

Well into the 1980s, though, women within the Campaign continued to be treated as 'totty', pressed into service modelling sweatshirts in awkwardly-posed photographs on the cover of *What's Brewing*, CAMRA's monthly newspaper.

When a full page of the 1985 Good Beer Guide was given over to a bawdy Bill Tidy cartoon which showed a stripper pushing over a pile of pennies with her breasts, it was the final straw for member Michelle McBride, who wrote a letter of complaint:

> I cannot be bothered to get angry… but must register my quiet disappointment that blatant sexism is still found amusing… It is difficult to believe that the possibility of increased female CAMRA membership is treated with such supercilious contempt.

This kind of issue fed into a greater anxiety about the Campaign's fortunes: it was increasingly seen as being dominated by middle-aged, middle-class, boorish, boring men, and membership remained low compared to the late 1970s. Things needed to change if it was to attract new, younger members.

Though Christine Cryne does not consider it to have been a political decision, the appointment of Andrea Gillies as editor of the Good Beer Guide in 1988 nonetheless sent a strong signal. A 27-year-old English graduate who described herself as 'a yuppie with principles', Gillies oversaw a complete overhaul of the GBG. Her arrival was announced in the 'How to use this guide' sample entry which opened the 1989 edition, describing an imaginary pub called 'The Woman's Touch':

> Lovely new theme pub of character, with delightful pastel floral décor in the English tea shop style. All original features lovingly ripped out. Charming plastic palms in the conservatory. Champagne snug and 'Pollyanna's Pantry' upstairs… Try also: The Blue Stocking, Gladys' Leap.

There was a woman pictured on the cover (sort of — the illustration is dreadful); there were new female contributors (Roz Morris, Virginia Matthews, Katherine Adams); and a fresh emphasis on food and dining, still regarded by many today as the key to making beer more appealing to women. Just to be entirely sure the message was being hammered home, Adams's contribution was a polemic entitled 'Women and the Pub: the bitter truth':

> Speaking personally, the biggest drawback with pubs is, to be blunt, that they were designed by and large for men… [Women] simply don't feel comfortable going into a pub alone… [Women] who actually like pubs are familiar with… the assumption of the assembled males that a woman who comes alone into a pub must be either a scarlet woman or a pint-swilling harridan.

This lurch into self-conscious female friendliness did not please everyone: 'I suspect I have a lot of enemies among the old guard members,' Gillies said in an interview in 1988. The point having been made, it was toned down for the 1990 edition of the Guide, which nonetheless retained an emphasis on food and on a more sophisticated approach to tasting beer, as opposed to swigging it.

When Gillies handed over the editor's seat to Jeff Evans for the 1991 edition, she left the GBG fundamentally changed — it would never go back to the days of sexist cartoons, and female writers such as Susan Nowak became a fixture, even if they did often end up writing about food and the daintier side of beer appreciation.

The following year, another high profile job within the Campaign went to a woman, namely Christine Cryne: 'When I became the first female organiser of the Great British Beer Festival, it created a great deal of media attention and, I hope, encouraged more women to become involved in the event.' In 1995, the theme for the festival was 'Women and beer', and the programme contained the following observation: 'No woman at any CAMRA beer festival will get a quip or an odd look if she asks for a pint. We just now have to wait for everyone else to catch up.'

In most manufacturing industries in the post-war period, women, if they were present at all, worked in offices or on production lines. In breweries, they worked as secretaries or in bottling plants, but not as brewers.

Of course, there were odd hangovers from an earlier age when many women brewed, such as the All Nations Inn 'homebrew house' at Telford, Shropshire, described by Frank Baillie in his 1973 *Beer Drinker's Companion*:

> Mrs [Eliza] Lewis does all the brewing and has done so for the last thirty-eight years… Once a week, when most good citizens are in the depths of their slumber, Mrs Lewis rises in the small hours and commences operations at 3 am…. The vats hold about 260 gallons and Mrs Lewis used to move the liquor from once vat to the next by means of a hand ladle.

More typical, however, was the reaction of the Daily Express in 1977 to the discovery that 23-year-old Fiona McNish was working as a beer taster at Paine's of St Neots: 'Fiona, long brown hair, topographical as the Alps, a very feminine lady, has worked her way deep into male territory…'

The new generation of less conservative, often very small breweries which began to appear from the mid-1970s onward offered far more opportunity for women to get involved, sometimes out of pure necessity.

When David and Louise Bruce opened the first of their chain of Firkin pubs in London from 1979, though David was the face of the business, and had experience in the industry, both consider it to have been an equal partnership. (Well, almost: 'Chauvinist bastard that I was back then, when we set up the company, I gave Louise 49% and I kept 51%, because I had to be in control,' David Bruce told us.) It was Louise who wrote the original business plan from David's rough notes, and, later, when she wasn't ferrying buckets of yeast around London from one pub to another in her car, she also did her share of early morning brewing.

Meanwhile, in Northern Ireland, Anne Scullion was the driving force behind Hilden Brewery, which she founded in 1981 with her husband, Seamus. She spent two months with Peter Austin at Ringwood learning to brew, before commencing work at Hilden with the assistance of Heriot-Watt graduate Brendan Dobbin. As well as hands-on brewing, she also drove the delivery van. A 1982 newspaper profile calls her a 'mother-of-three' and an 'engaging blonde' but otherwise treats her with respect. Women in brewing were beginning to be taken seriously.

It is a sign of progress, perhaps, that we have no idea whether Kim Taylor was 'engaging', blonde, pretty or a mother. She was appointed head brewer at the Orange Brewery, a Clifton Inns brewpub in West London, in 1983, at the age of 23. Ann Hills, writing for the *Guardian*, included Taylor as one of many examples of women finding paid employment in areas previously the preserve of men. Taylor eventually went on to be supervising head brewer for the entire Clifton Inns group of brewpubs, though what became of her thereafter is something of a mystery.

At Traquair House in Scotland, Catherine Maxwell Stuart had been helping her father in the tiny country house brewery since the early 1970s, when she was around ten years old:

> It was a great treat because I was allowed to stay up late and help with the cooling process which involved ladling the beer for up to three hours to help it cool to the correct temperature…Then we had to wait for a Customs office to come out and verify the original gravity so we would sometimes be up until midnight. The other job I did was cleaning the vessels – not so much fun but there was a huge amount of scrubbing to be done before and after every brew.

When Peter Maxwell Stuart died in 1990, Catherine not only became the 'lady laird' but also took charge of the brewery, which role she still performs today.

In the last 30 years, though brewing remains male-dominated, things have changed. There are now many breweries owned or run by women, such as Wilson Potter of Manchester, Mallinson's of

Huddersfield, and Waen of Powys. A number of them have formed a kind of promotional union, under the name Project Venus, and have brewed several beers together to date.

With the increased interest in producing lager and other European styles among newer (trendy) small breweries, there also seems to be an influx of female technical expertise from continental Europe, such as Italian brewer Giada Maria Simioni at Huddersfield's Magic Rock, and Swede Sarah Hjalmarsson at Cornwall's Harbour.

In the wake of Andrea Gillies, beer writing, too, has ceased to be the sole preserve of bearded, professorial men peering over the rims of their glasses. Melissa Cole's book *Let Me Tell You About Beer* was published in 2011 and is the first such general educational guide after the style of Michael Jackson or Roger Protz, as far as we can tell, by a female writer. 'Before [publisher] Anova came along, I was offered two book deals to write a woman's only guide for beer,' Cole told us. She rejected them. *Let Me Tell You* isn't a 'girls' guide', and is admirably gender-neutral in tone and design — no pink, no high heels and handbags, and no *Sex and the City* nonsense.

Another first in the last decade was the appointment, in 2003, of 44-year-old Paula Waters to the top job as chair of the Campaign for Real Ale — a position she would hold for six years. Though, inevitably, the press wanted her to talk about women and beer, and she was obliged to give soundbites on that subject, she always confesses to finding it 'exceedingly tedious' and something of a non-issue: 'I firmly believe that there are no real differences between men and women.' She is proud of her time as CAMRA chair, but not because of anything relating to her gender.

Why do we need a Project Venus? Why, when Harbour appointed a female brewer, did the local newspaper focus on her gender in the first line of the story? Why do some female beer writers feel compelled to call themselves sluts, beauties and babes? And why do women working in pubs and bars still report the kind of incident described by Rosie Pointon in a Tweet: 'Award for most patronising customer this week goes to the main who said "Obviously you don't drink real ale but what do you recommend?"'

The simple answer is that the presence of women in the world of beer is not quite regarded as completely normal, not yet. Melissa Cole:

I think there's a long way to go. Women have been disenfranchised from beer for thirty to forty years and it's going to take time, it's going to take effort, it's going to take commitment and it's probably not going to fully turn around in my lifetime.

She might be right, though perhaps Mrs Lewis at the All Nations would have been surprised to hear it.

A pint of Old & Filthy

First published on our blog in 2016.

Saucy beer names – Dirty Tackle, Piddle Slasher, Old Slapper – are a bit of fun to some, but off-putting to others. Either way, they are another battleground for debates over 'political correctness', censorship, good taste and sexism. One common argument in their defence is that they are traditional – but are they?

    First, to have saucy beer names, you need to have beer names — that is, other than in the format Bloggs Bitter, Bloggs XXX, and so on. The 1966 *Brewery Manual*, a rather dry industry directory, contains a reference list of trademarked brand names. It's not comprehensive, beer historian Ron Pattinson tells us, but it's still a good starting point: of the 650 or so provided, none are outright filthy and only about ten provide anything for a bar-room wag to get a snigger out of with enough mugging and winking, e.g. Big Horn, Cock o' the North, 'I'll take a Mild Maid please!' (And it had apparently not even occurred to anyone that there was fun to be had with 'Blonde' — no beers are listed with that name.)

    There's no real change by the time of Frank Baillie's *The Beer Drinker's Companion* in 1973, which catalogues every brewery in the country with notes on the beers in regular production. Only Shepherd Neame Bishop's Finger offers Mr Nudge-Nudge much to work with. And, in any case, the naughtiness there was in the eye of the beholder until a 2006 advertising campaign which featured a flirtatious *Carry On* style 'wench' with bedroom eyes.

    That brings us up to the beginning of the microbrewery boom of the 1970s when it was business as usual until David Bruce came on the scene with his Firkin brewpubs. The beers had silly names – Dogbolter, Earthstopper and so on – but the real giggle was in ordering 'A pint of Firkin bitter, hur hur!' Bruce, a compulsive punster and joker, claims not to have spotted the potential for this gag until customers at the Goose & Firkin latched on to it. We don't really believe him.

    There was also some influence from the world of comedy and journalism where real ale and its drinkers were often mocked with over-the-top fictional beer names such as Scruttock's Old Dirigible, for which Alexei Sayle seems to get the credit, or Old & Filthy – the title of a 1969 LP of music hall songs by comic actor Ronnie Barker.

By 1988, when Brian Glover's CAMRA-published *New Beer Guide* came out, there were quite a few breweries trying such stunts. There was Raisdale's Looby's Lust, Marston Moor Brewer's Droop, Rockside's Hewer's Droop, Wye Valley Brew 69 (it was our 69th brew! the owners insisted), Min Pin Inn's Brown Willy (it's named after a hill!), and beers called Ebony Bitch and Son-of-a-Bitch from the Bull Mastiff Brewery of Penarth, Wales. The logic for those? Well…

> Keen home-brewer Bob Jenkins blames his dogs for the odd names. He keeps Bull Mastiffs.

This defence – it's quite innocent, you've just got dirty minds! – was to become a common theme. In March and April 1994 there was an exchange of letters in CAMRA's *What's Brewing* which prompted one brewer to express his motives in plain terms. First, there was a complaint from Welsh CAMRA member Jeremy Vernon, titled 'Who Wants a Tosspot?'

> While agreeing with the criticism of renaming pubs by vulgarians… I can't help but notice a similar trend in the naming of beers… Old Tosspot springs immediately to mind as one of the most recent absurd names for a brew… There are many others (Crippledick, Roger Over and Out etc.), some admittedly quite funny, but the joke is beginning to wear a bit thin… I am not having a go at the likes of the excellent originally-named Old Speckled Hen or wonderful Wobbly Bob, but who needs Old Tosspot? Or is that only too clear?

We were mildly surprised to discover that the brewery responsible for Old Tosspot was Oakham, today best known for their more tastefully named JHB and Citra. A retort from John Wood, the brewery's original owner, was headlined 'There's Nothing Wrong With Calling an Ale Old Tosspot' and opens with the It's Quite Innocent gambit:

> While I sympathise to some degree with Mr Vernon's view that some beers have extreme names which could cause

offence (for example, Old Fart and Dog's Bollocks), I cannot agree that my brew has an 'an absurd name'... I do not know what connotation Mr Vernon is applying to the word 'tosspot' but I would like to point out that it is simply an old and well-used term for a drunkard — one who tosses the pot or tankard.

The more interesting part of the letter concerns the business incentives for naming beers this way:

I would ask Mr Vernon to spend just a few minutes considering the market from my side of the mash tun. He simply drinks the stuff – to me it's my livelihood. The cask beer market in this country is now immensely competitive and all the odds are stacked against the small independent brewer... [Maybe] the biggest obstacle... is the success of the independents in terms of the vast numbers of beers now on the market. It is no longer sufficient to name a beer simply Bitter, or Best Bitter, or Extra Special Bitter — the name has to grab the attention of the punter... A name that stands out and is memorable is surely fair game. I am sorry if this offends Mr Vernon's sensibilities.

We can conclude from all this that saucy beer names are a phenomenon that arose in the 1980s as a result of an ever-more crowded market and, at the same time, an increase in the tendency for DIY-inclined brewers to undertake their own branding and marketing. These days, the market is even more crowded, and deliberately provocative beer names are now just one way of grabbing attention. Compared to collaborations, unusual dispense methods, marked cloudiness, and stunt ingredients, it seems a rather passé approach.

Only a northern brewer

First published in this form on our blog in 2017.

When we wrote *Brew Britannia*, we researched and wrote about many small breweries that came and went in the hot foment of the 1970s and 80s. This is the story of a first-wave British microbrewery that didn't make the cut and about which little is remembered more than 40 years on: Pollard's of Stockport, in Greater Manchester.

A handful of small new breweries opened in the early 1970s, and the Campaign for Real Ale had come into existence, but it was only after 1975 that a kind of chain reaction seems to have been triggered. CAMRA membership kept climbing, hitting 30,000 by March that year, and specialist pubs sprouting across the country to cater for 'the real ale craze'. New brewers began to appear in ever greater numbers, too, and among the original set was Pollard's of Reddish Vale in Stockport, run by a towering man with a drooping moustache and thick sideburns – David Pollard.

Pollard left school and went straight into the brewing trade in 1950, working alongside his father, George, as an apprentice at Robinson's in Stockport. He went on thereafter to take jobs at various breweries across England, finding himself repeatedly shunted on as, one by one, they fell to the takeover mania of the Big Six. He became increasingly angry and frustrated, as expressed in a 1975 article in the *Observer:*

> The accountants and engineers had started running things. All the big firms wanted were pasteurised, carbonated beers with no taste or character.

In around 1968 he started his own business – a small shop selling home brewing equipment and ingredients, on Hillgate in Stockport. Until 1963 home brewing had needed a license but when Chancellor of the Exchequer Reginald Maudlin removed that requirement, a small boom commenced. Newspapers and magazines were filled with recipes and how-to guides, and Boots the Chemist began to sell brewing kits to a new band of enthusiasts. Amidst all that excitement, Pollard's shop was a success, and soon moved to larger premises on nearby Buxton Road.

Therapeutic as home brewing might have been for him, however, what he really wanted to be doing was making beer for sale in pubs and clubs. Buoyed by the rise of CAMRA, and perhaps aware of the recent small brewery openings in Litchborough and Selby, he bought £5,000 worth of new brewing equipment, and invested a further £5,000 in premises and ingredients. The site he chose, largely because it was cheap and the water was good, was a small unit in the recently-opened Reddish Vale Industrial Estate in the countryside south of Manchester, where the low, red-brick buildings of a substantial 19th Century printing plant had been converted into workshops.

As well as new equipment, Pollard also pushed the boat out when it came to selecting a strain of yeast. Whereas other small brewers were supplied with buckets of from the back doors of bigger regional breweries, or used dried home-brewer's yeast, Pollard approached the Brewing Industry Research Foundation at Nutfield in Surrey and arranged to be supplied with a pure sample of one of the strains preserved in their culture bank. Yeast is such an enormous contributor of flavour and aroma in brewing that this decision must surely have gone a long way to ensuring his beer stood out in the local market. Had he arranged with Robinson's to use their yeast, as might well have been tempting given his family connections, his beer would almost inevitably have been very like theirs. His mission was clearly to do something different – to give consumers some real variety.

Another sign that he was part of a new brewing culture was in the formulation of his recipes. Like Martin Sykes at Selby, Pollard made much of the quality of his ingredients, brewing with malt only rather than adding sugar to boost the strength, as was common in larger breweries. Sugar has been used in British brewing for centuries not only to increase alcoholic strength while saving on raw material costs, but also to thin the body of the beer (to make it more 'drinkable'); to add colour, in the case of dark sugars; and to add a range of often subtle flavours. Nonetheless, this was to become an important distinction between big, old-fashioned brewers and those that were smaller and more youthful in their outlook. Pollard, like many who followed, wasn't heeding the call of the SPBW to make beer as it used to be, but rather making beer as he wanted it to be, and as he thought the market desired. That is, wholesome, and pure.

He began brewing test batches of John Barleycorn (JB) best bitter in the summer of 1975, with launch scheduled for August. With a team of four working every day of the week, Pollard expected to produce the equivalent of around four casks a day, to be delivered in a dray which was actually a repurposed milk float. The venture was in immediate success.

He arrived, uninvited, at CAMRA's first national beer festival at Covent Garden in London in September 1975 with a cask of ale in the back of his Mini. After some negotiation, the team running the festival agreed to take it even though it hadn't been ordered. As it happened, the bar selling it was mobbed, and every drop sold out 'literally within hours', according to a contemporary report in CAMRA's newsletter, *What's Brewing*. Drinkers were desperate for something, anything, new.

The following month, a pub in Hyde, Greater Manchester, owned by CAMRA's new pub company, CAMRA Real Ale Investments, began selling Pollard's JB and reported that it was shifting almost as well as similar beers from better-established local breweries, Boddington's and Hyde's. It seemed people liked the opportunity to drink something different and, perhaps, to support an underdog.

By 1977, Pollard had expanded the brewery once, and had plans to do so again, up to a 100 barrel plant, to meet huge levels of local demand for his beer. The 'micro-brewery', as this type of set up would soon come to be known, was here to stay, even if Pollard's itself would cease trading in April 1982, foreshadowing the great shake out to come.

Nineteen-seventy-four: birth of the beer guide

First published in CAMRA's BEER *magazine in 2017.*

In 1974 the first edition of the CAMRA *Good Beer Guide* was published. We spoke to those who were involved in its genesis to find out how it came to be. Here is the story in their own words, gleaned from interviews and correspondence.

John Hanscomb (early CAMRA member, and first editor of the *Good Beer Guide*)
We all knew we liked proper beer but the problem was, we didn't know where to drink – we didn't know where the pubs were. There was Frank Baillie's *Beer Drinker's Companion* but that was all about the breweries, not the pubs, although it did give you an idea of their trading areas. And the brewers… The brewers wouldn't give me any information! I rang up one and asked them which were their pubs and which sold proper beer and they wouldn't tell me because they thought I was from Watney's or Whitbread: 'We don't know who you are.'

Michael Hardman (co-founder and first chair of CAMRA)
John Young [of Young's brewery] was championing cask ale in a very serious way, and had been holding out for a decade before CAMRA came along. He thought of himself as the only one left. Young's had never been a particularly profitable company. They had some pretty dingy pubs, and a very 'bitter' bitter that was going out of fashion. In 1963, he'd been approached by Derek Peebles, a former naval officer, who said: 'What you need is a PR campaign, and I'm the man to do it!' What he did was put together the first ever comprehensive list of Young's pubs under the title 'Real Draught Beer and Where to Find It'.

John Hanscomb
The Young's guide was undoubtedly an influence, very much so. With Young's you could guarantee that all their pubs would have proper beer. John Young deserves a lot of credit.

Terry Pattinson (journalist, early CAMRA executive)

[The Society for the Preservation of Beers from the Wood] were too cosy with the big brewers, they didn't want to rock the boat. They thought we were a bunch of hot-blooded young troublemakers. When we were putting together the *Good Beer Guide*, they were appalled at the idea. I remember one pin-striped lawyer saying 'Listen, old boy, if we have a list [of real ale pubs] we'll be sued by the brewers.' But we wanted the bastards to take us to court!

John Hanscomb
The first CAMRA Good Beer Guide, the 1972 edition, was a loose leaf publication with 300 pubs and 18 pages. We sold it in pubs for 25p.

Michael Hardman
It was typewritten and photocopied, and the pages were assembled in folders by half a dozen of us. The job was done on a wallpaper table in my flat in North Finchley.

Barrie Pepper (CAMRA campaigner and beer writer)
I paid about £11 for my copy at auction. It's a slim, blue, spiral-bound folder and it is titled *Where to find Real Draught Beer*. This original guide is a real mish-mash with only six pubs in the whole of Yorkshire and all of those in the Huddersfield area, which was the home of the first CAMRA branch. There were 16 entries in Henley-on-Thames all serving Brakspear's ales and other small towns well represented were Salisbury with eight and Amersham, Devizes and Great Missenden with six each. Even Little Missenden had a couple. London and Manchester had the largest number of entries but there were none at all for Bristol, Birmingham, Leeds, Liverpool and Sheffield.

John Hanscomb
We didn't have many branches then so I spent hours and hours of my life visiting areas trying to find pubs. I've sometimes said that I was doing so much of the work myself that I was a one man branch. In those days there was no breathalyser and there was little traffic compared to today so I'd get in my car and go out to fill in gaps myself. The only source of information I had was talking to people in pubs – where else is there that has good beer? It was a dodgy old situation back then. I went out one evening to Henley-on-Thames with my notebook and a few suggestions and visited no less than ten or twelve

different pubs. Then we missed a year in 1973 while we worked on the commercial version.

Michael Hardman

I read something about Beric Watson, managing director of Waddington of Kirkstall Ltd, a printing subsidiary of Waddington's of Leeds, which produced Monopoly and Cluedo, among many other board games. Beric was described as a beer lover and I arranged to meet him in The Guinea, a wonderful old pub in Mayfair. He immediately offered to publish the guide, which removed any financial risk for CAMRA. The Campaign appointed John Hanscomb to be the editor because of his amazing knowledge of real ale, pubs and breweries. I was the production editor, responsible for overseeing the guide's printing, and a Manchester-based commercial artist, Trevor Hatchett, was chosen to design it. In addition, Tom Linfoot, another passionate ale drinker from Kent, was assistant editor, helping Hanscomb to compile lists of suitable pubs. Coverage of some areas of the country was patchy and just before the deadline, we discovered that one county, Huntingdonshire, had no pubs recommended at all. With typical enthusiasm, Hanscomb and his wife Rose set off in their car on a Sunday morning to put matters right. They returned with seven pubs, six of them serving Charles Wells beers and one offering Greene King ales. A glance at the map in the guide shows that all the pubs were along a fairly straight line, corresponding to the A1 trunk road, which Hanscomb explained was the only way that he and Rose could complete their task in the two hours pubs were allowed to open on Sunday lunchtime back then.

Christopher Hutt (CAMRA chair 1972-73)

I was the outgoing chairman of CAMRA at the York AGM in spring '74. That's when the row with the publisher blew up: Waddington's were spooked by their lawyer telling them that the original Watney comment was actionable.

John Hanscomb

I penned that famous line about Watney's: 'Avoid like the plague'.

Gerald Milward-Oliver (PR executive at Watney Mann & Truman Brewers)

1974 started with the three-day week, lasting through January and February, when the Government mandated that businesses could only operate for three days a week, in order to save power. I well remember whole areas of London going completely unlit for hours at a time at night, including street lights. Obviously, the pub trade suffered. At one point, I think the share price for Grand Metropolitan [Watney's parent company from 1972] dropped to 19p, and I recall being told that Watney Mann & Truman Brewers was running at a severe loss. Quite a number of staff lost their jobs and there was a real feeling of not knowing if you would be next. The old Watney Mann marketing and PR people were vociferously opposed to CAMRA and everything it stood for, so it would not surprise me if the publishers were right to have concerns over the possibility of Watney Mann suing.

Christopher Hutt
Beric Watson, a bit of a stooge, was despatched by his brother Victor, who called the shots, to tell us that we needed to agree to change the comment or the GBG could not be published. Waddington wasn't an experienced book publisher and did not handle the situation very professionally. I always felt that they should have spotted the problem earlier or taken a stance to publish and be damned. But they didn't do either and instead made the hospital pass to CAMRA's National Executive. The situation was pretty gut-wrenching for us. On the one hand we felt that our freedom of opinion and expression were being curtailed and, in those early days, they were really the only campaigning weapons we had. On the other hand, failure to publish would have had serious campaigning and financial repercussions which might even have been catastrophic. There was as much heat as there was light in the NE's debate on what to do for the best. It was not a pleasant meeting to chair. When I left York, I remember feeling that it had been the most tiring weekend of my life. I don't think that feeling has been surpassed in the 42 years since. I was so relieved to give up the chair to Gordon Massey.

Trevor Unwin (CAMRA volunteer)
The plague edition *Guide* was delivered to the De Grey Rooms in York which was the venue of the 1974 AGM. I had agreed to help unload the van so that the contents could be made available on the morning of the first session. Waddington's had apparently agreed to reprint at their expense and would we mind awfully if we just loaded them all back

onto the van again so that they could be sent back to Leeds for pulping? In our annoyance and frustration it is just possible that some of the packets were 'accidentally' damaged and the contents liberated. I still have my extremely dog-eared copy and my wife the censored version, and I think that any other copies of the original version must have must have seen the light of day in the same way.

What's Brewing, April 1974
'But the following week, Watson presented new plans to CAMRA for rescuing the guide. These involved changing only one phrase in the whole book: advising drinkers to avoid Watney pubs "at all costs" instead of "like the plague".'

Christopher Hutt
Michael [Hardman] was our head of publishing. Ultimately, after much soul searching, he decided it was best to compromise and agreed the revised wording with Waddington's. I thought he was right and backed him, and the decision to run with the revised wording was ultimately agreed by the NE.

John Hanscomb
I didn't like the change at all. I was so upset at what Watney's were doing, out in places like Norfolk especially.

Michael Hardman
The disagreement, although tedious, resulted in a huge wave of publicity for the guide and when it was eventually released, it quickly began to sell out.

John Hanscomb
I had quite a few journalists from national newspapers ring me at home to ask, 'Why should we avoid them like the plague?'

Michael Hardman
The irony was that the disputed words were printed in newspapers and repeated on radio and television and not one of them was issued with a writ for defamation. The upshot was that Watney's *were* avoided like the plague.

Ron Pattinson (CAMRA member, beer historian)
Flicking through the 1974 guide I realise it was really crap for me locally [in Newark] and Nottinghamshire in general. No pubs listed at all in my bit of Notts. But I looked at it a lot, just to learn about the different breweries around the country. There weren't many sources at the time. It was great to have concise and reasonably complete information in one place. It opened my eyes to what was around – so many different beers around the country.

John Lamb (CAMRA member)
In 1974 I was working on a construction site – the M42 motorway in the Midlands. I recall being given a copy of the *Guide* by a colleague when I was 17-years-old. It was the first guide to pubs that I had seen. Coverage was far from comprehensive – there was only one pub in Birmingham – but I can recall that a pub near to my parents' house was listed, the Railway in Dorridge, which prompted me to visit.

Paul Bailey (CAMRA member)
I bought mine after seeing a friend's copy. I was a student at Salford University at the time and I couldn't wait to start using it. A friend and I went on a mission to track down and sample as many beers as possible. I was like a kid in a sweet shop! The often pithy, one-line comments were enough to convey all you needed to know about a pub.

Steve Barber (CAMRA member)
At the time I thought that it was wonderfully useful in spite of the relatively poor coverage by modern standards. There was nothing else worth having. By the time of its replacement in 1975 I had marked off quite a few pubs that had fallen victim to the ongoing fizzification of cask beers at the time.

John Robinson (CAMRA branch organiser, South Lancashire)
Locally the Guide was a bit of a disaster. I don't know who did the survey but the only pub in the centre of St. Helens referred to in the guide sold bitter from cellar tanks via electric pumps. Needless to say in was removed from the Guide almost immediately.

Richard Keal (CAMRA member)
I was a Medical Student in London and going out with a nurse. One weekend we were visiting her parents in Guildford with her brother

and his girlfriend. He was a [keg] Worthington E drinker and I was trying to convert him to real ale. I had the *Good Beer Guide* and chose a Gale's pub just outside the town, which we hadn't visited before. We set off at about 8 o'clock and as we drove through Guildford we heard a dull thump. We thought we had driven over a loose manhole cover and drove on to the pub. On leaving, we tried to drive back but the town was in lock-down and all roads were closed. We got home about an hour later to find our parents in an almost hysterical state knowing only that we had gone out for a drink in a pub in the town. I later worked out that we had driven past The Horse & Groom about five seconds before it was hit by the IRA bomb. If I hadn't had the *Guide* with its comment about Gale's – 'Good choice of excellent beers' – we may have well been in the town that night. I married the nurse and I have bought the *Good Beer Guide* every year since then.

James Lynch (CAMRA activist, chair in 1978)
It is easy for some latter day CAMRA members to knock what the very early years produced in terms of publications, beer festivals, and so on, but we were pioneers. There were no crib sheets, no owner's handbooks, no workshop manuals. When those first guides appeared they should have been hailed unreservedly as successes, not knocked. They paved the way for many more wonderful publications, and gave careers to beer writers.

John Hanscomb
I wasn't involved in editing the next edition. It was a difficult time in my life – I was working in the print trade and doing funny shifts – so I wasn't sad to hand it on to Michael Hardman. I knew him well and he was a good man and I knew he'd look after it. I still get it every year – I have a regular order and get one of the first copies off the presses though my door.

The pub crawlers

First published in CAMRA's BEER *magazine in 2018.*

There is a breed of British beer drinker for which CAMRA's annual *Good Beer Guide* is more than a reference book – it is a way of life.

Duncan Mackay bought his first edition when he was in his early twenties. 'I started ticking the pubs off in the '81 guide and have done so every year since,' he told us in an email. Pick up any old edition of the *Good Beer Guide* and the chances are you will find literal ticks scribbled in biro in the margins but it's usually only a few – every pub in a single town or village, perhaps. For Duncan, though, the aim is to have visited every single pub listed in the entire book at least once, even if only for a half-pint of ale. That doesn't mean he drinks in 5,000 pubs every year, only those of the 400 or so new pubs added to each edition he has not previously visited. In 2015 he actually achieved his goal but was foiled the year after: 'I still require three pubs in the 2017 Guide, two of which are in London and were closed on my visit, when they were supposed to be open, and one on the Isle of Man. (Sigh.)'

Martin Taylor started ticking *Good Beer Guide* pubs more than a decade later than Duncan, as he told us over a pint in a Bristol pub (chosen by him, of course, from a list of required 'ticks' on a flying visit to the city):

> My first Good Beer Guide was the 1996 edition but I started taking it seriously with the 1998 edition, the 25th, published in September 1997. If you drank in all 25 pubs that had been in every guide – the Silver Selection Pub Trail – you won two bottles of beer brewed at the Bass Museum.

He and his wife Christine did it, of course, and 20 years on still have the bottles and certificate to prove it. That gave him the bug.

Simon Everitt describes himself as a 'a young 38' and in photographs on his blog *The British Real Ale Pub Adventure* (BRAPA) does indeed resemble an impish teenager. He is a relative newcomer to *Good Beer Guide* pub hunting:

After first getting into real ale in 2001 me and Dad struggled to know where to find it before Hull City away games. Then, by chance I picked up a second hand 1999 GBG in Leeds and we used it to find a pub in Epworth before Scunthorpe away. It was really good with the best quality ale we'd had so far so I never looked back after that. Most lunch-times I'd go to Waterstones in Leeds and read the new editions making mental notes for future trips. I only started buying it religiously from 2012.

On what makes a good pub, these pub tickers are surely worth listening to, immersed as they are in the reality of the situation right across the country. All three share a frustration with pubs that aren't open during advertised hours – annoying at the best of times, of course, but when you've got one chance to hit every pub in some far corner of the country it is almost disastrous. None seem particularly enamoured of micropubs, partly because of their often limited opening hours; nor do they like 'smart' would-be gastropubs. Indeed the more pubs they visit the more they seem to fall in love with a particular type of traditional establishment, as described by Simon:

> I'd say a multi-roomed creaky old building that smells old; the staff is welcoming; food is limited to snacks like pork pies and scotch eggs; there's a pub cat; no children; and the locals are friendly but not intrusive, so you can either be sociable or hide with your pint in a dark corner depending on your mood.

It has become something of a mantra for Martin that pubs selling a lot of one or two cask ales, even 'boring' ones, are generally better than those with ten pumps dispensing more adventurous beers in lacklustre condition. Acknowledging that stance (Martin, Simon and Duncan correspond with each other frequently) Duncan quietly disagrees:

> I like a place with a choice of beers of different strength and styles. If the person running the pub is passionate about their beer they will probably make sure visiting there is a good experience overall. Beer quality is the single

biggest determinant for me. Keeping good cask beer is a labour of love.

Martin grumbles about the GBG from time to time, especially the space it gives to information about small breweries in which he has limited interest, but is at heart a true believer:

> There's no better pub guide. I would say that 90 to 95 per cent of the pubs listed that I've visited have had beer I've been happy to drink. And the system works – the pubs that stop being reliably good, because of a change of management or whatever, tend to get dropped in the next edition. It's only ever going to be a snapshot of which pubs were good last year when it was surveyed. And I'd ask people who aren't happy with the pubs listed in their town what they've done to contribute to the selection process.

Wondering what type of personality takes up such a hobby we asked Duncan if is obsessive about anything other than visiting pubs. 'Ha- the question to make me look like a complete anorak!' he replied. 'I am also a ground-hopper and have seen matches on over 2,000 football grounds.' He is a birdwatcher, too, and has also started observing moths: 'There is an extraordinary number and variety but don't get me started.'

Simon, on the other hand, insists he is generally the opposite of obsessive: 'But when I'm in full-on BRAPA mode it's like my personality takes a 360 degree turn.' He also concedes that there are times he wonders why he's doing it: 'Ahhhhhh, you know sometimes I'm on that 6am train from York to Kings Cross in the dark in the depths of winter, and I think "I could be in bed having a lie in, then go for a few quality local pints with friends or family – why do I do this?"'

Putting aside his tendency to dry irony for just a moment, Martin had a thoughtful response to this question, arguing that his interest in *Good Beer Guide* pub ticking is actually an expression of a deeper interest in maps, geography and place – a way into understanding Britain as good as any other and more fun than most. 'I hate staying in the same place,' he says. 'I *never* want to be at home.'

There is also a sense that, in a Britain apparently divided where all the talk is of 'metropolitan bubbles', that pub crawling attains a higher meaning. 'It gets you to places you'd never go otherwise,' says

Martin. 'How else would I ever end up in a Hungry Horse in Burnley, or at the Conservative Club in Maidenhead?'

Nineteen-seventy-five: birth of the beer festival

First published in CAMRA's BEER *magazine in 2015.*

In 1975, the Campaign for Real Ale invented the modern beer festival when it staged a five-day event with more than 50 beers, attended by 40,000 thirsty members. Forty years on, we asked those who were there – volunteers, Campaign leaders and drinkers – to share their memories. Here, they tell the story in their own words.

Chris Bruton (organiser)
A Cambridge branch member suggested a beer festival in the Corn Exchange at an early meeting in 1974. The main credit should go to the late Alan Hill – then a Personnel Manager at [electronics firm] Pye in Cambridge. The festival made a significant profit, and the donation to central funds was essential to keep the Campaign afloat during a difficult period.

Chris Holmes (CAMRA chair 1975-76)
Because of the success of Cambridge, someone had the bright idea of a bigger festival in London. I'd like to say that we were being very sophisticated and testing the market for a national festival but, really, we just had the opportunity and said, 'Let's do it!'

Chris Bruton
By this time CAMRA had employed a Commercial Manager, Eric Spragett, who was a Londoner. The main organising trio was Eric, John Bishopp, and me. For some time a huge warehouse at St Katharine Docks was the favoured site but the logistics proved insurmountable. Finally, we found the old Flower Market in Covent Garden.

Chris Holmes
This was in the days of the GLC (Greater London Council) and they were always, for some reason, always very supportive of CAMRA. Covent Garden was very different then, and they were very happy to do anything that would help bring the area to life – to bring *people* back. The Flower Market had just become empty so they gave us it rent free,

which is remarkable. The deal was put together fairly simply – we said we'd take it for a week and that was that.

Chris Bruton
The location was superb and the old stalls upon which the flowers had been displayed for sale were perfect for stillage.

Richard Sanders (volunteer)
I was 25 and had been a CAMRA member for about two years. I helped out at the festival for a week from the Saturday lunchtime until the following Saturday afternoon. The site had been provided on the understanding that we clean the place up. It took hours of using high pressure hoses to remove many years of dirt and old flower stalks.

Chris Holmes
The only brewery who said, 'No – no beer leaves our brewery until it's paid for!' was the Home Brewery in Nottingham, where I was living at the time. So, I got on a train from London with a cheque in my hand, went to the brewery, asked to see the MD, and said, 'There's your cheque – can we have our beer?' He said yes.

Richard Sanders
On the Sunday before the festival opened a Mr Pollard of Pollards Brewery arrived in his Mini with a wooden 36 Gallon of his beer. He was one of the new micro brewers who had just started. His beer hadn't been ordered but we decided that we could sell it.

Gill Keay née Knight (volunteer)
I became a beer drinker when I was at university in Manchester in the late 1960s. Later on, in 1973, my old university friend Denis Palmer signed me up for CAMRA after a visit to Becky's Dive Bar near Waterloo. I can't remember exactly how I got roped in to Covent Garden but I suspect that it was by getting to know Eric Spragett through the Cambridge Beer Festival and other CAMRA events in 1973-5. Eric was tall with a long pony tail – that was his trademark – and very jolly.

Chris Bruton
Eric, Michael Hardman [CAMRA co-founder] and HQ staff worked on the publicity. Richard Boston was writing an occasional 'Boston on

Beer' column in the *Guardian* on Saturdays in which he regularly mentioned the Campaign and close to the event, he pushed 'Covent Garden is alive with Real Ale' more than once.

Denis Palmer (volunteer)
The build-up period was hectic with a load of CAMRA members running around the West End like headless chickens, furiously improvising. There was much sweaty panic – it was a very hot summer – and many cross words were spoken, with frequent disruption because of security alerts.

Gill Keay
There were a lot of IRA bomb scares at the time. We were using an office just up the road – there were no mobile phones in those days so we had to have an office with a phone – and, one evening, when we were locking up, we left a briefcase in the street. The alarm went up and the police cordoned off the whole area.

Richard Sanders
John Bishopp had to run round to Bow Street Police Station, offer abject apologies, and explain that his briefcase was not a bomb and please would they not do a controlled explosion on it. As a consequence of the bomb scare, and because London was on high alert, CAMRA had to hire security guards to search all customers' bags and cases on entering the festival. I remember going out with Eric Spragett to visit a security firm and Eric beating down the price quoted for security.

Chris Bruton
Eric persuaded a Covent Garden landlord to get the necessary licence to sell alcohol on the premises on our behalf, but other local landlords put pressure on the licensee to back out, and so he did. All the beer had been ordered, and it was not all on sale or return. Unless we could get a licence, we knew the Campaign might fold. We approached Fuller's and Young's – the only two independent London brewers in 1975 – and Anthony Ansell, the Marketing Director at Fuller's, agreed to help.

Chris Holmes

On the *morning* – the very morning – that we were due to open, I had to go to the local magistrate's court with someone from Fuller's, and got the licence just in time.

Anthony Gibson
I was the publicity officer for the West London branch of CAMRA and was working in the press office the National Farmers' Union so I knew all the techniques, and that's why I was approached to work on publicity for Covent Garden. It was all done in quite a hurry. We were pretty good at publicity in those days, CAMRA, and a lot of people in the media were just beginning to wake up to real ale, so we got a lot of pre-publicity without having to pay for any of it. I think we were just in tune with the spirit of the times.

Chris Holmes
About 20 minutes before we were due to open. We were all standing there, slightly nervous, not sure if anyone was going to come, and someone said, 'Shall we have a quick look outside?' We opened the door and saw a queue stretching the all the way round the block. There was a Watney's pub right next to the entrance, doors open, and this queue of thirsty people, but they didn't have a single customer.

Denis Palmer
I was honestly tempted for a moment to run away and just enjoy a quiet pint in the pub over the road.

Gill Keay
I remember smartly-dressed city gents queuing round the block in long lines, waiting to get in.

Denis Palmer
I was manning the ticket machines as we threw the doors open for the first session and they all jammed solid in the first few minutes. I spotted a couple of friends from work, signed them up to CAMRA on the spot, and put them to work on the front entrance. They were still there on the last day and, so they claimed, loved every manic minute of it.

Richard Sanders
That first lunchtime session I served JW Lees bitter from 18 gallon wooden kilderkins, and the TV cameras wanted to film me. I was asked

to describe the beer and I said, 'It could not be described as not bitter.' Most people at the festival on that first day had never tasted northern bitters and it was a bit of shock to those who were used to softer southern beers.

Gill Keay
Lots of beers were in wooden casks. Those casks looked good but were heavy and difficult to handle.

Chris Bruton
Unfortunately the space between the stalls was insufficient to allow for normal bars so the bar staff stood next to the casks. Clearly cash was not an option so we had to use tokens.

Chris Holmes
On day one, I was manning the membership stall, a chap came up in his three-piece suit. I was astonished but I managed to splutter out, 'You're Kingsley Amis!' And he said, 'Yes, and I think you chaps are doing a wonderful job.'

Steve Barber (volunteer)
I was on the Arkell's stand, behind a high timber barricade. Each side had a serving aperture cut in it with a crude shelf for a bar with hand-pumps. Staff could enter and leave the 'stockade' via a bolted gate. It was as if we were expecting an attack from the Vikings! Initially, it was all very civilised but the pace increased until we were pulling beer as fast as we could, with punters shoving empty glasses and money at us through the serving holes. Quite frightening, really.

Richard Sanders
On the first evening I served Home Ales Bitter and I managed to sell a whole 22 gallon container in just over 20 minutes. There was only one size of glass, a half pint straight fluted glass with the logo at the top, and I don't think I ever turned the tap off except when I had a quick half that a customer brought for me.

Ron Pattinson (drinker)
I'd joined CAMRA on my 18th birthday and one of my friends, Martin Young, had joined, too. I think it was him who suggested that we take the train down to London from Newark for the day to attend. It was

only the second or third time I'd ever been to London, so it was pretty exciting.

Paul Bailey (drinker)
I had only recently turned 20 and I did have a feeling that I was part of something special and exciting, and the excitement grew as we queued to get in. The customers were a mixed bunch but there was little evidence of the T-shirt and sandal brigade that characterised CAMRA during the 1980s and 1990s. As we attended the event on the Friday, there was a good sprinkling of office workers, including quite a few city gents, but I don't recall there being many women at the festival.

David Davies (photographer)
I worked in a nearby photo lab and a colleague and I managed to pay a couple of extended lunch breaks at the Beer Ex, enjoying more half pints than we should have done. What I found interesting was the mix of City Gents, Office and manual workers, and I remember the smell of wet wooden barrels and spilt beer.

Keith Flett (drinker)
I was 18 and just heading off to University. A beer festival then was an extremely unusual event -- radical even. There were beers on offer you hardly saw in London then -- Courage Directors, Ruddles County and so on. I think it was my first taste of Directors. I also remember the food being interesting -- Stilton and bread, I think.

Gill Keay
My role at Covent Garden was organising food – probably because I was one of the few women involved! My challenge was to set up a preparation and serving area in the Flower Market, and to find staff who didn't mind buttering a mountain of bread rolls.

Chris Holmes
Eric Spragett had signed a contract with Pork Farms in Nottingham so we had an enormous delivery of pork pies. As far as I can remember, that was the sum total of the catering.

Gill Keay
I'll never forget the cheeses because they were all different colours. They were Cheddar (yellow), Sage Derby (green), Stilton (blue)

and Red Windsor (guess…). They used to get all mixed up on the preparation surfaces. We weren't very organised.

Richard Sanders
I believe on the second day of opening some money from the front desk where customers bought glasses and tokens went missing. Chris Holmes had been running the membership stall, but after that, he went and sat on the money, so to speak. He had also been looking after the festival licensee from Fullers Brewery and I took over Chris's duties. My abiding memory of that was Mr Fuller [Antony Ansell] asking if I could stop people urinating in one corner of the hall. The toilets were grim to say the least.

David Harrison (drinker)
I was really impressed by the scale and number of breweries. I hadn't really travelled about much and beers didn't seem to be traded round the country then, so the sight and taste of beers from up North and the West Country was very exciting.

Paul Bailey
There were beers whose names I had only read about, and now they were presented right in front of me. I wanted to try them all – talk about a kid in a sweet shop!

Ron Pattinson
Oddly, I can remember one of the beers I drank: Yorkshire Clubs Dark Mild. Black as coal and a lovely drink. I think I remember it because the brewery was taken over and closed a few weeks later.

Keith Porter (drinker)
Myself and two pals turned up at around 6.30 pm to find long queues around the entrances and lots of people sat on the pavement of The Anglesey. Having given up hope of getting in to the event we decided to go somewhere else but, as we walked away, I noticed an unmarked door with a steward in attendance. I asked him was this an official entrance and he said, well, no not really, but come in anyway. As Saturday went on the hall got noisier and singing broke out.

Chris Bruton

By Saturday, much of the beer was sold out. The public were sitting on the stalls as the empty casks were taken down and a group of West Ham United supporters led a rendition of 'If you hate Watney's, clap your hands'.

Denis Palmer
There was a staff party after the last punter but most of us were too stunned to celebrate in any style.

Chris Bruton
My overwhelming memory at the close on Saturday night was of tiredness. I had in the past run five marathons in under three hours, but I'd never been so exhausted.

Chris Holmes
CAMRA was on this incredible roll – membership going up, press coverage – we had the wind in our sails. But when I look back at Covent Garden now I think, how did we get away with it?

Denis Palmer
I walked home across Waterloo Bridge in the early hours thinking. 'What the hell have we just done?'. Then two years later it was Ally Pally and the Great British Beer Festival and we did it all again, and again...

The above material was gathered from telephone conversations, interviews and emails and has been edited for clarity.

The Campaign for Unreal Ale

First published at allaboutbeer.com in 2015.

From the 1970s, the Campaign for Real Ale (CAMRA) dominated the conversation around beer in Britain and cask-conditioned 'real ale' was all but synonymous with good beer. Then, in the mid-90s, a band of industry insiders began to question that orthodoxy, suggesting that beer in kegs and bottles, filtered and carbonated prior to packaging, might be the key to increasing stylistic diversity and overall quality in the UK. They found their voice through a niche industry magazine called *The Grist* and especially in the November/December 1995 issue which amounts to a manifesto for the next 20 years of an emerging UK craft beer scene. Its editor was the young London-born, German-trained brewer Alastair Hook.

Alastair Hook: *The Grist* was an independent magazine run by Tony Williamson and Elisabeth Baker. When I first set up the Packhorse Brewing Company in Ashford, Kent, in 1990, they made contact and said they'd like to do a feature. The magazine was their passion.

Peter Haydon (beer historian and brewer): In 1994, I'd just published my book, *The British Pub*, and Lizzie was looking for someone to help Tony, so I became a sort of freelance jobbing journalist contributing articles. When Tony became ill, Alastair stepped into the editor's chair and changed the magazine's direction. He was evangelical.

Mark Dorber (manager/landlord at the White Horse 1981-2007): In 1994, Roger Protz suggested I should talk to Alastair Hook. I spoke to Alastair on the phone and we got on well and then met at a pub in Greenwich and spent Sunday afternoon drinking and talking. We shared the same beer values – we wanted to get people looking internationally rather than being narrowly parochial. We had a very strong feeling that the UK beer scene needed shaking up.

Alastair Hook: When I was 17 or 18, I was very gung-ho about CAMRA – cask ale was the be-all-and-end-all, all that – but by the mid-90s, I'd lost my fascination. The editorial line at *The Grist* became more and more critical of CAMRA. The more dogmatic they became, the more we reacted against it.

Mark Dorber: We love cask ale – we adore it, and I made a career out of it – but what we were critical of was the idea that, if it wasn't cask, it couldn't be worth drinking. That all-or-nothing mentality was a negative drag.

Peter Haydon: We took the view that the British brewing industry had failed to represent itself. If a journalist wanted a comment on something beer-related, they went toddling off to CAMRA. If you had a story about roads, you wouldn't go to the Reliant Robin Owners' Club, would you?

A particular bone of contention was the 'cask breather', a device that allows traditional casks to work in their usual way except that, instead of permitting air to enter as the cask empties, it fills the void with a light blanket of CO_2, extending the life of the beer.

Mark Dorber: CAMRA's refusal to support the use of cask breathers made them seem, to us, like inhibitors of change. If your pub was found to be using cask breathers, you were seen as being somehow not a true supporter of cask beer, which is ridiculous.

Alastair Hook: Oxidation kills flavour and the idea that oxygen improves beer is just absurd.

Peter Haydon: CAMRA would rather you drank shit beer as long as it was 'correctly' dispensed.

Mark Dorber: I first went to judge in Denver in 1992. By 1995, it was certainly where all the thoughtful English beer people were going. Being on those professionally-run blind-tasting panels with like-minded people eager to explore tradition, eager to explore flavour – the best of your peers in the world – was hugely uplifting. There was a buzz, a sense of energy, of unbounded optimism, a feeling that anything was possible.

> "Vibrant flavours stood out in many of the beers judged and sampled. (Alas, much of the UK brewing industry, by

contrast, seems reluctant to offend any portion of the beer market with its bland (aka 'balanced') beers.)" – Mark Dorber, 'An Uplifting Experience', the *Grist*, Nov/Dec 1995.

Alastair Hook: From those American trips, I learned that tasty, flavourful, consumer-attractive, choice-providing beer didn't have to be cask-conditioned.

> "American microbrewed beers are rich in character, flavour, diversity and in the case of the more successful micros, consistency… CAMRA take the credit for revitalising the magnificent art of cask conditioned ale brewing, but they fail to see how their puritan approach is a threat to the emerging microbrewing scene." – Alastair Hook, 'All guns blazing in the USA', the *Grist*, Nov/Dec 1995.)

Mark Dorber: Meanwhile, in the UK, micros seemed to lack aesthetic judgement… They weren't interested in keg or bottle, only in paying homage to the great god of cask-conditioned beer.

> "For the small brewer to survive, a quality product is needed at the point of dispense, albeit from a cask with or without the breather, bottled or, dare I say, filtered and kegged." – Keith Lark, Hook's former school teacher, under the pseudonym Keith Laric, 'Thoughts of a Beer Drinker', the *Grist*, Nov/Dec 1995.

John Cryne (Chairman of CAMRA 1989-98): What Mr Dorber and his cohorts may have done in 1995 must have passed me by. Clearly the ripples they intended to create were something of a damp squib… Judging by the plethora of US beer styles, presumably they won their argument and CAMRA lost. Oh wait a minute – CAMRA has a 170,000 members and the *Grist* has presumably gone to the mill?

Alastair Hook: [My criticism of CAMRA in the *Grist*] didn't necessarily chime with the heart-chords of SIBA members who were mostly cask ale brewers. In fact, it wound them up. The late Michael Jackson told me, 'Only ever talk good things of beer', and that's what I try to do, so, for all their ills, CAMRA have spent decades promoting good beer. (I'm just not sure they know what it is.) I don't have a problem with CAMRA – I don't think about it. It's irrelevant. What was strange was when I gave a talk at the Great British Beer Festival but my own beer, from Meantime, got stopped at the door by some jobsworth who wouldn't have it on the premises because it wasn't real ale. Isn't that weird? Absurd.

Peter Haydon: [The *Grist*] was a bit ahead of its time – there weren't really the number of breweries around then to support it with advertising – but it was a bloody good little magazine.

Alastair Hook founded Meantime Brewing in 1999; it was taken over by SAB Miller in May 2015. Peter Haydon succeeded Alastair Hook as editor of the Grist, *which ceased publication in 1998, and went on to run a brewery in South London. Mark Dorber now runs the Anchor at Walberswick and was a co-founder of the Beer Academy.*

Craft before it was 'a thing'

First published on our blog in 2015.

The quintessentially Scottish brewery Williams Bros began its life in 1988 when an elderly woman walked into a home-brewing supply shop in Glasgow and approached the young man behind the counter with the recipe for a long lost style of beer with a legendary status – heather ale.

      A famous poem by Robert Louis Stevenson tells the story of how the Picts, defeated by a Scottish king, took to their graves 'the secret of the drink' – a brew 'sweeter far than honey… stronger far than wine', with semi-magical properties. It concludes:

> But now in vain is the torture,
> Fire shall never avail:
> Here dies in my bosom
> The secret of Heather Ale.

      In a 1903 book entitled *The Heather in Lyric, Lore and Lay*, Alexander Wallace considered various stories and tales of heather ale – 'a liquour greatly superior to our common ale' – dating back to 1526. If it had not died out, he concluded, then it had certainly become hard-to-find, with only a handful of doubtful reports from people who claimed to have tasted it in the latter half of the 19th century, as brewed by 'shepherds on the moor'. He also cited, for balance, the view of one authority that heather ale might never have existed at all.

      And yet, there she was, the wise old woman, with the secret in her hand, and Bruce Williams, the young man behind the shop counter, was intrigued.

      This fairy tale-tale origin story sounded, to us, too good to be true – almost like something from a Dan Brown novel – but in a telephone conversation, Bruce's softly-spoken younger brother, Scott, insisted on its veracity, and put it into context:

> We used to get a lot of customers from all parts of Scotland and they'd give you bottles of nettle beer, beer with bog myrtle, and tell you about these recipes their families had been using for years. The recipe she gave

Bruce didn't have much detail so he spent a lot of time at the Mitchell Library in Glasgow researching recipes, looking at old sources like the Book of Kells.

Bruce did not have a particularly academic background and never went to university. 'Bruce has always been…' said Scott Williams, hesitatingly, 'Well, he's more distracted. He's always looking for the next thing to be interested in. He's very practical and gets on and does things, whatever it is, like building an extension on his house or researching an ancient beer recipe.'

The Williams family came from Dunfermline where Bruce's father worked at the dockyard, eventually becoming an engineer with a more comfortable and secure job. Scott recalled a 'fantastic upbringing' spent in various places around the world, from Bahrain to Mauritius, and wherever else his father's specialist line of work took them.

In the 1970s, when the family had moved back to Scotland, Mr Williams opened a shop in the small town of Crossford in Dunfermline. It sold both baking and brewing supplies because, as Scott Williams remembered, the only suppliers of malt in bulk were bakery wholesalers, and most home brewers were using baker's yeast. Then, after a short while, he moved the business to Partick in the city of Glasgow.

For his part, Scott managed a year of university before quitting and heading off to London to sell photocopiers: 'I still flagellate myself over that – knocking on people's doors, a bit of a wide boy… But it was good experience; it teaches you resilience, knocking on 90 doors and being told to go away 89 times.' When he came back to Scotland, he took a job working at a company that made malt extracts and kits for home brewers.

It took several years of research and experimentation for Bruce to come up with a recipe that, in Scott's words, 'people would actually want to drink'. With a shudder, he said, 'A couple of the early versions Bruce brewed were awful.' Eventually, he hit upon a blend of the mainstream — malted barley and wheat, with hops – and the quirky, with heather, ginger and bog myrtle as additional aromatics.

In 1992, four years after its first conception, Bruce Williams's heather ale, now named Leann Fraoch, pronounced 'Frook', was first brewed commercially, in the railway station waiting room at Taynuilt, Argyll. 'There was a little brewery there run by a guy called Dick Saunders,' recalled Scott. 'Dick was a jack-of-all-trades, very charming, but not much of a salesman. Bruce had been helping him out with his brewing.'

They used an entire batch of heather, picked by hand by Bruce and gangs of locals who he paid £2 per gallon bucket. His son, Chris, who now works at the brewery but was then a small child, recalled the experience in an email:

> I think we spent more time playing hide and seek or chasing the massive, beautiful dragonflies about the heather. I remember the evenings with the pickers, sat round a fire, playing/jamming folk songs, drinking beer and eating stews…

They brewed enough to fill several casks (borrowed from Dick Saunders) and put them out to the trade. 'It sold really quickly,' said Scott.

At this point, the slow life cycle of heather ale became a problem, as Scott recalled: 'We had to kick our heels for a year before we could pick any more heather and brew it again, in 1993.'

The next batch was just as popular, and lured famous beer writer Michael Jackson to Scotland, where Bruce Williams made him nibble on heather: 'Now try this one. The bell heather is sweeter, but the ling heather has more perfume. Do you get the spiciness, the astringency?'

Fraoch, with its off-kilter herbal oiliness, offered something genuinely unusual at a time when British drinkers were beginning to grow weary of endless ranks of bitters and best bitters. The burgeoning number of beer writers, hungry for good stories, wrote about it in articles and books, ensuring that, almost from the off, beer geeks were lusting to taste it. 'Some of our success has been because of the story and the image,' Scott Williams acknowledged. 'Michael Jackson and some of those original beer writers were genuinely interested because what we were doing was quite literary, well-researched, and all about provenance before that had become a popular idea.'

Scott, meanwhile, took on the role of Heather Ales' chief salesman, drawing on his experience in London. 'I found restaurants tended to have the open doors,' he said 'but pubs and bars weren't interested, except some of the CAMRA pubs.'

After a couple of years at Taynuilt, they needed to increase production. Refused a loan by the bank, Bruce Williams sent them a copy of Robert Louis Stevenson's poem, which, astonishingly, did the trick. With three months to pay it back, they approached a more traditional Scottish brewery, Maclay's of Alloa. 'We went with them because they were only people who were really interested in what we were doing,' Scott Williams said. 'They didn't really get it, but they were tremendously supportive. And Roger Ryman – he was a laugh!'

Roger Ryman is now head brewer at St Austell in Cornwall but, in 1995, had just joined Maclay having graduated from Heriot-Watt two years before. When we interviewed him at St Austell's brewery, he told us about his time working with the Williams brothers:

> Bruce used to turn up with these sacks straight off the hillside – heather, bog myrtle, ginger… He was wild, off the wall – full of energy and enthusiasm, bursting with ideas. But he also knew what he was doing and played the part, to an extent. He had wild hair, and always looked like he'd just come down from the mountainside.

Though the Maclay brewery was old and in poor repair, it also offered technical advantages when it came to brewing Fraoch, as Scott Williams recalled: 'They had this huge underback which we could fill with heather – 300-400 litres solid heather in volume — and let the beer filter over it, picking up aroma as it went.'

In that first year working with Maclay, the brothers only produced one batch because they were still dependent on a seasonal supply of heather. We wondered whether they had ever been tempted to find a more reliable source, which idea Scott dismissed: 'You can buy heather from Poland, but it smells like potpourri – it's sieved to get just the flowers. Heather is all about provenance, all about Scotland.' And picking it cannot be automated – as Scott put it, 'It's a pain in the arse.' They spent several years perfecting a system, still in use today, whereby they blast-freeze the heather at -35 and then store three-years' worth in case there's a bad harvest.

Roger Ryman recalled how quickly their range of beers expanded:

> Eventually, Williams Bros started to look at producing some secondary brands. They were selling niche beers into a broad market, which was really unusual at the time. It was a strong brand – selling the Scottish dream. I helped to

develop Grozet, Ebulum and Alba. It was about finding the right balance between interest and authenticity, and practicality. Using spruce tips instead of hops [in Alba], for example, meant you had no natural filter in the hop back, so we had to find a way around that, using spent hops just for filtering. Alba was parti-gyled off Maclay's 80 Shilling. I was aware of how unusual these beers were but I don't think I had any sense that we were being 'revolutionary'.

Scott Williams did not mince words when Alba came up in conversation: it was even more of a 'pain in the arse' than Fraoch.

You've got a very short window in which to pick the spruce tips – shorter even than heather. If you look at the trees, from March to April, you'll see the new growth, a little brown bud; that grows a little cap, bright green, before it opens up fully. When it opens up, it goes dark green, and you can't brew with it because it's full of chlorophyll. It's like cotton-picking only much more difficult, in the dark of the forest, with most of the tips way up out of reach.

Again, there was no way to automate this, or to buy in suitable materials from elsewhere.

In 1996, Hollywood star Mel Gibson won five Oscars for Braveheart and celebrated by ordering 20 cases of Fraoch for a party in Los Angeles, which led to a rush of demand from American drinkers. In 1998, Heather Ales acquired its own brewery at Strathaven, but also continued brewing at Maclay in order to meet ongoing demand from the US market.

When Maclay's finally announced that they intended to retire the increasingly decrepit brewery, Duncan Kellock, Maclay's Head Brewer and Roger Ryman's boss, proposed to the brothers that they go into business together running a contract brewing plant using the old Maclay kit at a new site in Central Scotland. 'It had been an old Younger's depot, defunct for maybe 60 years,' recalled Scott Williams. But the joint operation went into receivership after a couple of years at which point Heather Ales took it over, under their new company name William Bros.

Scott Williams told us, with what perhaps seemed a touch of regret, that it was at this point that things got serious:

> We've never really had a grand plan or a strategy, or looked much at what anyone else is doing. We've been like a dog sniffing its own arse for 20 years. Not interested in politics, just making something and hopefully finding a market for it. We did it because it was fun and interesting. We started to become more of a business when we got our own brewery and some overheads to worry about, a bottling line and so on.

This prompted their beer range to expand yet further but with an emphasis on, as Scott conceded, 'more commercial products — things with malt and hops'.

Their current best-seller is not, as we assumed, Fraoch, but Joker IPA, of which Scott said, 'It's like a gateway drug for a lot of people. Balanced, not in your face like BrewDog Punk – a sessionable IPA.' The next most popular beer in their range is Caesar Augustus, an easy-drinking lager-pale-ale hybrid. These products might be less superficially oddball than the beer that started it all, but there is still a streak of freakiness behind the scenes, and Scott became suddenly enthused explaining the hidden principles that guide their brewing:

> We like all our beers to have to have some kind of story or history behind them. So all the Williams Bros beers are brewed to golden ratio proportions – the same way the universe expands, the divine proportion. Do you know the number Phi? 1.618, the golden ratio. Look up 'Phiness'. It's the shape of your credit card, the proportions of the human body.

He grew yet more animated as he went on:

> What that means with our beer is that if I use seven malts, the first malt makes up the bulk of the brew, but the second malt is added according to the golden ratio, and the third is in proportion to the second, and so on. It's a pain in the arse for the brewers because it means the seventh

malt is something like 0.07 litres of rye. I always say, this is how God would have made beer.

At which point, he turned coy, muttering, 'But we don't really mention this in marketing because it was a bit much for people.'

As he had brought them up, we wondered how Scott feels about the new kings of Scottish craft beer.

I think BrewDog are damn clever – I take my hat off to them. I remember when they used to come down to our place dropping things off, picking up casks, and I thought, gosh, it's amazing beer, but I just didn't think their strategy was going to work. I was wrong. I guess I'm too conservative. To a certain extent, we've grabbed on their coat tails as they've whizzed by. They've dragged the whole industry along with them. They've been critical of fellow brewers sometimes, including us, but sometimes what they say, it's for an audience, and we don't take offence.

He is perhaps too harsh in declaring himself conservative. Williams Bros released a mixed case of single hops beers some years ago, much like BrewDog's current IPA is Dead project, but to little acclaim. 'Retailers didn't get it,' Scott said with evident frustration. 'They'd say, "Why would anyone want this?" It's like Leonardo da Vinci inventing the helicopter – right idea at the wrong time.'

We didn't write about Williams Bros in *Brew Britannia* because we weren't convinced that, though well-respected, they were particularly influential — there was no flood of heather ales or breweries using hyper-local ingredients in the late-90s — but if they have a place in the narrative of the 'rebirth of British beer' it's this: they showed that brewers without a brewery, but with interesting ideas and a story to tell, could do very well for themselves selling mostly bottled beer. Perhaps they weren't, as some have suggested, a proto-BrewDog so much as they were the Mikkeller of their day.

The beer hunter was human

First published in Beer Advocate *magazine in 2017.*

The world's most famous beer writer, Michael Jackson, died in 2007 at the age of 65, leaving peers and disciples bereft. Obituaries, reminiscences and tributes poured forth, highlighting his contributions to a global craft beer scene which arose in tandem with his career, and for which he is given much credit. He was a hero to many, a friend to others, and his 30-year pre-eminence is hard to deny. This makes it difficult to assess him critically or even objectively but, a decade on from his passing, perhaps it is time to try.

First, the obligatory biography in a nutshell: Michael Jackson was born in Leeds in England's industrial north in 1942. His mother was English through-and-through while his father was the son of Jewish immigrants from Eastern Europe. Jackson spent his childhood in Huddersfield, a grand but fading town between Leeds and Manchester, where he developed an interest in rugby league and, as a teenager, in drinking beer. And here is where we find our first point of query.

Legends of Great Men often include tales of prodigal behaviour, signs of the genius yet to come. Mozart, for example, is said to have composed his first music at the age of four. Michael Jackson's life as a beer writer began with a similar feat: at the age of 16, the story goes, before he was even legally permitted to drink, he started writing about pubs for a newspaper in his native Yorkshire. Jackson himself was vague about exactly which organ he wrote for perhaps anxious even 50 years on that he might get someone in trouble for sponsoring under-age drinking. Some third-parties name with apparent authority the *Batley & Morley Gazette* but if you travel to Huddersfield and pay a visit to the local studies library hoping to read back issues, you will be disappointed: it doesn't seem ever to have existed. And if a column entitled 'This is Your Pub' appeared in the *Huddersfield Weekly Examiner*, the *Batley Reporter* or any other likely outlet between 1958 and 1960 we were unable to track it down.

It is certainly true that he entered a career in journalism straight out of school, starting as a cub reporter on the *Huddersfield Daily Examiner*, before moving to Edinburgh, and then onward to London's famous Fleet Street, the home base of most of the biggest English newspapers at the time. He was an old-fashioned journeyman journalist who learned the craft by tramping the streets with notebook in hand which equipped him perfectly for the less romantic but more lucrative world of trade journalism. He was involved in the establishment of the KLM airline's long-running magazine *Holland Herald* and also oversaw the creation of *Campaign*, a British magazine covering the advertising industry, including coming up with the attention-grabbing name. He worked in television, too, producing episodes of gritty documentary series *World in Action*, including one in which he escorted the prudish pro-censorship campaigner Mary Whitehouse around free-and-easy Copenhagen. By the early 1970s, and still only in his early thirties, he had made a name for himself as much more than a mere reporter.

His move into publishing, as a co-founder and editorial director at Quarto, seems a natural move with hindsight. According to Quarto's official company history, Jackson was already in partnership with Bob Morley and it was they who went to New York in 1975 with books ready to pitch including *The English Pub* and *The World Guide to Beer*. They met American academic Laurence Orbach and the three formed a partnership dedicated to producing lavish, large-format, heavily illustrated coffee table books. Reading between the lines, that partnership eventually went sour, which is perhaps why Jackson seems to have been reluctant to mention it in later interviews, instead telling a version of the story which suggested he was a mere jobbing wordsmith who was asked to finish *The English Pub* when someone else failed to deliver. Whatever the truth, that book, published in 1976, became Jackson's first substantial piece of what we now recognize as Beer Writing. Though it is a decent book with many examples of the artful prose which so elevated his writing – 'The sensuous procedures of brewing don't die easily' – it is no classic. Had he stopped there and moved on to writing about rugby or some other subject it is unlikely beer enthusiasts would remember his name any with any more reverence than those of Mike Dunn, Frank Baillie, or the pub-crawling duo Warren Knock and Conal Gregory. In the mid-1970s, indeed, the most revered British beer writer was Richard Boston. His anarchic, witty weekly column for the *Guardian* newspaper was a major driver in the rise of the Campaign for Real Ale, and his book, *Beer and Skittles*, is better than *The English Pub*, even though it is far plainer to look at than Jackson's photo-laden prestige publication.

It was with his next book, *The World Guide to Beer*, that Jackson trumped Richard Boston and every other pretender to the throne.

Even now, though so much of the content is out of date, it has much to offer, not least as a perfect time capsule of the pre-craft-beer world, and because the writing is so often brilliant – at turns playful, precise, romantic and startlingly evocative. With a true beat reporter's instinct Jackson visited as many countries as practical and then bombarded his readers with detail and colour. At that time, it was quite possible for him to taste, or at least record the existence of, a good number of beers in production anywhere in the world. There were few meaningful tasting notes, however, beyond the top level – hoppy, malty, sweet and dry. Instead, a sense of each brew was given by comparison to others – Newcastle Brown Ale is like Vienna lager, Russian stout resembles German Doppelbock, and so on. A beginner beer blogger would get sneered at for this kind of thing today but, in 1977, this put Jackson ahead of the game.

It was from that approach that emerged an embryonic global taxonomy – the first convincing, comprehensive, wide-reaching attempt to explain to consumers how various types of beer relate to each other. Of course there were similar exercises before Jackson – categorising things is a natural instinct – but they were either industry focused, obscure, or lacked the wider view, as in the case of British writers who tended to add something like '…and lager' to cover everything else. In a section headed 'Classical beer styles' covering a mere two pages, Jackson listed 24 distinct styles of beer from Münchener ('dark-brown, bottom-fermented… malty without being excessively sweet') to Steam Beer ('a hybrid between top and bottom-fermentation'), each categorized as either top-fermented, wheat beer, or bottom-fermented. He was attempting to record what he observed, not to lay down the law, but when he says of, say, Kölsch, 'Alcohol content by volume just under 4.5 per cent', in the context of a book that throbs with encyclopaedic authority, it feels like a rule.

He also drew a distinction between 'types' (broadly similar beers) and 'styles' (fixed classical models). It is prototypical and muddled but, even so, this brief bit of introductory matter was arguably more influential than the prose that fills the rest of the book. To novice beer geeks (and there weren't many veterans in 1977) it was like being presented with a map, or perhaps a training regime. For those whose enthusiasm led them into home-brewing, and from there to commercial brewing, it was a playbook.

Since it was first published, Jackson's style guide has formed the basis of judging regimes at beer festivals and homebrew competitions. It has been ripped off, expanded upon and debated by multiple generations of beer writers. And, less positively, it has also led to a kind of straitjacketing which says every beer must belong to a style, the parameters of which against it will then be judged: 'Not true to style. Zero stars.' Jackson's influence is sometimes overstated, but that's not Jackson's fault. His own claims in this regard were modest and carefully worded: 'I think I was the first person ever to use the phrase beer style' is how he put it in one 1996 interview.

Another angle from which Jackson's work has come under tentative scrutiny in recent years – tentative because criticizing him, even respectfully, can make his acolytes bristle – is the question of journalistic ethics. In recent years, Andy Crouch has made journalistic integrity something of a personal crusade, putting him at odds with many of his peers who still operate in the cosy Jacksonian mode of collaborative bonhomie and only gentle criticism, if any. In 2010 he spent several days mining the Michael Jackson archive at Oxford Brookes University and was among the first to break ranks when in a blog post he just barely criticized Jackson, in the mildest possible form: 'Michael counted many brewers (not just crafts) as among his "clients", an interesting revelation to say the least.' And this is true – while he was the world's foremost beer *critic* he was also employed by breweries in various capacities, such as giving opinions of products prior to launch, hosting tasting events on their behalf, or even appearing in advertisements for their products. He was also personally friendly with many brewers, partly no doubt because as a journalist it was necessary to keep channels of communication open, but also because it is hard to maintain a distance from affable people who like to talk about beer, and drink it, as much as do you.

Of course standards and practices were different a decade ago, or two, or three, and it seems to us that, with some hesitation, he worked for, and was friendly, with brewers he respected, rather than making a show of respecting breweries who paid him – quite a different proposition. He demonstrated objectivity through the quality of his recommendations rather than by simply declaring it. To some extent we can't help but suspect that barbs directed at Jackson on this basis today are really a proxy for criticizing active players whose partnerships with breweries can seem opaque and confusing. Nonetheless, it is likely that if Jackson was still around and operating like this in 2017 he too would be being 'called out' far more frequently.

Another related but lesser complaint is that Michael Jackson gave the industry as a whole an easy ride. For the first 30 years the nascent profession of beer writing and the embryonic micro-brewing industry had the same priorities: they wanted to get people excited about unusual, distinctive, interesting beers, and to challenge the dominance of large multi-national companies. If they were to sell articles and books, beer writers needed a constant flow of new breweries and beers; and, if they were to grow, breweries needed to gain the attention of potential customers. Michael Jackson put his philosophy into words for CAMRA in 1987:

> If I can find something good to say about a beer, I do. Any merit or unusual aspect is, I believe, of interest to my readers. That is why I choose to write about it in the first place... Nor since I have the whole world from which to choose, can I be comprehensive. If I despise a beer, why find room for it? This poses a problem only when a beer is too big to ignore.

This is the approach that most beer writers subscribed to until recently, and many still do: focus on the positive, and avoid revelling in the kind of hatchet job that so often characterizes food or art criticism. But readers have grown cynical, like the enthusiast who recently said to us, 'The problem with beer bloggers is, they never have a bad beer.' An increasing number of readers expect to hear about both good and bad and roll their eyes in exasperation at what is sometimes called the 'cheery beery' tendency in writing. Fundamentally, the idea that a writer might be on the side of the industry rather than the consumer troubles them.

And, yes, the industry still venerates Michael Jackson. Influential British brewers such as Alastair Hook (Meantime) talk about his 1982 *Pocket Guide* as a kind of holy text which set them on the path to righteousness while in the US he is given even greater credit: Brooklyn Brewery's Garrett Oliver has called him 'the spiritual father of the early [American] micro-brewing movement and the greatest champion of the craft brewer'. Hyperbolic as this might sound, it is not unjustified. By giving space to Anchor in his best-selling *World Guide*, to begin with, and then by tracking the growth of US micro-brewing in subsequent editions, spin-off books and numerous articles, he all but talked the American craft brewing scene into being. He reported first-hand, visiting various parts of the US regularly, conveying the sense of a red-hot, developing trend. Then, finally, in 1990, he did the same on television in the cult show *The Beer Hunter*. Charlie Papazian has also always been generous in crediting Jackson for his part in establishing and supporting the Great American Beer Festival (GABF), a turning point in American beer culture.

There are occasional individual pieces of Jackson's writing that haven't aged well. For example, a 1987 article in the Campaign for Real Ale's monthly newspaper *What's Brewing* in defence of the GABF prompts a cringe with 30 years distance. In it Jackson reacts sharply and sarcastically to the then current controversy over breweries fielding flirtatious 'booth babes' in their pursuit of the popular vote in the GABF's best beer competition. Elsewhere, especially in his earlier work, he was prone to lamenting the disappearance of the stereotypical buxom barmaid, and to casually sexist asides in otherwise innocuous articles. As he said himself: 'Not only does beer inflame lust if taken to excess: heavy-beer drinkers are often male-chauvinists.' But he was, after all, a man of his time, with the love life to match – that is, more complicated than acknowledged in the officially sanctioned versions of his life story. He was according to those who knew him often to be found surrounded by women at beer festivals, charming them with eloquent talk of beer, and more than one girlfriend attended his funeral.

Does any of that matter? Yes, insofar as it highlights his humanity.

With that in mind we asked Geoff Griggs, a New Zealand-based beer writer who worked with Jackson on numerous occasions to reflect on Jackson the man rather than the legend. '[Contrary] to those who have commented on Facebook about his apparent haughtiness… I was always impressed by Michael's humility and approachability', he told us by email. 'Despite his 'rock star' image… I always found Michael to be somewhat shy and retiring. And despite his unquestionable eloquence with words in their written form, he wasn't the most gifted public speaker.'

Owen Barstow was Jackson's assistant for 12 years and recalls him as a frustrated novelist who started many but, as far as we know, never finished one. A starkly honest autobiographical piece Jackson wrote for *Slow Food* in 2003 shows what he might have achieved in this field. It commences with a delicately observed passage written from the point of view of his hungry refugee grandfather: "'Hay is for horses,' Chaim told himself in a desperate whisper.'

The Beer Hunter was a persona. Michael Jackson, on the other hand, was a complex person, scrambling like the rest of us to meet deadlines and organize his life, with faults, foibles and doubts. Those who treat him as a bland cipher onto which to project their own desires, prejudices and, yes, criticism, do him a disservice.

Belgophilia

First published in CAMRA's BEER *magazine in 2017.*

The waiter at a bar in Manchester carelessly places a bottle of Saison Dupont in front of retired lorry driver Des Fisher. When the waiter has gone, Des sighs and shakes his head, muttering in a warm Lancastrian accent: 'See, this annoys me. In Belgium, they always turn the glass and the label to face the customer. And there's none of this pouring half the beer into the glass! And it's always the right glass, too.'

To Des these details matter because he is one of a hard core of British beer lovers which has made Belgium its second home, travelling there at every opportunity and forming a community around a shared obsession.

An appreciation for Belgian beer is an important but sometimes forgotten step in the development of Britain's current vibrant and varied beer culture. It began back in the 1970s when, before people talked about 'craft beer', there was 'world beer', and Michael Jackson. It was largely under his guidance in the form of the 1977 *World Guide to Beer* and numerous other works that British drinkers were first made aware of Trappist beers, sour Lambic beers, and other curiosities that seemed so strange to palates brought up on bitter and mild. Belgian beer has been a special guest star at CAMRA's Great British Beer Festival since the late 1970s and through the 1980s specialist shops and distributors popped up. Bottles of Belgian beer began to appear in the kind of pubs frequented by enthusiasts and then, in the 1990s, dedicated Belgian bars arrived including, perhaps surprisingly, in the small market town of Leek in Staffordshire.

It was there that Martin, a softly spoken civil servant from Stoke-on-Trent who is as obsessed with cycling and good coffee as beer, and known online as @6townsmart, first had his head turned. 'Den Engel opened my eyes in around 2000-2001,' he says. 'Westmalle Dubbel was the first thing I remember really exciting me. I tried everything on the menu with one of Tim Webb's early guide books for Belgium and Holland [for guidance]. I went virtually every weekend, sometimes on the odd weeknight.' But he also mentions another key development: 'What prompted me to actually go to Belgium was Eurostar – it was so quick and easy.'

Jeremy, better known online as Jezza or under the handle @BonsVoeux1, lives in London and works in the charity sector. For him, the opening of the Channel Tunnel was also a key turning point, tempting him and his wife to make their first trip in January 1998. 'We had always been interested in beer but not Belgian beer,' he recalls, but Bruges won them over. 'Well, it was this cold, empty, beautiful place, with (this being Belgium) the Christmas decorations still up. It was just wonderful. And then we found Brugs Beertje which is the best bar in the world.' So entranced were they that they went back to Belgium for the next 13 Januarys in a row and he estimates that the trip from which he had just returned before our meeting was their 109th – an astonishing average of six trips a year.

At around the same time as Jeremy was discovering Bruges, Des was being bitten by the bug closer to home, up in the North West of England. 'It started for me at beer festivals in around 1999, probably at a CAMRA festival,' he recalls. 'I tasted Belgian beer and thought, "Oh, yes, I could get used to this!"' So enamoured is Des of Belgian beer almost two decades on that most people know him simply as @DeDolleDes – an online identity chosen in honour of his favourite brewery, 'The Mad Brewers' of Diksmuide. After taking his interest as far as possible at home he and his late wife started travelling to Belgium regularly, at first staying in hotels which they found expensive and exhausting.

Nowadays, sadly widowed, he explores in his very own motorhome – a piece of Belgium that is forever Greater Manchester. 'I go where I like,' he says. With an avuncular manner and a knack for remembering people he gives out samples of English beer, making friends along the way. He receives gifts in return that often end up in his private cellar of more than a thousand bottles. 'I like to share them with other people,' he says. 'Take a few along to tastings or festivals.' Dina, a fellow enthusiast based in Edinburgh, confirms this: 'He may not remember where he saw you last, or even your name, but he will remember exactly what kind of beer you discussed. He'll find the perfect bottle of it – the best year, best condition – and he'll make sure your glass is filled with it.'

Jeremy also has a substantial collection that started out on a shelf in a cupboard in his south London flat, then spread to fill the entire space, then the fireplace next to it, and now has a room to itself, decorated with Belgian breweriana. A precise, intellectual type, he has a programme of buying beer in bulk and maturing it systematically. 'I've had some great results already with ageing Lambic,' he says, growing animated at the thought. 'I've got bottles of De Dolle Stille Nacht going back to 1989 – just a few of those – and I'm now into buying huge quantities at a time to help with the project.'

These three are only a small part of a substantial number of British Belgophiles who got to know each other online in the pre-Twitter days of social media, as Jeremy recalls: 'A lot of this started with the Burgundian Babble Belt which was a classic old-school message board that started in about 2000 and had its heyday around 2006. Lots of people who are into Belgian beer used to hang out there, including Tim Webb from time to time.' The message board, according to the *Good Beer Guide Belgium*, is 'cliquey but never outfoxed'. Steve Hannigan, AKA @birkonian, recalled in an email how things developed from there:

> Gradually, our internet interactions became real friendships as we arranged to meet up at Beer Festivals in Belgium. You can still find a group of us from Britain, Belgium, Luxembourg, Denmark and U.S.A. huddled together.

When we asked Jeremy if he often ran into other British beer geeks on his travels in Belgium, he laughed: 'Oh, I'd be surprised *not* to meet people I know in Belgium. It happens more often than not. There are maybe 20 or 30 people I know who go regularly, five or six times a year, often around the same festivals and holidays so, yeah.' He reeled off a long list of their names, often paired in couples, as in the case of Simon and Jackie, who goes by the name 'Lambic Queen' online.

Steve Hannigan believes there is a three question test to identify a hardcore Belgian-beer geek:

> One, does Daisy Claeys, the legendary (recently retired) owner of t'Brugs Beertje bar in Bruges know your first name? Two, have you ever been on one of Podge's organised beer trips to Belgium? Three, have you been acknowledged in the Good Beer Guide Belgium by the author, Tim Webb?

('Podge', AKA Chris Pollard, was famous among enthusiasts thanks to guidebooks and guided tours on which he collaborates with Siobhan McGinn. He died in 2018.)

Jeremy is proud of his contributions to various editions of Tim Webb's book over the years: 'He would send me a list of leads and I'd go around checking out cafes for him, reporting back.'

We asked Tim Webb about this gang of disciples – what does he think drives them? 'These are people of immense good taste who in my experience are also attracted to the food, the museums of obscure subjects, the extraordinary range of small family-run hotels and the sheer bloody oddity of small-town Belgium', he told us in an email. Like Jeremy he cites the importance of the Brugs Beertje bar, declaring it ground zero of the Anglo-Belgian love affair, among other things:

> The [*Good Beer Guide Belgium* was invented [there] at about 03.00 on a Thursday or Friday morning… during the same conversation that created CAMRA's first publishing company and ordained the British Guild of Beer Writers. Not a bad night's work. I reckon it was October 1987.

But this 30 year period of back-and-forth may be about to change drastically. There was a note of anxiety in several of the conversations we had in early 2016, between the result of the EU Referendum and the formal declaration of the UK's intention to leave the EU under Article 50. Martin, not a man who revels in confrontation, described an incident during a recent by-election:

> I live in Stoke and this morning a UKIP canvasser knocked on my door: 'Will you be voting for our candidate?' I said, 'Well, I spend five weeks a year in Belgium and the Low Countries so… No.'

But he remains philosophical. After all, as he observes, 'The English beer scene is so good now.' He certainly has no plans to move to Belgium permanently.

Jeremy and his wife are similarly minded: 'Bruges is a little retreat for us – an escape. We drink and eat stupid amounts, and then we're glad to be home by the end. If we lived there it wouldn't be as much fun, not least because we'd have to navigate Belgian bureaucracy.' He does confess, however, to a compulsive habit of looking at houses on the Belgian property website *Immoweb*, indulging a daydream.

Panic on the streets of Woking

First published on our blog in 2017.

In 1988 the British government faced a now forgotten domestic crisis: previously placid towns, villages and suburbs up and down the country were suddenly awash with mob violence – the kind of thing people expected in forsaken inner cities, but which seemed newly terrifying as it spread to provincial market squares and high streets.

The police panicked, the public fretted, and politicians were pressed to take action.

What was causing this rash of insanity? Who or what was to blame for this descent into madness?

In September 1988 at an informal press briefing John Patten MP, Minister for Home Affairs, pointed the finger: the chaos was a result of what he called 'the Saturday night lager cult' and 'lager louts'.

Lager. Lager was to blame. A type of beer that had arrived in earnest in Britain only thirty years before as the upmarket, sophisticated, sharp-suited Continental cousin of the traditional pint of wallop.

Where did it all go wrong?

Lager was first brewed in Britain as far back as the 1830s and had its first boom in popularity, primarily as a hip, high-price imported product, from the 1860s until World War I. (See our e-book *Gambrinus Waltz* for more on that.) For the next 40 years or so it sat in the background, very much a minority interest, represented by imports from the Continent and the occasional attempt by British brewers such as Barclay Perkins. In the 1950s it had a less than two per cent share of the total UK beer market.

The 1950s were an unsettling time for British breweries. They could no longer rely on armies of industrial workers tramping to the pub on a regular basis to drink ale in substantial quantities. Young people seemed less interested in pubs and beer and drawn rather more to burger bars, coffee shops, Coca-Cola and pop music. Mild was definitely passé – a relic of the slum era – and though sales of bitter were surging, it too lacked glamour: bitter drinkers wore blazers and smoked pipes. The tiny handful of lager drinkers, on the other hand...

Lager was chic. Lager was beer's answer to Swedish cutlery, Danish chairs, and Italian scooters. There was no suggestion of soot or grit in lager, which spoke of clean living and the cool grey north of Europe. Lager was smart. And so were lager drinkers.

The problem for British brewers was that lager sophisticates, those who knew their stuff, were drinking imports. Ind Coope had a British lager in its roster, Graham's, but it was Carlsberg that had the credibility. In 1959, though, Graham's was relaunched and rebranded, as explained by Martyn Cornell in a 2012 blog post:

> Ind Coope... spent £1 million over four years from 1955 rebuilding its two lager plants, Arrol's in Alloa (which received a new Swedish-made brewery) and Wrexham in North Wales (acquired in 1949), and in 1959 it launched a new brand: Graham's Skol Lager... The 'Skol' part was supposed to be derived from the Danish/Norwegian/Swedish toast word 'skål', equivalent to 'cheers'... The 'Graham's' bit was soon sidelined, with 'Skol pilsner lager' being promoted in what Ind Coope called 'the biggest advertising campaign Britain has ever seen for any lager', which was deliberately pitched at young people in a way that would not be allowed today.

At around the same time Guinness was in the process of launching its own lager brand in Ireland. In a recollection published in *The Guinness Book of Guinness* in 1988, Guinness executive Arthur Hughes recalled that brewing in Ireland was always a test for roll-out into the UK market. And if Skol was brewed on Scandinavian kit, Guinness's new lager was to be brewed by an imported German, Hermann Münder, for reasons Hughes explains:

> No British lager had the cachet of Danish, German, Dutch or Czech lagers. We decided on Germany, as the ancient home of lager... S.H. Benson, our advertising agent, went to work and produced some thirty names and draft labels for some of them... I recall Atlas, Alpine, Alpha, Cresta, Dolphin and Lancer... None seemed to suit.

Eventually they settled on the name 'Harp' which referenced an image associated with Guinness but was distinctive enough to avoid confusion with the draught stout. No expense was spared in the equipping of the brewery, the marketing, or the distribution network, and it was an immediate success in Ireland. It was launched in England in 1961, in the North West exclusively at first, and soon other major British brewers, including Courage and Scottish & Newcastle, had bought into the brand as partners.

The third of the new national lager brands was a Canadian import, Carling Black Label, inserted forcefully into the UK market by entrepreneur Eddie Taylor. To push Carling he took over several British breweries until his firm, United Breweries, eventually became part of the colossus that was Bass Charrington.

By 1967 those three – Skol, Harp and Bass (Carling/Tennents) – had the bulk of the rapidly swelling UK lager market carved up between them.

You might think this is when lager started to lose its cool or slide downmarket but apparently not. It remained about as expensive as in its import-only days and retained an air of Continental exclusivity, despite domestic mass production. But perhaps this was an illusion, the damage already done below the waterline. Writing in *The Times* on 9 December 1967, John Graham suggested that publicans were maintaining the premium because they enjoyed 'fantastic margins'. A bottle of Harp, Graham said, cost about the same for a publican to buy as bottled bitter but sold in the lounge bar for almost twice the price.

In the following decade, though lager's share of the market continued to rise (4 per cent in 1968, 10 per cent in 1971, 20 per cent by 1975), competition grew with it. More brands emerged – genuine imports, foreign brands brewed under licence in the UK (Carlsberg, Holsten), and home-grown 'faux' lagers such as Greenall Whitley's Grünhalle.

Draught lager became more common after 1966. Harp was supplied in bulk to regional brewers who packaged it on their own lines, increasing its reach but surely diminishing its stature, and perhaps its quality.

At the same time lager's image began to change in line with a general cultural shift which saw the first wave of 'new man'-ism – only subtly sexist, and knowing his way round an omelette pan – give way to the hairy-chested, unrepentant machismo of the 1970s. Instead of the Scandinavia of walnut coffee tables and Ibsen, lager adopted Viking imagery — Hagar the Horrible for Skol, Norseman from Vaux.

As Edward Guinness put it in The Guinness Book of Guinness...

> [Lager] became a man's drink; in the words of one observer, 'the 'cissy' connotations of lager became a thing of the past'... For, almost overnight, it became possible for the customer to order a pint, which was always cooled, rather than fiddle around with half-pint bottles, which invariably were not.

And the Australians arrived, too. Foster's Lager was an import brand throughout the 1970s associated in British eyes with a particular kind of larrikin stereotype. When Barry McKenzie arrived in London with his aunt Edna Everage in the 1972 film *The Amazing Adventures of Barry McKenzie*, he brought with him a suitcase loaded with cans of lager. A 1975 episode of gritty crime drama *The Sweeney* starred Patrick Mower and George Layton as two Australian armed robbers who swig Foster's throughout the episode in lieu of convincing accents. And when Watney's launched UK-brewed draught Foster's in 1982, the attendant advertising campaign was fronted by comedian Paul Hogan, swaggering and frank, in T-shirt and jeans — the ultimate Australian male. The message by now was explicit: lager was unpretentious, laddish, good fun.

But perhaps it was also more (or less) than that, because the word 'lager' had begun to crop up in a certain type of news story, like this from the *Guardian* for 11 May 1984:

> John Foreman is a postman and, on the face of it, not much to write home about. He is light, slight, with neat blond hair and a downy moustache. He seems meek — and each Saturday afternoon on the streets of some football town, he inherits the earth... In his terrace tribe there is a ritual and a sort of code. Each 'good day out' follows a similar pattern; invariably the violence is fuelled by a mixture of lager and cider. Fist fights are acceptable, knife fights are not.

A similar pen portrait from *The Times* for 22 July 1981, of an 18-year-old east London skinhead called John O'Leary, mentions his habit of drinking lager from the can in the very first line. When

England football fans returned home after an outbreak of violence at a match in Copenhagen in September 1982 journalists felt the need to mention that they arrived at Heathrow 'drinking lager from cans'. Lager's symbolism had become potent, the mere word a shortcut for a certain type of troubled, troublesome youth.

But that was just the beginning of lager's growing image problem.

One night in March 1987, it kicked off in Witney. A small town in Oxfordshire with a population then of c.18,000, it was the unlikely setting for a battle between 70 drunk youths and police. This, by some people's reckoning, was among the first incidents in what came to be regarded as a wave of 'rural violence' that seized headlines in the following years.

It just so happened that the Member of Parliament for Witney was the Home Secretary, Douglas Hurd. That perhaps meant that he was paying particular attention when similar violence fired up in places like Gloucester, Milton Keynes, Berwick-upon-Tweed, High Wycombe, and Lincoln where 170 young people rioted in November that year. And on New Year's Eve 1987, the Lincoln mob did it again, this time 300-strong, smashing windows and looting as they went.

Television presenter Robert Kilroy-Silk, formerly a Labour MP on Merseyside, captured the hysteria when in August 1987 he wrote a rather hysterical op-ed for *The Times* entitled 'Riots That Go Unremarked':

> Let us be clear what we are referring to. We're talking about gangs of hundreds of drunken white youths, often wielding knives and machetes, rampaging through otherwise peaceful towns and deliberately seeking battle with the police.

In 1988 the problem only seemed to escalate and the baiting and assault of police officers attending such incidents apparently intensified, as reported by David Leppard in the *Sunday Times* on 27 March that year.

In January, Leppard wrote, PC Paul Seymour was attending an incident in the village of Kingfield near Woking at 11:45pm on he was set upon by a pack of 30 teenagers. His commanding officer heard his screams over the radio. Seymour survived, just, and was awarded a special commendation. Leppard also told the story of 26-year-old WPC Elain Gostelow who was repeatedly kicked in the face and had her hands crushed as she attempted to help a fellow officer outside a pub in the village of Somercotes, Derbyshire. She was permanently disabled in the attack and had to leave the police force.

The police, understandably, did not like this trend, and so the Association of Chief Police Officers (ACPO) commissioned a report which they summarised in a press release in June 1988. It contained some scary statistics: more than 2,000 people had been arrested in 250 separate 'serious public order disturbances' in the preceding year. The anecdotal evidence was scarier still, as in this piece from the *Guardian* for 10 June 1988:

> One of the most ferocious incidents occurred in Crowborough, East Sussex, last weekend. More than 100 youths rioted after police tried to close a wine bar... Youths began pelting police with beer glasses while chanting 'Kill the Bill'. One officer was pushed through a shop window cutting both tendons in his right wrist.

The ACPO report itself wasn't made public – they thought a list of towns where violence was a regular occurrence and where the police were struggling might act as a kind of catalogue for mobile yobs – so we can't know if it mentioned lager. Certainly the attendant newspaper coverage based on the press release does not seem to have flagged lager as a particular problem, and wine, as in wine bars, got mentioned more and more often.

In the months that followed, though, the phrase 'lager lout' began to crop up frequently in quotes from senior police officers and politicians. With its alliterative lilt it had a certain snappy quoteability that rendered its accuracy irrelevant. Where did it come from?

It almost appeared in print in a strange centre-spread feature in *What's Brewing*, the monthly newspaper of the Campaign for Real Ale (CAMRA), in December 1987. It was credited to 'Chris Thompson', actually a pseudonym for left-wing activist and pub designer George Williamson. The article amounts to a manifesto in the Travis Bickle mode. In a section entitled 'Chasing the sloanes and clones' he wrote:

> It is the image of lager, exuding its message, 'Stay young; stay with the herd', which is so malign. It is the content

and colour of the product which allows it to be used this way – uniformly banal in taste and texture, and brewed as a lowest common denominator mass product. But then herds are all given the same feed... When the lager lad says that beer is an old man's drink, the reply is to ask if they have ever thought of growing up? ... Lager is a candle to the moth for these people. It lubricates the louts as they lurch to the football terraces...

Lager lads, who are louts – so close. This, at any rate, is probably the ultimate source of the phrase as it began to appear during 1988. (John Patten, the Home Office minister, was known to be a real ale drinker, and probably read *What's Brewing*.)

What did people think a 'lager lout' was in 1988? The ACPO report suggested that the majority of the troublemakers were not poor, unemployed or socially excluded, but white, well-off and in work. Douglas Hurd, the Home Secretary, called them 'young people with too much money in their pockets, too many pints inside them, but too little self-discipline'. And in a parliamentary debate in November 1988 Robin Corbett, MP for Birmingham Erdington, described them as 'loadsamoney lager louts'.

Loadsamoney was a character played by comedian and impressionist Harry Enfield and written by Paul Whitehouse and Charlie Higson. It was the breakout hit from *Saturday Live*, the UK's own short-lived answer to *Saturday Night Live*. It was a parody (rather snobbish with hindsight) of the vulgar nouveau riche – a charmless working class man with little education, no manners, and the frightfully vulgar habit of mentioning how much he had earned through the dreadfully menial business of painting and decorating. (It's worth noting that Whitehouse and Higson had themselves worked as painters and decorators, though.) What the character captured most accurately was the class confusion of the time, which saw money and purchasing habits cease to be reliable barometers of social class. As one contemporary commentator put it, 'all the surface indicators have gone to hell'.

By October 1988 suited officer workers in the City of London were also being described as 'lager louts', accused of terrorising fellow commuters at Liverpool Street Station. The perception that middle and even upper class youths were forgetting their manners under the influence of lager seems to have been particularly alarming, suggesting perhaps that the inner-city rot was spreading not only outwards but also upwards through the very timbers of the social order.

The Government had to do something, or at least be seen to do something, so it commissioned Mary Tuck of the Home Office Research and Planning Unit to conduct an investigation into 'rural violence'. She and her team chose three areas identified by the ACPO as being particularly prone to post-pub violence, and then for each one a control area of similar profile but where no such trouble had been reported. Then they went out on the streets to observe what was really going on.

Like the Mass Observation team in Bolton 50 years earlier they must have stood out. Though the report is dry there is one brief telling moment when the fieldworkers report being heckled by drunks: 'One little group of five males... made fun of everyone walking past, including us, calling one of us "Jeremy"!' Elsewhere they describe, in cold officialese, running away from trouble and hiding in their parked car.

Nonetheless, they did often get stuck in, and what they reported rings true to anyone who has been out town centre drinking in Britain. They saw groups of young people (very young, often underage) getting drunk (eight or more pints in a session starting at around 9pm) in pubs with loud music. The youths they observed got hyped in each other's company before being suddenly turfed out of the pubs at bang on 11pm, made all the more angry by the rudeness of their ejection. They then hung about in large groups in the street or in and around late night take away restaurants, too excited to go home, but with nothing particular to do. They flirted, squared off, shouted and sang. It did not always turn violent. In the troubled towns, though, it did sometimes escalate:

> At 12.15 am there was a loud noise and shouting coming from the Hamlet Road direction, and people ran from the Chinese towards the noise... As we rounded the corner into Hamlet Road we were confronted with a group of approximately 200 people moving towards us... The group walked up to the Chinese take-away and re-gathered outside the Job Centre. At this point the large police van arrived... The mass divided into smaller group and some made their way home. Two remaining large groups were herded towards the Wimpy and the Pightle, with one

police officer on each side of the road, walking slowly behind them. This took another 15 minutes, and involved a lot of jeering and baiting of the police officers.

The arrival of the police, the observers noted, was sometimes greeted with cheers from crowds simply excited that something was happening.

They also interviewed young men actively involved in street disorder, some on the street at night, and others in their homes later on. They found that most of them did have jobs but only (this sounds rather snooty) 'of a very basic kind – postman, caretaker, labourer, forecourt attendant'. They tended to feel hopeless and take a short term view, daydreaming about great wealth and idolising or envying public figures who were seen to be successful:

> Prince Charles (attractive wife, lots of money), Don Johnson (star of Miami Vice, cars, pretty girls, expensive clothes, money), Rod Stewart and Peter Stringfellow (for the same reasons).

A second group of youths — those who stood around adding bulk to the intimidating mobs but simply watching while their harder peers actually put the boot in — were quite different: smarter, more articulate, actively pursuing careers, and sometimes even public school educated.

Though the report was sensible and far from fearmongering it made clear that the problem was real and that something worrying was going on Britain's towns on Friday and Saturday nights.

What was really happening, we can see from 30 years on, is that a whole lot of unconnected social problems, most of which had nothing in particular to do with lager, were being lumped together.

One so-called 'lager lout' riot, for example, actually involved 600 middle-aged line dancers scrapping with local gypsies in the foyer of a village hall. Others were the kind of town centre scuffles that have been happening since long before lager came on the scene, and will probably continue for as long as young men get bored, drunk and randy. It's hard not to think that it simply suited police authorities, lobbying for funding increases and greater power, to present all this as a surging, terrifying trend.

And of course others with their own agendas leapt on the bandwagon. Anti-drink campaigners, for example, saw an opportunity to protest newly extended pub opening hours, to call for tighter restrictions on pubs, and to argue for regulation of alcohol advertising.

The Campaign for Real Ale, of course, had a field day. For some time it had been re-orienting its guns from keg bitter, the great scourge of the 1970s, towards lager, and in an article for *What's Brewing* in December 1988, activist Tony Millns gloated over lager's new image problem:

> *Blitz* magazine, the stylesheet for the image-conscious, summed up the reversal: 'Lager is the official drink of Yob Britain'... The hype which has promoted Britain's lager boom now looks to have boomeranged on the brewers... Suddenly, order a pint of lager and you're socially badged as a lager lout, not as a trendy style-setter... The anti-lager PR campaign is being managed, free of charge, by CAMRA, by Home Office Ministers, the media, and Crown Court judges.

Andrea Gillies, the new bright young editor of Campaign's annual *Good Beer Guide*, spoke yet more harshly of lager brewers at the launch of the 1989 edition of the book, as quoted in the *Guardian* for 25 October 1988:

> They must take a lot of blame for the promotion of lager and its violent consequences... My argument is not with lager itself, but with the big boys who are marketing ruthlessly to the wrong people... You can make even more [money] if you convince boys that drinking 10 pints makes them even more macho, but this results in the violence we have seen in the shires.

Rob Walker, CAMRA chair from 1988 to 1989, reflecting on this time told us in an email that

> the lager lout phenomenon did, over time, work in CAMRA's favour in that it provided an opportunity for us to make a clear distinction between the discerning cask ale

drinker in the pub environment versus the loutish 'down-market' behaviour of those fuelled by strong, cheap lagers.

In the long-term this opportunism probably did CAMRA more harm than good, making it seem snobbish and puritanical, and perhaps alienating those who enjoyed lager and ale.

But this moment passed. Woking, one of the towns worst hit by town centre mass scrapping during 1987, declared the problem solved in early 1989. Lager retreated from the scary pint and back into its dainty bottles, re-emerging as designer lager, boutique lager, even craft lager. Tarnished, sure, and Skol and Harp were to all intents and purposes dead brands in the UK, but the once Canadian Carling reinvented itself as a solidly British standard, while Stella Artois surged with adverts that resembled French films, reassuringly expensive once again. (Well, for a few more years at least.)

The hysteria in the papers died down and the police moved on to fretting over ecstasy and illegal raves, and then alco-pops, and then happy-slapping and then...

None of this was really lager's fault – it just happened to be the drink of the day. Although perhaps it was, and is, just a touch too easy to drink – crisp, sparkling, cool, light on the palate. The most eight-pintable of all beer styles.

Reflecting on moral panics and the need for scapegoats in government and the media as we worked on this piece we got an uneasy feeling. Surely craft beer will get its turn in the doghouse, won't it? There is, after all, a cycle new beer styles or market segments seem to go through:

Upmarket, exclusive
Mass-market, everyman's
Down-market, cheap

(Further reading: Pete Brown is particularly brilliant on this subject, with Stella Artois as his case study, in 2003's *Man Walks into a Pub*.)

Craft beer is currently in the process of moving from the first stage to the second, from specialist bars to mass-market venues, from boutiques to supermarkets. Punk IPA is a 5.6% ABV beer marketed more or less explicitly at young people. It is available in high-street

Tesco mini-marts for less than £2 a bottle, and in Wetherspoon's for not much more. We keep seeing empty BrewDog bottles lying in the street on Sunday mornings, or among the lager tins in the park — a sure sign, we think, that the drift has begun.

We're not saying that's a bad thing — again, remember, lager didn't really do anything wrong. It's just that it's only a matter of time before someone works out an alliterative name for mischievous young people who prefer India pale ale to lager and, when they do, the panic will begin all over again.

Swanky beer: a lost Cornish style?

First published in Beer Advocate *magazine in 2015.*

Cornwall is officially a county of England but, jutting out into the Atlantic in the far west of the Britain, sparse and windswept, it feels every bit the Celtic nation in its own right.

When we moved to Penzance in 2011, we began researching indigenous beer styles straightaway. Devon, Cornwall's nearest English neighbour, has its legend of White Ale, and we hoped to discover something similarly exotic. Naturally, mentions of a mysterious brew known as 'swanky' among lists of Cornish recipes online, generated considerable excitement.

One particular set of instructions is repeated in various corners of the internet, usually verbatim, without any original source. The earliest version, posted on *RootsWeb* by someone called Jan Gluyas in May 1997, calls for boiling four pounds of brown sugar in five gallons of water for 45 minutes with hops, ground ginger, raisins and salt. It is to be fermented for around two days and then bottled with a single raisin in each bottle for priming.

It's ready to drink 'when the head is about to force the cork out of the bottle,' explains Gluyas. The recipe text also states that Swanky was 'always made by the Cornish about six weeks before Xmas.'

The only problem about discovering the kind of 'beer from a place' we were looking for: no one in Cornwall seems to have heard of it.

Nineteenth century Cornish dialect dictionaries lack a single mention of Swanky, and no Cornish language word or phrase seems to relate to it. Swanky does not appear in any of the numerous written histories of Cornish culture. Nothing with a name even similar to Swanky is listed in a handwritten collection of 17th and 18th century Cornish recipes held at the Morrab Library's archive in Penzance, though it does contain instructions for two varieties of wine made with raisins. Nor is Swanky included among the alcoholic beverages like Metheglin (spiced mead) and Mahogany (gin beaten with treacle, or molasses) found in the book *Cornish Recipes* published by the Women's Institute of Cornwall in 1930. Questions put to local historians and archivists were met with blank looks and variations of, 'It doesn't ring any bells.'

So, where did the name come from? The etymology of the English word swanky, meaning expensive or ostentatious, is obscure and seemingly at odds with its use in the 19th Century, in parts of the country other than Cornwall, to refer to poor quality small beer. Perhaps there is a connection with the words for 'weak' in Danish, Dutch and German—respectively, svag, zwak and schwach—which might also explain how an obscure American style, Pennsylvania swankey, another small beer, got its name.

The answer to how the word swanky came to be connected with Cornish culture, meanwhile, can be found on the far side of the world, in Australia. From around the end of the Napoleonic wars until the turn of the 20th Century hundreds of thousands of Cornish people set out to find their fortune, most often as miners and engineers. They took soccer to Mexico and pasties — savoury pastries stuffed with vegetables and meat—to Michigan. In Australia, they built entire villages of Cornish-style cottages, with pubs named The Ancient Briton, the Redruth Arms, and so on. Slowly, though, evidence of this and other distinct migrant cultures began to fade as a new Australian national identity was forged.

In the period after World War II, however, many Australians became interested in rediscovering their roots. One nostalgic 1945 newspaper column from the *Kadina and Wallaroo Times* mentions Swanky as a lost pre-war Christmas tradition, calling it 'the real spirit of the people' which 'used to take pride of place in the homes.' 'It was often heard going off "pop,"' the paper observed, as the corks 'flew off up the chimney.'

The best-known account of Swanky is a passage in Oswald Pryor's tremendously popular 1962 book *Australia's Little Cornwall*. In it, the then 81-year-old author and cartoonist recalled life in the migrant Cornish communities of South Australia around the turn of the 20th century, including passing mentions for some of the recipes prepared by Cousin Jenny (the name given to Cornish migrant women) in their cottage kitchens:

> Swanky was a brew of sugar, hops, ginger, wheat, malt, and yeast. It had to be allowed to work for three days in the bottles before the corks were tied down with string.

Pryor also notes that it was popular with teetotalist religious groups who 'believed—or made a pretence of believing—that it was non-intoxicating.'

Whether the recipe he describes definitely came to South Australia with Cornish migrants is unclear. It is somewhat different to Gluyas's recipe in that it includes grains, where hers is all sugar. At any rate, whatever its origins, for a generation of Australians of Cornish heritage, Pryor's publication became a kind of handbook for the reconstruction of something they had lost. Though he did not claim it was Cornish, only that Cornish-Australians brewed it, Swanky was seized upon and made, in effect, the national drink of the Copper Coast.

In 1973, a great festival of Cornish culture was held for the first time on the Yorke Peninsula under the Cornish-language name *Kernewek Lowender*. Brass bands played traditional Cornish tunes, people ate Cornish pasties by the ton, and, to wash them down, Cooper's Brewery supplied a thousand bottles of Swanky beer.

Roslyn Paterson was on the organizing committee and recalls that they gave the Adelaide brewing company a handwritten recipe for the kind of beer enjoyed by her great-great-grandfather. It called for rainwater, hops, sugar and a handful of raisins in each bottle. Cooper's didn't want to use raisins and, instead, 'grogged' a more standard ale with port and added a label featuring an iconic Oswald Pryor portrait of Cousin Jack, a stereotypical Cornish miner.

'The resultant drink had a kick like a mule,' remembers Ms. Paterson. Cooper's, Roslyn Paterson says, eventually refused to brew it again because the port had contaminated their fermenting vessels, and the batches were too small. Various breweries have since been commissioned to fill the void. Most recently, Copper Coast Wines of Moonta Bay, a side project of local businessman Richard Davis, has taken up the mantle, occasionally brewing a fairly mainstream (malt and hops) version of Swanky and selling it at the Patio Restaurant in Moonta Bay.

We created our own recipe for swanky by comparing ingredient lists from Jan Gluyas, Roslyn Paterson and Oswald Pryor, omitting anything that did not appear in more than one list. That meant leaving out malt, wheat and salt, and using only sugar, ginger, raisins and hops. We decided on white sugar because, though brown sugar might seem more rustically authentic, refined white 'loaf sugar' was actually the most commonly available variety in the 19th Century. Various country beer and wine recipes in archival recipe books helped us come up with the method.

This a homebrew in the true sense of the word, so don't get worked up about temperatures, equipment, specific ingredients, or process—imagine yourself thousands of miles from home and improvise with what you have at hand. The batch we brewed on Saint Piran's Day, the national day of Cornwall, was ready to drink less than a week later and sat somewhere between true beer and a soft drink: fizzy and refreshing, with a powerful herbal dryness from the hops which set it apart from straight-up ginger beer. It was perhaps a touch bitter. Next time we'll use 60 grams (about 2 oz) of hops. It won't keep long, so if you brew some, have a party.

- 2.5 gallons (11 litres) water
- 2 lb (1 kilo) white sugar
- 4 oz (100 g) ground ginger
- 2 oz (60 g) raisins
- 4 oz (100 g) old hops (such as East Kent Goldings)
- 2 oz (60 g) fresh baker's yeast

Boil everything together for 45 minutes. Allow it to cool completely before transferring to a fermenting vessel and adding the yeast. After about 48 hours, decant into 750ml Champagne-style bottles, add a bruised raisin to each, and, using standard corks, seal loosely. After a few days, the corks will begin to work loose, at which point, it's ready to drink.

The quiet one

First published on our blog in 2015.

Peter Elvin isn't a rock star brewer. He doesn't stand up on countertops and give talks so that people can 'engage with his brand' and he isn't likely to have his own cable TV series any time soon.

You might not even spot him in his own pub, the Star Inn at Crowlas, in the far west of Cornwall – he does not hold court. You won't find him behind the bar much these days but he can sometimes be seen shuffling in through the door behind the counter, in well-worn polo shirt and Crocs, from where he slips quietly onto a stool at the end of bar, or makes conversation with a few regulars in a corner, a half-smile under his drooping white moustache. Unless he's talking directly to you, you won't hear what he's saying: he is, as the cliché goes, a man of few words, and those words are spoken softly when they come.

We've been admirers of the Penzance Brewing Co. beer at the Star for years but have only spoken to Mr Elvin on a couple of occasions. Once, in around 2013 we had a brief chat about the hop shortage. Then, a year or so later, we caught him in animated mood during Penzance's yearly vintage bus weekend when hordes of real-ale-drinking public-transport-spotters from the Midlands make the pub their home. He spoke then with quiet enthusiasm about the suspension systems of heavy vehicles, which was rather lost on us.

The lack of desire to stand in the spotlight is, we think, exactly what makes him interesting: he is to some extent representative of the vast majority of the almost 1,500 brewers in Britain today who rarely get interviewed or profiled. Though they might like to sell a bit more beer, they can't quite be bothered, or lack the ego, to elbow their way into the conversation. They are interested in pipework, the cell counts of yeast, and fermentation temperatures – not the stuff of which soundbites are made.

A couple of times we've pitched a somewhat 'high concept' article about these low-profile brewers to magazines under the title 'The Quiet Ones' but editors ask, quite naturally, 'What's the story?' But the story is that there isn't one: Peter Elvin didn't get there first, he isn't doing anything 'innovative', and he hasn't got (or concocted) a dramatic origin story. He's a relatively contented bloke with a talent for brewing decent beer and just gets on with it.

Actually, that's not fair.

Mr Elvin's beers, as regular readers of this blog will be tired of hearing, are, at their best, not only faint-praiseworthy – 'decent for a regional microbrewery' – but just as boldly, brightly, expressively hoppy as anything from hipper breweries such as Thornbridge or Magic Rock. And he has worked hard – perhaps harder than many of his peers – to get where he is today, which is highly-regarded by local beer geeks, by other brewers and, perhaps most impressively, by regular pub-goers in the village where his brewery is based.

The interview that follows was edited together from transcripts of two sessions on consecutive days at the Star Inn. The first time, Mr Elvin leaned on the back of a chair for 30 minutes, not quite committing to the conversation, somewhat self-conscious. The next day, we had a more in-depth, longer discussion. He arrived for that meeting straight from the nearby semi-derelict house he is renovating – himself, that is, with hammer and nails in hand, not supervising hired builders. He bought us drinks, and made himself a big mug of tea, and we sat in the pub's relatively quiet lounge.

He is a practitioner of what you might call Cornish Polite, a habit similar to Minnesota Nice, with a dose of the 'So Very British' tendency. At no point did he raise his voice above a warm, softly-accented murmur (beers aren't hoppy, they're 'oppy) but we could tell from the raising of his eyebrows and a suppressed grumble here and there that a couple of our questions struck him as odd, daft, or perhaps even a touch annoying.

First, can you give us the basics: when and where were you born, and what's your background?
Oh, uh, now... When was I born?

[Scratches head]

Er... 1958, on Scilly. St Mary. I grew up there, joined the Merchant Navy in 1979, mostly round northern Europe, then went back for a year-and-a-half on the pleasure boats. But it was sort of... claustrophobic. I'd had too much freedom, I suppose. So I left again went up to Budeleigh in Worcestershire.

Why?
Well… Chasing after a woman.

You'd be surprised how often that's what people say when we interview them.
I did all sorts up there – building work, lorry driving.

So when did you make the move into brewing?
I'd always home-brewed for, well, as long as I can remember, really. From kits, 'cos on Scilly, you're limited with what you can get. I moved to Wiveliscombe in Somerset in 1983 – I bought a knackered old house that needed doing up, totally rebuilding. I was still lorry driving and I needed more money and more time. My next door neighbour at the time was working for Exmoor Brewery and I thought, yeah, that sounds good, so I got a job at Cotleigh Brewery. I did deliveries, barrel washing, and had more time to work on my house. But I was watching… I could see straightaway that things weren't right.

How so?
Just… [Squirms] General inconsistency. One batch wasn't the same as the next. It was hit and miss. I'm not technical or academic, whatever you want to call it, but whatever I'm doing, I am a practical sort of person. Whether it's mixing cement or putting up a roof or brewing, I want it to be consistent, and done proper. I'm a do-er. So I got some books out of the library, read up on a few things, and within three months, I'd taken over the brewing. And I just absolutely loved it. It was a lucky accident, I suppose you'd call it. I upgraded the brewery twice, moved it down the hill – when I first came in, it was up at the old Hancock's brewery, with Exmoor in the old Hancock's loading bay. Then we moved to an old Dutch barn. I basically built that, too.

And how did you start to really get into hops? Was that at Cotleigh?
That was where I first realised that I'd always drunk real ale. I was never a CAMRA type of person but I'd always drunk real ale, never lager, never anything fizzy. In the Merchant Navy, I hardly ever went ashore, but if I did and all they had was lager, I didn't bother. On the ships it was something like Tennent's Export in cans and I've never been one for drinking whatever's there for the sake of it. I'd rather have a mug of tea. So I hardly drank at all at sea. At Cotleigh, we

always used English hops – East Kent Goldings, Fuggles, bit of Northdown occasionally. In the eighties, it was all the Hop Marketing Board – you used what they promoted and what you could get. And I don't mind English hops – there's Fuggles in Number 9. [Potion 9, his signature pale'n'hoppy session ale.] But then, in the early 1990s, mid-90s, we started to do some single-hop beers with American hops – one-offs so it didn't matter if you couldn't get a regular supply. Guest beers. But to be honest with you, I always find single-hop beers a bit boring.

Going back to Cotleigh – why did you leave?
I'd split up with my wife but didn't want to move away while the kids were at school so I stayed there from 1983 to 1999, until they went to uni or whatever. By the end, though, I'd taken it as far as it could go, and it was getting to the point where the brewery needed another upgrade. The fun had gone out of it, I suppose.

So then you came back to Cornwall?
I had no ties in Somerset and I wanted to be nearer home, near the Old Man. I bought this place with brewing in mind — I never wanted to run a pub. I always had my eye on the outbuildings, not this. [Gestures around the bar.] I'm a do-er, not a seller – I've never been a pushy person. I wanted a place in Falmouth but this came up first, and we came in 1999. It was an old Courage pub that Usher's had taken on and it had had sixteen tenants in nine years. People had come in, taken the free six month's rent, then gone, and they hadn't done any work on the place at all because they weren't staying. No-one had done anything so it was in total disrepair.

Another old wreck for you to fix up?
Yeah! Time and money again. We had to get it trading straight away because we needed the money. I spent all my time and money getting it straight, and buying bits of brewing kit when I could afford it. I didn't want to start brewing on rented kit. Me and Tracey [his partner] spent three years running a kitchen until I got the accounts early one year and looked at it and thought, 'I can't see my making anything out of this.' We were working our asses off but getting nothing out of it. I enjoyed being a landlord. Yeah, I quite enjoyed it, even though it wasn't what I wanted to be doing.

Some people are naturals at dealing with people every night, being sociable…
I did find it very tiring. I wanted to brew which I eventually did start in 2008. That's a totally different ball game. I'm normally out there at five in the morning, a few nice hours on my own. People come out sometimes during the day, stick their head round the door, give you feedback, tell you how great the beer is, and that's nice.

Some small breweries are in an old barn next to a pile of manure… Yours, from what we've seen, is always spotless, which perhaps makes the difference in the quality of your beer?

[Bemused.]

It's not that clean. It needs dusting. I need to find someone who's really passionate about cleaning. But it ain't rocket science, is it? You clean it the minute you've finished brewing, hose it down, lock the door. I bought two fermenters from another brewery and they'd obviously never been inside 'em the whole time they had them because the pen marks from the bloke who made them were still on the inside. Dirty bastards. And it's the same with casks – people sanitise inside but then the outside is covered in mud and shit and spiders. I won't rack into something like that, dropping mud and shit all over the other casks, all over the cellar. It takes five minutes to clean the outside. That's why I don't dry hop: why take all that care and then bung in a hand of dirty hops covered in bird shit and god knows what?

How did you develop the pale hoppy beers like Potion and Trink that you're known for?
I didn't really know anything about hops when I came here but I knew what I wanted – that grapefruit taste. So I read a few things and tried brewing with some of the varieties of hops that are meant to give you grapefruit and… nothing. Right, fine. So then I started trying others in different combinations, and discovered that Amarillo and Chinook gave me what I wanted.

The first time we spoke to you a few years ago you were a bit stressed because you couldn't get hold of Amarillo.
Back then, I didn't know enough about hops to cope with the shortage. I'd got this recipe and I liked it and everyone was happy and then,

suddenly, I didn't have what I needed to make it. I managed to experiment and find a couple of other hops that I could substitute, sort of bodge it, that got close and that's what I'm still using today. Now, I used a blend of different hops in all my beers so that, if one of them disappears, it's less important. I try to keep a stock in so that I can phase a hop out over ten or fourteen brews, too, so it's not so jarring. But Trink is predominantly Citra, and there ain't no Citra, so that's on the way out.

We're big fans of your beer, as you know, but especially when we drink it here. We've had it Falmouth, or even just across the way in Goldsithney [the next village over] and it hasn't tasted quite as good.

[Shakes head.]

Can't see why. Shouldn't be a problem.

Well, we've wondered if it's that, here, you fuss over the cellar, and you're on hand to see and taste the beer.

I wouldn't say I was a control freak but here, yeah, I am in full control. I have pulled my beer from a few pubs when I've heard they're not looking after it, or not getting through it quickly enough. Scilly Stout will just keep getting better the longer you hang on to it but Number 9 or the other fresh, hoppy beers have got to be drunk. They can't be sitting around. I don't care what people think, really, but if I'm putting out a beer with a specific name, I want it to be the same beer every time people drink it. But then I know pubs up north where they sell my beer, and festivals, and there's never any problem with it at all.

Is it true that when you go back to Scilly on holiday you send your own beer over beforehand so it will be ready to drink when you arrive?

[Sighs.]

I did that *once*. The pubs over there are alright but I get fed up of Doom Bar and Tribute and the brewery over there's OK too but... I only did it once!

Finally, this is a question we always ask: are there any particular beers you've found especially inspiring?

[Shrugs, bemused at the question.]

Not really.

Well, are there any desert island beers – things you really admire?

[Still bemused.]

St Austell Proper Job is a good reliable thing if I'm out in town. And Roger [Ryman, St Austell head brewer] is a good lad – he's given me lots of technical advice over the years. Bottled beers... It would have to be Sierra Nevada Pale Ale, I suppose. That's a lovely beer.

[Long pause.]

Well, that's about it—

[Sigh of relief.]

Good. Do you want another drink? Crows-an-Wra's just come on.

* * *

As our second conversation wrapped up Ray pulled out a camera and asked Mr Elvin if we could take some photos. He said yes but (Cornish polite again) really meant no, and so we got nothing useable before he slipped out and headed back up the hill to continue his building work. A quiet man he may be, happier in the peace and quiet of one type of workshop or another, but the two glasses of gloriously hoppy, golden ale with which he left us made us say, once again, 'Wow!'

Newquay Steam: Cornwall's own beer

First published on our blog in 2013.

In 1987, a pub-owning entrepreneur looked at British brewing and decided it wasn't working.

Stylishly packaged ranges of bottled beers trumpeting their purity and quality are easy to find these days. Back in 1987, though, bottled beer meant, in most cases, brown or light ale gathering dust on shelves behind the bar in pubs, with labels that appeared to have been designed before World War II. If you wanted to know their ingredients, or their alcoholic strength, tough luck, because the breweries didn't want to tell you.

A cult beer from Cornwall would play a major role in changing that scene.

Having weathered the brewery takeover mania of the nineteen-sixties and seventies, West Country family brewery Devenish was a strong presence in the region, with more than 300 pubs from Wiltshire to Penwith.

It was also a household name, at least amongst anyone who had ever taken a seaside holiday in Dorset, Devon or Cornwall. Nonetheless, in 1986, the company was struggling. They had been forced to close their brewery in Weymouth, Dorset, late in 1985, thereafter concentrating operations in Redruth, Cornwall. At the same time, they had also closed fifteen pubs. Profits continued to tumble.

Depending on how you look at it, Devenish was either in need of rescue, or vulnerable to predators.

Michael Cannon was born in Bedminster, Bristol, in 1939, and left school in the 1950s (according to most accounts) 'barely able to read and write'. He worked as a poultry farmer in Avonmouth before entering the hospitality industry as a chef with the Berni Inn chain. Then, in 1975, he bought a stake in a pub in the centre of Bristol – the Navy Volunteer – and began his ascent to the rich lists. By 1986, he was the boss of Inn Leisure, which owned around 40 pubs in Bristol and surrounding areas.

Cannon saw in the struggling Devenish, and especially their large estate of West Country pubs, a perfect opportunity. In February 1986, Inn Leisure and Devenish 'merged'. Cannon's company put

£35m into Devenish to secure a controlling share, with the support of Whitbread's investment arm. After some initial confusion, it became apparent to most people that this was a takeover by the smaller operation which, in one swoop, took the total number of pubs under Cannon's control to almost 400.

People who worked with Cannon talk about him being 'a dynamo', 'dynamic and intense', and he has described himself as having a 'low boredom threshold'. Journalists call him 'colourful'. Looked at as a whole, his career in pubs and brewing suggests a complete focus on achieving profit, without the slightest sentimentality. Newspaper headlines, perhaps inevitably, tend to refer to Cannon Fodder or Cannon Fire.

On taking over Devenish, he set about rejuvenating the company with vigour. First, he evicted many sitting pub tenants, feeling that they were paying too little rent, and replaced them with his own managers. Then, in July 1986, news came of the resignation of board member Bill Ludlow, a member of the former controlling family, in the wake of a 'clash over policy'.

Having asserted his dominance, Cannon also set about revamping the uninspiring range of rather too-similar, middle-of-the-road beers produced by Devenish. Cornish Best and Wessex Best, both the same strength, were made weaker and stronger respectively, while the latter was given a saucy new name: Wessex Stud. It was joined by a much bigger beer called Great British Heavy. West Country branches of the Campaign for Real Ale very much approved, though they remained anxious about Cannon's plans for local pubs.

But that wasn't enough for Cannon: he wanted a slice of the burgeoning 'designer beer' market, and knew that the name Devenish, with its suggestion of dusty old country pubs and deckchairs, was never going to cut it. In the first instance, he renamed the brewing arm of the company (the Redruth operation) 'The Cornish Brewery Company', and there was more to come.

According to Paul Hampson of design agency the Hampson Partnership, who worked closely with Cannon on the design of this new brand, it was a trip to America, and exposure to the growing US 'craft beer' scene, that provided the necessary inspiration. Cannon was particularly impressed, Hampson believes, by Anchor Steam, the flagship beer of Fritz Maytag's revived Anchor Brewing.

Anchor Steam was one of the first US 'craft beers' to find favour in the UK from the late 1970s onwards, primarily among

CAMRA members, and under the influence of Michael Jackson. Despite its attractive packaging and interesting brewing process, Anchor Steam is not overly aromatic and is a familiar brown colour – in other words, exotic and yet also accessible to British drinkers brought up on best bitter and Fuller's ESB.

Having decided that, somehow or other, 'steam' needed to be part of the story of his new beer brand, Cannon next decided to imply a more glamorous place of origin than the mining town of Redruth where it was actually to be produced. In the late nineteen-eighties, Newquay, in North Cornwall, was about as near as the UK got to the Californian beach culture. It was famous for its world-class surfing and increasingly popular with young holidaymakers. And so the name Newquay Steam Beer was born.

But what, apart from a snappy name, would be its unique selling point?

Unsure where to direct its energies after the Big Six brewers had relented and reintroduced cask ale to their ranges in the late 1970s, CAMRA had been campaigning on various fronts.

One particular hobby horse was 'pure beer', brewed without additives. Founder member Michael Hardman's 1978 coffee table book *Beer Naturally* set the agenda. The 'pure beer' baton was picked up by fellow founding member Graham Lees who, having moved to Germany, became convinced that Britain needed a version of the German *Rheinheitsgebot* beer purity law; and also by beer writer Roger Protz, who published something of a pure beer manifesto, *Pulling a Fast One*, in 1978.

In 1986, 'pure beer' was finally made a CAMRA priority, and, throughout that year, the Campaign renewed its efforts for clearer labelling of beer ingredients and the banning of 'additives'. Then, either in response to CAMRA's lobbying or simply reacting to the same external influences, towards the end of 1986, Samuel Smith's of Tadcaster launched 'Natural Lager'. Acknowledging the influence, a spokesman for Devenish said: 'There's a growing market for healthy foods. Sam Smith's have produced a bottled natural lager, but why not have a complete range?'

This 'health food' image might have been sufficient to make a success of Newquay Steam, but Cannon was also determined to go all out on the packaging and presentation. Paul Hampson:

[Cannon] had very firm ideas as to how the label for his new Steam Beer range would look and there were very few of the graphic devices associated with beer labelling that were left out. Had we been handed an open brief, we might well have created a label less complicated, but this wasn't the time for that. We did, however, ensure that all the elements of the design were beautifully crafted, from label cut-outs and bottle shape, to the woodcut illustrations, hand lettering and typography.

One design feature that would come to define the image of Newquay Steam Beer was its ceramic 'Grolsch-style' swing-top:

I recall presenting our first bottle top sketches to Michael, the result of which was a long silence. Didn't I know how much more expensive the ceramic top would make this new product and wasn't I aware of the potential cost saving of a standard metal cap? He then approved our ceramic top design and instructed us to forge ahead with production without delay.

Cannon's nose for what would make money was infallible. Those stoppers, and complete transparency about ingredients and alcohol content, helped the brand stand out in a market place where beautiful-looking bottled beers were then few and far between.

Will Wallis worked at the Redruth Brewery from 1984 to 2004 and was involved in quality assurance on the Newquay Steam beers. He recalls that the workforce was enthusiastic about the product and just as determined as Cannon to make it succeed:

As a proud Cornishman I felt proud to have our 'own beer'. There was a lot of hard work put into the beer by a very excited workforce. We believed that Steam Beer was unique on the market and stood a good chance of being a success. Personally, I can remember working twelve hour round the clock shifts with my colleagues who really believed in the product and put in a lot of effort to help launch the brand and make the whole thing a success.

Head brewer Tony Wharmby spoke to CAMRA's *What's Brewing* in July 1987:

> [We have] had to completely reorganise our operation... The water isn't Burtonised, no additives to help clarification or speed the process, and the need to double ferment all have their challenges. The major operational factors are the maturation time, which is weeks rather than days, and the new labelling plant to accommodate the bottle shape and complexity of the labels.

As Will Wallis recalls it, it was a sign of Wharmby's genuine belief in Newquay Steam that he allowed his image to be used to market the beers (though it is also possible that Cannon insisted on it as part of his marketing strategy). Since then, many head brewers have put their names, signature and even faces on 'premium' products, but it was distinctly unusual at the time.

At launch in 1987, the range included bitter, strong bitter, brown ale, strong brown ale, lager, strong lager, and a stout—an unusually diverse selection at a time when most breweries in the UK restricted themselves to brewing bitter and best bitter, with perhaps a 'strong ale' at Christmas. A full-page advertisement appeared in CAMRA's What's Brewing under the heading 'Announcing Britain's First Range Of Entirely Natural Strong Beers... No Preservatives, No Additives':

> In response to an ever-increasing demand for additive-free products, The Cornish Brewery Company is delighted to announce the launch of their unique range of natural beers. A unique choice of Lager, Bitter, Brown and Stout: a unique choice of strengths: a totally new concept in drinking which will appeal to all beer drinkers. Don't miss your chance to join the New Age of Steam.

Though some have suggested retrospectively that the beers were 'bland' at the time they offered refreshing alternatives to the market leading stout (Guinness) and brown ale (Newcastle). As such, they found cautious approval from the new class of beer critics, including Michael 'Beer Hunter' Jackson, who, in his *New World Guide to Beer* described 'a range of well-made all-malt brews':

They are not Steam Beers in the American sense, and the term was clearly conceived as a marketing device.
However, they are made in a way that it unusual in Britain. They have a two-stage primary fermentation, and they are cold-conditioned. The whole range is malt-accented and notably clean-tasting.

That same year, it seems Anchor Brewing in San Francisco got wind of Newquay Steam and took, or threatened to take, legal action. (We have not been able to find specific details.) In response, Cannon's 'Island Trading Company', which owned the Newquay Steam trademark, took Anchor to court. The intention was to block Anchor's plan to launch its own Steam Beer on draught in the UK. With breathtaking nerve, Cannon's lawyers argued that British customers were used to ordering a 'pint of Steam', meaning Newquay Steam bitter, and that another draught beer of the same name would be confusing to them. It was at this time, it seems, that a story for the origin of the name Newquay Steam was contrived: in Cornwall, the lawyers claimed, 'steam' is slang for strong beer. We can find no evidence to support that suggestion, and have certainly never heard the phrase in use. Island Trading won their case, holding back the arrival of draught American 'craft beer' in the UK.

The success of Newquay Steam took many by surprise: from a standing start, the equivalent of 35,000 barrels was sold in 1988. (For comparison, London Pride sold 89,000 barrels in 2012-13.)

Cannon put that success down, in large part, to the popularity of Newquay Steam with other UK brewers who wanted to provide a choice of interesting bottled beers in their pubs without importing or buying from their more heavyweight competitors.

John Spicer, a leading drinks market analyst at the time, told us: 'Everyone in the City of London had high hopes for Newquay Steam and there was a lot of interest in it.' In their 1989 report on the *The Supply of Beer*, even the Government's Monopolies and Mergers Commission recognised that, though beer generally was struggling in the marketplace, Newquay Steam seemed to be bucking the trend.

It couldn't last and, in 1991, Boddington's of Manchester made a hostile takeover bid. Whitbread sold their 15 per cent stake to Boddington's without a moment's hesitation, much to Cannon's annoyance: 'The cosy relationships of the past have been shattered,' he told the press. As Will Wallis recalled, 'The widespread belief was that as we were a direct competitor, they wanted to purchase us and shut us down to remove excess brewing capacity in the trade at that time.' Michael Cannon, however, saw them off with his customary vigour, though it was a close shave, and left the company reeling and in need of cash. In May 1991, the Newquay Steam brands were finally sold outright to Whitbread, and Will Wallis recalls uncertainty at Redruth:

> All artwork, recipes, brewing and processing procedures were passed on to the new owners. At that time we believed that the Newquay Steam range would continue, produced elsewhere in the country using the premises, and raw materials of the new owners.

Then, in July the same year, head brewer Tony Wharmby and a Devenish director, Paul Smith, bought the Redruth brewery for £700,000 and went into business as contract brewers and bottlers.

Devenish continued as a pub company and distributor until, by 1993, Cannon had achieved his aims, and was ready to sell up on his own terms. He had bought his stake of Devenish for £35m in 1986, turned a failing company into one of the hottest brands in the industry, and sold it to Greenalls (Whitbread) for £214m. He ploughed his share of the profit (£26m) into a new pub company, capitalising on changes in the industry following the 1989 'Beer Orders'.

The Newquay Steam brand name lived on for short while, but the distinctive swing-top bottles were ditched in favour of cans, with the beer being brewed at Whitbread plants elsewhere in the country. What was a great hope for the industry in 1989 was, by the end, a tarnished brand and a lost opportunity. It seems to have disappeared completely in around 1996.

The brewery at Redruth closed for good in 2004, though there are currently plans to redevelop the site, including proposals to install a microbrewery.

Michael Cannon made yet more money running and selling pub chains, and went on to gain notoriety for his purchase and sale of another failing brewery, Eldridge Pope of Dorchester, in 2004. He remains a permanent fixture on 'rich lists'.

Newquay Steam Beer is fondly remembered by many who popped those ceramic stoppers on beach holidays in the West Country in the late 80s and 1990s, and also by those who appreciated the opportunity to buy a 'premium' British lager, stout and brown ale produced by someone other than the 'Big Six'.

Mellow Brown vs. the Amarillo Kid

First published on our blog in 2014.

A brewery has operated from the rear of the Blue Anchor, a rambling granite-built pub on Helston's main drag, since at least the turn of the 20th century, and to say it has a cult reputation among enthusiasts of traditional British beer would be an understatement.

It was as we were winding up an afternoon drinking session that we first met the head brewer, Tim Sears, in the back yard of the pub and asked whether he would mind telling us which variety of hops were used in Spingo Jubilee IPA. (We were obsessing over East Kent Goldings at the time.)

'Amarillo,' he said, with a just-noticeable curl of his lip.

An American variety noted for its pungent pop-art tangerine aroma, Amarillo was first released to the market in 2000. There are pint glasses at the Blue Anchor that have been in service longer.

'That's Gareth's doing,' he continued. 'He's the brewery manager. See those sacks of spent hops?' He pointed to a corner by the gents' toilets. 'That little one's mine; his is overflowing! I tell him he uses too many.'

'Fascinating,' we thought, Spock like.

A few weeks later, we got hold of Tim's email address and explained that we were interested in finding out more. 'Tension is a bit strong!' he replied, 'But I know what you mean.' And so, on a paint-peelingly hot afternoon in July, Ray took a trip to the brewery.

As he lives in Penzance, Tim agreed to pick me up and save me a bus fare, 'As long as you don't mind me smoking, and Dutch music… Gezondheid, tot dinsdag!'

Sure enough, as we hurtled along the coast road, weaving around tractors and convoys of German tourists, the car stereo played a stream of oompah-ing Nederlandse pop-rock.

'What's the Dutch connection?' I asked.

'Belgian beer,' he replied. 'About ten… twelve… ten or twelve years ago, we went on a trip, a coach trip, to Belgium, and I loved it. I got on well with the bloke who ran the hotel where we were staying and now he's sort of a pen pal. I write to him every week, in Dutch.'

Tim isn't a native Cornishman but has been brewing Spingo Ales at the Blue Anchor in Helston since 1981. 'I'd been home-brewing for a while and winning awards,' he said, lifting a hand from the steering wheel to circle his cigar in air for emphasis, 'so when I saw that they were advertising for a new brewer I said, "Yes, please! I'll have some of that."' The landlord gave him a six week trial: 'I never did find out if I'd got the job.'

People sometimes talk about the Blue Anchor as if it's been exactly the same, and brewing the same beer, for 400 years. It's more complicated than that, but 'Middle', its flagship beer, is certainly nearing its 100th birthday, having first been produced to celebrate the return of Helston boys from the First World War, in 1919. 'As far as I know, it's the same recipe,' Tim said, 'but the original paperwork isn't available. It's been 1050 OG, Goldings, as long as I've been brewing it.'

Elsewhere, there have been tweaks: Spingo Special went from 1060 to 1066 to celebrate the marriage of Charles and Diana in 1981, and at some point, crystal malt got added to the recipe. 'Devenish [a defunct regional brewery] used to supply the malt and they weren't too careful cleaning out the chutes for our order, so we got pale malt with a bit of crystal mixed in, which I used for specials. Nowadays, we mix it ourselves.'

To put some space between it and the amped-up Special, Christmas Special went up to 1076. (It's now back down to 1074, to avoid the higher duty bracket.) Spingo Best, too close in gravity to Middle, got quietly dropped, as did a 1033 'Ordinary': 'We called that Mrs Bond, because she was the only one that drank it.'

Tim is clear about his own tastes: 'I don't like a hoppy beer. I prefer that malty sweetness – that sort of Cornish traditional taste.'

(We have long felt that West Country ale is almost a style in its own right – less attenuated, heavier in body, with barely any discernible hop character. If you've tried the bland, sweet Sharp's Doom Bar, or St Austell's HSD, then you'd recognise Spingo Middle from the family resemblance, though it's less smooth, and less consistent, than either of those bigger brewery brands.)

'Obviously, you've got to have hops,' he conceded, 'but they're there for bitterness. They shouldn't make your beer smell of fruit. I can't stand when people say they can smell lemon or citrus or passion fruit, or whatever.'

A couple of years ago, his colleague Gareth, and Ben, a son of the Blue Anchor's licensees, went on a three-week course at Brewlab in Sunderland. They came back with new ideas. The stout Ben designed for his coursework is now a regular at the pub, and is called, obviously, Ben's Stout. Cornwall isn't stout-drinking country, but it ticks over.

'Ben doesn't drink it, though,' said Tim. 'He drinks my Bragget – no hops, malt, honey, apple juice, first brewed to commemorate the town's charter, granted by King John in 1201.'

But it was Gareth upon whom the course had the most profound effect.

'The IPA, that was my beer originally, brewed for the Queen's Jubilee in 2002. But then Gareth got hold of it and now it's all—' A faint shake of the head. 'Amarillo.'

At the pub, Tim, in sleeveless T-shirt and wellies, disappeared up the granite staircase into the steam of a brewery which is cramped and hot on the best of days, and handed me over to Gareth, who was just concluding his morning shift.

We had developed a picture of a maverick young hipster obsessed with 'craft beer', perhaps riding around the brewery on a skateboard. In fact, though he is younger than Tim by some years, he is softly-spoken, practically-minded, and, in his black working t-shirt, more mechanic than artist. A Helston local, he worked his way up to the post of brewery manager from cleaning barrels and the occasional stint behind the bar.

'I do like hoppy beers,' he said, sipping instant coffee from a chipped mug at a plastic table in the pub's garden, 'but I mostly drink more mellow things, if I'm honest. Middle, St Austell HSD – things like that.'

This did not bode well for our hopes of finding a British version of the feuding Bjergsø brothers of Mikkeller and Evil Twin fame: Tim and Gareth do not hate each other; they are definitely not 'at war'. So I decided to poke the nest with a stick: what did Gareth think of Tim's assertion that hops should really only be used to add bitterness?

'I disagree with him about that,' he said, with something just approaching roused passion. 'Hops should be there to give flavour. Definitely.'

Another new Spingo ale for which Gareth takes the credit (or perhaps the blame, from Tim's perspective) is the 4% golden Flora Daze. When we first tried it on the weekend it was launched, in March 2012, it seemed startlingly different to its stable-mates, and we observed conservative regulars at the bar recoiling at its lemon-zestiness.

'We have our beer distributed through Jolly's – LWC – and they wanted something lighter and hoppier,' Gareth said. 'I'd just learned recipe formulation at Brewlab and Flora Daze is what I came up with.'

A short while later, we all three reconvened at the top of the steps by the brew-house, where Tim was stirring the mash with a wooden brewer's paddle. He finished it by swinging a great wooden lid onto the blue-painted tun dating from the 1920s, and covered that with eight old malt sacks, for insulation.

Perspiring and out of breath, he leaned on the stable door and took a long draught from a cool pint of Spingo Middle. 'Jolly's wanted something under 4%,' he said, picking up the Flora Daze story, 'but we just can't go that low. Spingo Ales are strong – that's what makes them special.' He admitted, though, that he did roll his eyes on first seeing the recipe. 'Gareth usually brews it, but I can do it, and have. I follow the recipe and stick to the spec.' He paused before delivering the punchline: 'I just don't drink the stuff.'

In the quiet tug of war, Tim seems to be slowly getting his own way, and Gareth acknowledged that both the re-vamped IPA and Flora Daze have, at Tim's urging, become less intensely hoppy. 'I'm happier with them as they are, though,' Gareth said. 'They're more in balance now.'

Gareth's real influence is in the pursuit of consistency, as he explained showing me around the crowded pub cellar which doubles as a home for six hot-tub-sized fermenting vessels. 'Our beer is slightly different every time,' he acknowledged, with a mix of pride and anxiety. 'It's a small brew-house, we do everything by hand, and the malt and hops vary from batch to batch. The weather, too – that can have an awful effect. Oh, yeah – a big effect.'

But he is working on these problems and has instituted lots of small changes. In the last year, for example, he has taken the radical step of having lids fitted to the fermenting vessels so that the beer is no longer exposed to the air. Nothing fancy, though – just sheets of Perspex. There's a sense that, with too much steel and precision, it would cease to be Spingo.

But perhaps this most traditional of British breweries will see more change yet. Tim, not perhaps as conservative as we thought, confessed that he had sometimes wondered about brewing something to reflect his interest in Belgian beer. And Gareth, wistfully, and almost embarrassed, muttered: 'I have... Well, I have thought about a single-hop beer, Amarillo – something a bit stronger.'

A US-inspired Spingo IPA?

'Yeah, I suppose that's the kind of style I'd be going for…' He shook his head. 'But, no, we've got enough different beers for now.'

In the end, what we found at the Blue Anchor wasn't high drama or a bitter feud, but a kind of dialogue, and our original choice of word, tension, feels about right. We suspect that similar debates are occurring in traditional breweries up and down the country, and around the world, perhaps not always in such a civilised manner.

Ordinary, Best, Extra Special

First published in Beer Advocate *magazine in 2015.*

Bitter is the quintessential English beer. Low in alcohol, light bodied, typically amber-brown in colour, it seems to represent the essence of a country where pubs are Victorian and emotions are kept in check. Bitter is also, however, what overseas observers have in mind when they dismiss British beer as 'warm and flat' and, for a generation of British brewers inspired by the US craft beer movement, it is merely 'boring brown bitter'. That is a shame because the subtleties of bitter can be a delight for the beer geek willing to learn, and because craft beer as we know it was built on its back.

In his essential book *Amber, Gold & Black* (2010) Martyn Cornell examines the origins of every major beer style and explains how 'bitter beer' and similar terms emerged in 19th century Britain to described various forms of draught pale ale. A widely reprinted 1855 parody of Charles Greville's controversial memoirs has Queen Victoria serving the Duke of Wellington 'a foaming jug of bitter' and this form, without modifiers, became common in the 20th century. By the 1930s, for example, advertisements for Yorkshire brewery Tetley headlined two types of beer, 'Mild and Bitter'.

After WWII bitter really took off as pub-goers began to reject mild ale, the previously dominant draught beer style. It had grown darker in the preceding 50 years and had also become a dumping ground for spoiled beer both at the brewery and in pubs where so-called 'slops' were returned to the casks. Bitter had long been a 'premium' product and, during a period of prosperity and optimism in which Prime Minister Harold Macmillan could say 'most of our people have never had it so good', quality became more important than price.

At the same time, British brewing was increasingly dominated by a handful of conglomerates keen to develop brands that could be advertised nationally. Mackeson Stout was one such product, as was SKOL lager, but most were bitters. Because their marketing nationwide relied on them being consistent and clean-tasting, these particular beers were not cask-conditioned but instead filtered, pasteurised, force-carbonated and shipped in airtight containers. The most famous of this new breed of so-called 'keg bitters' was Watney's Red Barrel, first launched in the 1930s but pushed heavily from the sixties onward.

Consumers began to fight back against monopoly brewers in 1963 with the establishment of the Society for the Preservation of Beers from the Wood whose constitution described keg beers as 'blown up out of sealed dustbins'. This battle escalated when, in 1971, a similar and more successful organisation was founded by four young men from the North West of England – the Campaign for Real Ale (CAMRA). They too were especially enamoured of the products of the hundred or so surviving regional family brewers such as Adnams and Theakston's and one of the founders, Michael Hardman, was particularly fond of the intensely dry bitters from London's Young & Co and Boddington's of Manchester. Beer writer Frank Baillie, an early CAMRA activist, said in his 1973 *Beer Drinker's Companion*:

It is probably the bitter beers that give the most satisfaction to the beer drinker and which exhibit the most marked variation in palate from different breweries.

CAMRA's battle with Watney's, Whitbread and the other colossal brewing concerns was fought largely over bitter and it was with the introduction of a new cask-conditioned bitter that Watney's signalled its capitulation in 1975.

Alongside CAMRA in the 1970s came the very first microbreweries, most of whom had bitters as their flagship brews. Litchborough Bitter, brewed by former Watney's employee Bill Urquhart near Northampton, first appeared in 1974. It was followed by bitters from similar operations such as Godson's (London,1977) and Butcombe (Bristol, 1978).

As Britain's micro-brewing revolution took off, the wonders of cask-conditioned bitter inspired key players in the nascent US craft beer scene. Home-brewing guru and craft beer champion Charlie Papazian recounts in his 2005 book *Microbrewed Adventures* a passionate affair with Brakspear Bitter of Henley-on-Thames during an early trip to England, marvelling at an earthiness and astonishing complexity delivered at less than 4% alcohol by volume. Brooklyn Brewery's Garrett Oliver has frequently spoken of the moment when his eyes were opened to the wonders of beer, drinking a pint of bitter in an anonymous pub near Victoria Station in central London in 1983. In his 2003 book *The Brewmaster's Table* he noted that 'it exploded in layers of flavour – hay, earth, newly mowed grass, orange marmalade, and baking bread… my beer odyssey had begun'. The creation of what is arguably the world's first American-style IPA, Anchor Liberty, was directly inspired by a visit Fritz Maytag and Gordon MacDermott made to the Timothy Taylor brewery in Keighley in West Yorkshire where they tasted Landlord, a notably stronger and more aromatic interpretation of bitter still marketed as 'pale ale'. (Historically, the terms are interchangeable.)

American drinkers, unless they travel frequently to the UK, will struggle to get to know bitter. It doesn't translate well into bottles and the best examples derive their character from the gentle carbonation and almost-but-not-quite imperceptible funk imparted by cask-conditioning; from subtle variations between house yeast strains; and, crucially, from context. Adnams's Bitter tastes better drunk in a wind-battered maritime pub in Suffolk within sniffing distance of the brewery than it does even a hundred miles away in London.

Though bitter is drunk all over England, those seeking true enlightenment should consider visiting Yorkshire, a particular stronghold where names such as Samuel Smith, Joshua Tetley and Timothy Taylor are still spoken with respect. Leigh Linley, the author of the 2013 book *Great Yorkshire Beer*, says:

> Many breweries here still retain a honest-to-goodness bitter in their portfolio and there's a legion of publicans and landlords who would be loath to stop selling it. There's plenty of typical Northern boasting of being able to brew 'a proper Yorkshire bitter' in the brewing scene – it's a badge of honour, a due to be paid.

In the UK today, bitter is not a strictly governed style and beers bearing that appellation might be golden to red, drily bitter or with honey-sweet, rich in hop perfume or rather austere. It is easier, perhaps, to say what bitter is not: it was once the classy alternative to mild, then the conservative alternative to trendy lager, and it is now the preferred choice of the anti-hipster – not double IPA, and definitely not fruit-infused barrel-aged saison. Dedicated bitter drinkers are sometimes to be heard lamenting its decline and their concerns are not entirely unfounded, as Adnams head brewer Fergus Fitzgerald explains:

> Southwold Bitter is still our best-selling cask beer and its place as number one is probably secure for some time yet, but it has been caught up by Ghost Ship [a hoppy golden ale] in the last few years. When I joined Adnams 10 years ago Bitter was about 70 per cent of what we did but it's

now closer to 40 per cent as we have expanded the range of styles we brew, and as tastes broaden.

Among younger drinkers in the UK, old-fashioned bitter is not popular, and it is likely that it will lose yet more market share in the coming decade, but perhaps in 10 or 20 years, it may be possible for it to be appreciated by a new generation of drinkers without prejudice as an expression of place and of identity – as something to be cherished.

Watney's bleedin' Red Barrel

First published on our blog in 2018.

You can't have cops without robbers, or Batman without the Joker, and so the story of the revitalisation of British beer needs its bad guys too. Enter Watney's.

Watney's (or Watney Mann, or Watney Combe Reid) was the Evil Corporation which sought to crush plucky small brewers and impose its own terrible beer on the drinking public. It acquired and closed beloved local breweries, and it closed pubs, or ruined them with clumsy makeovers.

Its Red Barrel was particularly vile – a symbol of all that was wrong with industrial brewing and national brands pushed through cynical marketing campaigns.

This, at least, was the accepted narrative for a long time, formed by the propaganda of the Campaign for Real Ale in its early years, and set hard through years of repetition.

But does it stand up to scrutiny? What if, contrary to everything we've heard, Red Barrel was actually kind of OK?

We've been writing about Watney's seriously since 2012. At first, we were interested because it was the 'baddie' in the origin story of the Campaign for Real Ale, which we were attempting to tell in *Brew Britannia*.

But then we began to find Watney's fascinating in its own right, as an example of the kind of company that dominated Britain in the 20th century: big and acquisitive, sure, but retaining a quirky, paternalistic tendency at least up until the 1970s.

CAMRA, and Christopher Hutt especially, regarded its consistent, pervasive brand style as a problem – identical pubs, with identical fascias, in the same shade of red, wherever they were in the country. A visual manifestation of the uniform blandness of Watney's beer, and the keg bitters of the Big Six more generally.

To those less engaged in the politics of beer, however, that brand is something to celebrate – a mid-century classic. Conceived with input from the Design Research Unit, an organisation with a cult following of its own, it has featured in gallery exhibitions and books as an example of the best 20th century design had to offer.

Even now, more than 40 years after the DRG brand design was abandoned, it is possible to recognise an old Watney's pub by remaining scraps of lettering and, if you're prone to nostalgia, to feel moved by the direct connection to a brief period, roughly between the Festival of Britain and the Wicker Man, when bold modernism was baked into everyday life.

And with hindsight, those derided pub makeovers look pretty cool.

As for the red barrel itself, it truly deserves that overused description 'iconic'. Whether in the form of a keyring, in Perspex over the back door of an abandoned pub, or sitting as decoration on the bar of a bar with retro tendencies, it prompts recognition, delight, or derision.

The sticking point, though, is the beer – a byword for the horrors of 20th century monopoly brewing, the butt of endless jokes. But can it really have been that bad?

"They can't have set out with an intention for it to be vile", wrote brewer Henry Bealby in an email. He is a childhood friend of beer historian Ron Pattinson and his brewery, Cat Asylum, based in Newark on Trent, specialises in historic recreations, including a cask ale based on a 1963 recipe for Red Barrel.

The history of Watney's Red Barrel, which also happens to be the story of keg beer in Britain, has been told a thousand times, but here's a short version: it was launched in 1931 as an alternative to cask beer for venues not equipped to dispense it and then, after World War II, became a flagship product, marketed nationally in print and on television.

In 1970-71 the beer was reformulated and relaunched under the name Red. This is the beer, evidence suggests, that really did turn people against Watney's, being sweeter and fizzier again. A contemporary internal training film unearthed by industrial historian Nick Wheat put a positive spin on the change, but acknowledged it nonetheless:

> What we've done is to give the beer a new smooth pleasant taste. We've also given it a much better head and altogether a more attractive appearance. Gone is any suggestion of bitter after palate; instead, there is a pleasant malty mealiness.... We've studied flavour, studied people's

reaction to flavour, and produced experimental beers, testing out all the variations we can think of in such things of sweetness or bitterness.

A pervasive advertising campaign that drew on the imagery of totalitarianism didn't help either – TV ads that aped the cold war grimness of TV spy series *Callan*, and billboards featuring lookalikes of Chairman Mao and Nikita Khruschev.

It was at this time that Watney's became the focus of the nascent Campaign for Real Ale. Christopher Hutt, CAMRA's second chairman, boosted CAMRA's profile by engaging in a battle with Watney's head of PR, Ted Handel, on the letters page of the Financial Times, and the first edition of the Good Beer Guide advised drinkers to 'Avoid like the plague'.

The Watney's Red (Barrel) brand was finally all but retired from the UK market in the late 1970s, a move widely seen as a retreat in the face of CAMRA's relentless battering. It lingered on as an overseas brand, though, in markets where the politics of 'real ale' were less potent.

When we were researching *Brew Britannia* we spoke to many veteran drinkers and observers and few had kind words to say about Watney's beer. One exception was Nick Handel, Ted Handel's son, who even more than 40 years on bristled at the rough treatment his father, and the beer he represented, got at the hands of CAMRA in the early 1970s:

> My father was working for a go-ahead brewing concern at a time of changing tastes and consumer needs. The battle with CAMRA was a small part of everything he had on his plate, but I did get the impression they were a bit of a pain. I think they used Watney's as a platform for their own propaganda and he had a tricky old time with them.

We also filed away a letter to the journal of the Institute of Brewing magazine (brought to our attention by brewer and beer writer Ed Wray) from a veteran brewer annoyed at what he regarded as lazy repetition of the myth of Red Barrel's awfulness:

> I have just read my copy of the October 2013 edition of B&DI The article which describes Watney's Red Barrel as

'infamous' is truly crass. I worked for Watney in the late 60s and early 70s and remember that brew as a decent bitter, albeit in keg form... At Mortlake laboratory, we taste-testers prided ourselves in being able to detect which brewery the Red Barrel came from; all had characteristic nuances. A touch of diacetyl from Norwich, a hint of SO_2 from Trowbridge or a slight whiff of DMS from Manchester. Alfie Gough's Brighton version was as well hopped as Tamplin's use to be, in true Sussex style.

All this only deepened our fascination: could there ever be a way to establish with any objectivity – that is, from sources without their own axes to grind – how Red Barrel tasted?

And then, one day in September 2014, such evidence did arrive, in the form of a black ring binder: the *Watney Mann Quality Control Manual*.

For more than 40 years, this document had sat in the personal collection of Stewart Main, a retired brewer best known for his time in charge at Shepherd Neame. We had emailed him hoping for a few titbits of information, little expecting that he would have in his possession the motherlode.

The binder was packed with tables, lists, recipes, diagrams and detailed notes on how to brew and package each beer in the Watney's portfolio circa 1965. What's more, it came with a sheaf of loose-leaf additions bringing the manual up to date for the 1970s.

At last we had something concrete to go on.

Unfortunately, we are not brewers, or even terribly technical, so it took every ounce of our concentration to derive anything at all from the raw data. It certainly seemed to support the idea that the beer itself, the basic recipe, was perfectly respectable – around 3.8% ABV, 30-32 units of bitterness, and made with almost 90% pale malt.

We scanned the document and sent a copy to Ron Pattinson hoping that he'd be better equipped to interpret it than us, which he was, and did, most notably in *an article for Beer Advocate* magazine, cross-referring to a set of brewing logs from the Watney's (Usher's) brewery in Trowbridge:

> I've seen thousands of brewing records from several countries, but these were the first to shock me. And the first where I haven't thought, 'I'd really like to try that

beer.' CAMRA was right to tell readers to 'avoid like the plague' in the first *Good Beer Guide*. Because Watney's products were up to 20 percent muck: beer returned from pubs, sludgy stuff from the bottom of tanks and other crap lying around the brewery.

In the same article, though, he admits to having little first-hand knowledge of how Watney's beers tasted "having taken CAMRA's advice to heart".

Keen to hear from some people who had tasted Red Barrel, and/or Red, and hoping that perhaps the passage of more than 40 years might offer some fresh perspective, we emailed some of the veterans in our address book and asked them one simple question: was Red Barrel as bad as everyone says?

Roger Protz, beer writer:
I don't think I ever sampled Red Barrel. It was the revamp, Watney's Red, that I drank. I was working on a newspaper in East London and had two pubs nearby, one selling Young's Bitter, the other Charrington IPA. I was bowled over by Young's Ordinary and it turned me into a cask beer devotee. When ads for Watney's Red were plastered all over London I thought I should try it and went to the nearest Watney's pub. I thought it was dreadful and later described it as 'liquid Mars Bars' – 'sweet, gassy and lacking any noticeable hop character. In fairness to Watney's Red, I think Tartan Keg was worse!

Sue Hart, campaigner and pub crawler:
In reality, it was no worse than Double Diamond or Whitbread Tankard, but it appeared to be everywhere and much more visible with its trademark than the others. They also did a beer called Starlight which was also keg but a tad more drinkable. It may even have been top pressure rather than keg.

James Lynch, chairman of CAMRA in 1978:
In truth it was neither any worse nor any better than any of the other national keg brands. Bland, brown, devoid of any character and ridiculously fizzy. That said, I can clearly

remember – just like I can remember where I was when I heard the news of JFK's assassination – where I was when I first decided, after just one mouthful, that I was going to drink no more of a particular pint. That was in London in 1964. That wasn't because of the condition it was in because, as a keg beer it would have consistent, albeit consistently characterless, but because it had nothing to offer. And that wasn't Red Barrel but Double Diamond.

As it happens, we have tasted a *version* of Red Barrel ourselves – two versions, in fact, one pasteurised, the other not. It was brewed for us in 2016 by Ed Wray, a professional brewer who, at the time, had access to a small pasteurising unit. He followed a recipe derived from the Quality Control Manual and handed over the finished products during a brief encounter at Paddington station.

Tasting those beers, with due ceremony, in the appropriate vintage glassware, was among the most thrilling experiences we've had in our many years beer-geeking. Of course it should have been kegged, not bottled, and Ed didn't add slops, or drive the beers around the country in tankers, but, still, it was hard to find fault with either version:

> It was delicious like a nice sandwich, not like five courses at the Fat Duck. Chewy, satisfyingly malty, fresh and definitely on the right side of the bland-subtle border. There was a slight cooked flavour, we thought, although maybe that was down to the power of suggestion. We imagine warmer, or if left sitting around in a pub cellar for six months, it might get a bit nasty. But, like this, we'd happily drink it every day.

This take on Red Barrel, at least, was a satisfying, decently-hoppy pale ale that could certainly hold its own against Doom Bar or Butcombe Original.

With similar curiosity, Ron Pattinson approached his old friend, Henry Bealby, with a worked-up recipe for Red Barrel as it was c.1963. We didn't get to taste that version but Henry shared some thoughts by email:

> It was a beer I hardly ever drank in the seventies, except perhaps in a Party 7 can, but it fitted well with our mission of bringing back beers from the dead. I figured that they can't have set out with an intention for it to be vile and thought the original recipe also might reflect the southern bitter style of the times. And indeed it did, reminding me and others of our first impressions of bitter when we strayed away from Nottinghamshire into the southern half of the country... There was a lot of scoffing about our intention to brew it but it all sold. Double Diamond next?

Henry Bealby isn't the only brewer risking ridicule by dabbling in these dark waters: in 2016, Brands Reunited, which specialises in acquiring expired brewery names and applying them to contemporary products, brought Watney's back to market.

When the news broke, the reaction was mixed. Some either remembered Watney's grim reputation, or remembered it indirectly through folk memory, and were appalled at the idea. Others found the idea hilarious, regarding it as a distinctly provocative, mischievous move at the height of a craft beer revolution led by the likes of BrewDog, and two fingers up at CAMRA at the same time.

The interesting thing is, though, that the new Watney's is using the name, and the stag logo, but not the red barrel, or any of the DRG typography. And among its roster of beers, there is no Red Barrel – only a set of modern pale ales, brewed at Sambrook's.

In an exchange of emails with Nick Whitehurst, one of the co-founders of Brands Reunited, we asked about the challenges of promoting beers with such an infamous name attached:

> It's true that Watney's had a bad rep in its latter years, but if you go back a bit further you find an amazing brand that was innovative and market leading... Many under the age of 40 haven't heard of Watney's so they evaluate us like any new brand, many over 40 remember the brand as something their dad or grandad drank and remember it fondly, and some even worked for Watney's back in the day and remember it as a great business...

Is there any chance of Red Barrel making a comeback?

It's not in our immediate plans but you never know… I think if we do we need to get it absolutely spot on as we will be inviting the world to judge us. For now, we are a small business trying to prove ourselves and to establish Watney's as a credible craft brand in a very competitive market… One thing we have just done is made some Red Barrel memorabilia. I get more requests for keyrings than anything else so we have just made some of those, and some Red Barrel pin badges.

There's a tension in the way Brands Reunited markets its Watney's branded beers: on the one hand, it wants to capitalise on nostalgia, but on the other it recoils from the negative connotations of the old name. The slogan 'We're back…. And taste nothing like we used to' is intended as self-aware self-deprecation but betrays doubt.

The stink around Watney's remains pungent.

Where the Boddies is buried

First published on our blog in 2014.

In its heyday, Boddington's Bitter was among the most highly-regarded of British beers, and the pride of its home city of Manchester. These days, it is rather unloved and rootless. Where did it all go wrong?

When we interviewed him in 2012, Michael Hardman, one of the founders of CAMRA, mentioned Boddington's, alongside Young's Ordinary, as typifying the 'intense bitterness' that, as a young man, he sought in a pint of ale: it was what those early campaigners were fighting for. Beer writer and CAMRA stalwart Roger Protz has similarly rosy memories, as he recalled in an article on his website in 2012: 'The first time I drank it, in a pub in Hyde, Cheshire, I thought I had died and gone to heaven: I couldn't believe beer could taste that good.' John Keeling, head brewer at Fuller's and a native Mancunian, named it as his number one 'desert island beer' in a 2012 interview for the Allgates Brewery blog: 'In 1974 at the start of my brewing career there was no better drinking beer than Boddington's.' And Manchester-based CAMRA activist Peter Alexander, who blogs under the name Tandleman, told us in an email:

> It was a very dry beer, yet intensely bitter throughout, though not greatly hoppy. I'm guessing early hop additions to give that intensity of bitterness throughout. Good mouthfeel too – not thin at all.

But it isn't just a matter of nostalgia. Contemporary 1970s sources note, albeit without waxing lyrical, that Boddington's was 'well hopped' (Frank Baillie's *Beer Drinker's Companion*, 1973), 'One of the best' (the first edition of the CAMRA *Good Beer Guide*, 1974) and 'exceptionally bitter' (*Good Beer Guide* 1977). A more evocative description of how Boddington's tasted in its prime comes from a letter to *What's Brewing* from Mike Field of Batley, published in May 1984: '[It had a] bitterness that clawed at the back of the throat and took you back to the bar for another one.'

It owed some of its reputation to what the 1978 *Good Beer Guide* called its 'distinctive straw colour', and Ewart Boddington, brewery chairman from 1970 to 1989, is said (by Mr Field) to have put the beer's popularity down to the fact that it 'looked like lager'.

Somewhere along the line, however, even as Britain was in the midst of the late-1970s real ale craze, Boddington's edge began to blunt. The story is told by the brief entries in successive editions of the *Good Beer Guide*: by 1983, it had ceased to be 'exceptionally bitter' and had become, instead, 'A popular light quaffing bitter', and the 1984 edition noted that 'locals are concerned that the bitter has lost some of its distinctive character'.

While it is possible that politics might have coloured local perceptions to an extent – when Boddington's took over the nearby Oldham Brewery in 1982, it caused a serious falling-out with CAMRA – there are many accounts like this one from blogger Paul Bailey (no relation):

> [As] far back as the late 1970s, when I was still living in Manchester, rumours abounded that Boddington's had reduced the hopping rate of their most famous product to make it less aggressively bitter (blander), so as to increase its appeal to a wider audience. This was confirmed by someone we knew who worked at the brewery, although the company strenuously denied it (they would, wouldn't they?). We ended up voting with our feet and switched to drinking in Holts' pubs, where the bitter still tasted like bitter, and was also quite a bit cheaper as well!

Mike Field's letter to *What's Brewing* quoted above, along with complaints at the 1984 CAMRA AGM, prompted the brewery liaison officer, microbiologist Kevin Buckley, to look into the matter. In a report in the April 1984 edition of *What's Brewing*, he concluded as follows:

> The traditional bitter was fermented to a very low final gravity – around 1000 – removing all fermentable sugars. Now fermentation is allowed to stop at an earlier stage... This affects the palate of the beer, increasing the 'palate fullness' or 'body' of the beer, so the light, slightly thin palate becomes smoother... In combination with the reduction in 'bitterness' and the use of less fragrant hop, the net effect is to produce a beer with a 'smoother mouthfeel', less after-palate, less alcohol and less hop-

aroma.... The colour of the beer has also apparently increased – to mimic the more commonly accepted 'national' bitters.

And it worked, eventually: 'blanded out', Boddington's did indeed become a national brand, in the 1990s, after the brewery was sold to Whitbread. Launched in cans in 1990, it was the bestselling canned bitter for almost a decade, supported by glossy but self-mocking adverts capitalising on its Mancunian roots in the era of the Happy Mondays and Oasis.

But it wasn't really Boddington's – it was an impostor, especially when, after 2004, new owners Interbrew moved production out of the city. Some Mancunians continued to drink it out of habit or nostalgia, while CAMRA members and other beer geeks wouldn't be seen dead with a pint of its 'smooth' keg incarnation. They weren't interested in 'creaminess' – instead, they yearned for that dry, golden, truly bitter beer of 30 years before.

The first to attempt to plug the gap was Manchester brewery Marble which launched 'Manchester Bitter' in around 2001. Never intended as a clone, MMB started from the idea that Boddington's Bitter in its prime was actually a single expression of a localised style. In 2011, head brewer James Campbell was quoted by journalist Will Hawkes: 'It's a pale, mid-strength, hoppy bitter beer, as was drunk in Manchester 30 years ago. That's the tradition here.'

Clone or not, how close does it come to its inspiration? According to Tandleman, 'It does reflect... the dryness and colour of the original Boddington's Bitter, but not the strength – it is much stronger.'

When we drank it at the gorgeously tiled Marble Arch pub in May 2014, we found it hard to distinguish from any number of other 'pale'n'hoppy' beers from the north of England, though perhaps less flowery or perfumed than some examples. If we could arrange for a pint of 1970s Boddington's Bitter to be transported through time and space, would it strike us the same way? We suspect so.

In 2013, another Manchester brewery released a beer inspired, at least to some degree, by Boddington's. J.W. Lees is a large family concern founded in 1828, with a rather conservative image. Their Manchester Pale Ale (MPA) at 3.7% on cask is an attempt to do something that, by their standards, is rather 'out there' – that is to say, not brown. MPA is the name of this particular beer, but, again, seems to imply that there might once have been an entire set of beers in this style – golden, dry, and 'sessionable'.

Perhaps partly because we're suckers for context and cues provided by packaging and branding, we fell hard for MPA as consumed in a Manchester pub. While its bitterness didn't claw at the back of our throats, it did trigger that pleasant chain reaction: pint-thirsty-pint-thirsty-pint... The crusty-bread character we've previously noted in the same brewery's bitter is present and correct, but complemented with more and brighter hops. It won't excite green-nostriled lupulin addicts frantically seeking their next fix, but as a beer to settle on for a few hours, it would be hard to beat.

Our own contribution to this nascent sub-style was a set of notes emailed to Matt Lovatt at Kirkstall Brewery who produced a beer under the name Revitalisation! for our appearance at North Bar in Leeds to promote *Brew Britannia*. We referred to a 1987 Boddington's Bitter recipe supplied by Ron Pattinson and Kristen England which suggested all pale malt and a touch of sugar, and then lots of Goldings hops to achieve dry bitterness without much aroma.

Matt put a lot of thought into interpreting our suggestions and came up with a beer that, as a beer inspired by Michael Hardman's memories of Boddington's or Young's, was probably not quite right. It was, however, very clean, pleasingly austere, and extremely drinkable – a very 'beery' beer.

We couldn't leave the North without drinking at least one pint of the real thing – or at least, the beer that bears the brand of the real thing these days. We found 'smooth' keg Boddington's Bitter on offer at a pub in central Manchester alongside a 'super cold" variant. (Hardly necessary, surely, as the standard version makes your teeth chatter.) It came with an inch of shaving foam on top – weird-looking even in a part of the world where a 'tight creamy head' is the norm – and bubbles clustered on the inside of the apparently slightly grubby glass. It tasted... well, not bad, really. Extremely bland, of course, with a touch of sweetcorn, and reminiscent of, say, Estrella Damm, but, for all that, not *terrible*.

None of the beers mentioned above are the best or most exciting you will find in Manchester – it is a city crammed with great bars and pubs – but we think they do tell you something about its culture and history, and drinking three beers that aren't quite Boddington's can certainly help you discern its outline in the void.

A final tip from Tandleman: 'If you want a beer that tastes pretty much as I recall the original Boddington's Bitter, I'd suggest Linfit Gold Medal from the Sair Inn near Huddersfield. It is as near as I've ever had.'

The secret of Doom Bar's success

First published on our blog in 2018.

How did a beer born on an industrial estate in Cornwall in 1995 become a ubiquitous national brand in just 20 years? And what about it inspires such loyalty, and such disdain?

A few incidents made us really start thinking about Sharp's Doom Bar. The first was a couple of years ago on a research trip to Manchester, having travelled all the way from Penzance, when we walked into a pub – we can't recall which one – to find two cask ales on offer: St Austell Tribute, and Doom Bar.

The second was at a pub in Newlyn, just along the coast from Penzance, where we met two exhausted cyclists who'd just complete the John O'Groats to Land's End run. They wanted one last beer before beginning the long journey home to the Home Counties. When we got talking to them, one of them eventually said to us: "You're into your ales, then? I'll tell you what's a good one – Doom Bar. Do you know it?"

People love this beer. They really, genuinely, unaffectedly find great pleasure in drinking it.

Sales statistics support that: from somewhere around 12 million pints per year in 2009, to 24m in 2010, to 43m by 2016, Doom Bar shifts units. So what is, or has been, Doom Bar's secret? And is there something there other brands might imitate?

There's a trend in Hollywood against repeating origin stories and the tale of Sharp's birth and metamorphosis has been told too many times, but here are some key dates, and a little context:

1994 – founded in Rock, Cornwall, by businessman Bill Sharp
1995 – Doom Bar first launched (a blend of Cornish Coaster and Sharp's Own)
2002 – Stuart Howe joins Sharp's as head brewer
2003 – Joe Keohane and Nick Baker buy out Bill Sharp
2010 – c.24 million pints of Doom Bar per year
2011 – Molson Coors buys Sharp's
2015 – Coors admits to brewing bottled Doom Bar in Burton-upon-Trent

2017 – c.43 million pints of Doom per year

When we were living in London in the noughties, Sharp's beer was ubiquitous, especially in pubs whose clientele skewed middle class, with Cornish Coaster as likely to show up as Doom Bar.

Once we'd started blogging about beer, after 2007, we recall Sharp's having a mixed reputation. Beer writers were schmoozed aggressively (they once invited us to go for a ride on a speedboat on the river Camel) and Stuart Howe, for reasons we'll get into shortly, was a favourite of the BGBW. Beers such as the strong golden Chalky's Bite, a commercial tie-in with celebrity chef Rick Stein brewed with Belgian yeast, stood out as interesting in those pre-BrewDog days.

At the same time, there were grumblings about the 2003 takeover. First, there was a sense that the new slickness of its marketing and ever-growing scale of its operation was, frankly, uncool. And, of course, the beer wasn't What It Used To Be. Finally, there was the fact that everyone knew, or suspected, that the brewery was being fattened for sale to an even bigger player.

The 2011 sale to Molson Coors was the first time we really noticed the familiar arguments around brewery takeovers being played out: it was terrible news, it was brilliant news, what did ownership matter, how could ownership not matter, and so on. Commentators attacked Sharp's, or defended it, as Doom Bar (already a big brand) gained the weight of a corporate sales and PR operation.

Bar-room wisdom has it that Doom Bar's ubiquity after this point was the result of cynical sales tricks such as offering television football licences to publicans in return for taking the beer. It certainly became part of the total package of Molson beers, often seen alongside Coors Light lager and Worthington keg bitter in social clubs and pubs.

The shift of production of some Sharp's branded beers from Cornwall to Burton did further damage to the brewery's reputation, not least because it took prodding for Molson Coors to admit it. (Where a beer is brewed doesn't matter, except for marketing purposes when it suddenly does.) In 2015 the claim was the only bottled Doom Bar was being brewed in Staffordshire and that cask production continued to take place solely in Rock. When we checked in with Sharp's in 2017, we were told that continued to be the case, but for whatever reason, many drinkers, based on conversations we've had in pubs, simply don't believe this to be true.

In our early days as beer bloggers, Sharp's then head brewer, Stuart Howe, was a somewhat intimidating figure.

He was invariably pictured with biceps on display, or looking fit to burst out of a standard issue head brewer's blazer, barely smiling. In his interviews and writing from the time we detected a certain defensiveness over Doom Bar; how could everyone have so many good things to say about BrewDog and so few positive words for his award-winning, technically perfect, extremely popular cask ale?

Mr Howe left Sharp's in 2015 and is now the head brewer at Harbour, another Cornish brewery, where we emailed him in November. He was happy to answer our questions, including the big one: what is the secret to Doom Bar's appeal?

> Doom was always characterised by being subtler than most of the cask ales on the market with a softness on the palate, a gentle fruity bitterness, and a clean finish. It was a great deal more accessible than the harder, drier tasting cask beer which dominated the category back in 2002. It used to convert a lot of drinkers to ales from lager. I've found that in beer preferences there is a continuum which runs from people who don't like beer because it's bitter to people who like beer that feels like someone has pulled out your tongue and nailed it to a plank.
>
> Humanity has evolved to avoid bitterness, rottenness and dryness because substances which have those taste properties are often harmful. Most people therefore are at the end of the continuum closest to the low bitterness/dryness/rottenness and Doom Bar appeals to them. Geeky drinkers tend to choose challenging beers at the opposite end.
>
> When Doom was growing at 40% per year, every pub we sold the beer into ordered more beer each week as more drinkers converted to Doom.
>
> At the time we had no one in marketing and the marketing budget just about covered a few bar towels and beer mats so there was no manipulation of the gullible, people just enjoyed drinking the beer.

One complaint levelled against Doom Bar by real ale purists is that it barely counts as cask-conditioned. That's because it ships from the brewery with relatively little live yeast in the cask, relatively little expertise required to handle it in a pub cellar and, correspondingly, there is little of the mystique of Bass or Landlord. Stuart Howe confirms that this ease of handling was vital in Doom Bar's popularity with publicans, which in turn was a key step in its popularity with drinkers:

> Doom was popular with landlords because it was racked with a lower yeast count and the correct CO_2 level for dispensing. This meant you could put the beer on about 4 hours after it was delivered and it would be crystal clear and full of condition. To achieve this, the beer was conditioned in the brewery before racking and of course the elements which affect how it would perform in trade were measured and controlled. There weren't many breweries in the UK doing this at the time.

If some subtle variation is all part of the fun for cask ale drinkers – again, that mystique – then Doom Bar's rigid consistency is a mark against it for that audience, but a significant plus for casual drinkers. Stuart Howe describes achieving uniformity from one brew to the next, and from one year to the next, as an exhausting battle:

> Doom is a difficult beer to manage because of its subtlety. The hardest thing a brewer has to do is to maintain a beer's palate in the context of continual change.
>
> Every year the hops are different, the malt is different and there are changes in the hops and malt from the day they are harvested to the day your stocks run out and you change on to the next year's crop.
>
> Also, yeast varies from generation to generation and can do strange things in response to nutritional changes in the wort.

> As a brewer you need to continually make small changes to the process to maintain the consistency of the beer. The more subtle the beer, the greater the impact of change and hence difficulty in maintaining the balance.
>
> Add to this getting the beer to be the same from two entirely new breweries, the crop of the main hop variety failing, and the barley variety being changed by the supplier twice and you've got a tough job.
>
> That's why I didn't take a holiday for five years at Sharp's and why I've got a heart condition!

Jason Merry is now sales manager for Devon brewery Otter but spent much of the noughties as Sharp's regional sales manager for the West Country, based primarily in Bristol. We spoke to him over a pot of tea at a central Bristol cafe in late November, and it was evident that he remains proud of the part he played in making Doom Bar a star. He began by offering a useful reminder of what Doom Bar was 15 years ago: a hip, upmarket product associated with surfing and sport, second homes and music festivals:

> At Sharp's, we hated that image of the old man in the flat cap drinking warm, flat bitter. We were young, we liked surfing and the beach, so we had hoodies and all that. The national appeal of the beer was based a bit on 'posh Cornwall' – the Rock crowd, up in London.

He also believes that the sales team had a certain youthful vigour missing from better-established rivals which had dominated the market:

> We were very aggressive on the ground, almost to the point of where people thought we were arrogant. We were all in our twenties and just really up for it. I think some of the older local and national brands commonly seen around the region at that time had got a bit lazy and complacent, and whereas their sales people would be in the pub chewing the landlord's ear for half an hour, telling anecdote after anecdote, we were more like, 'Right, let's do

some business, let's sell some beer.' Publicans are busy people.

He echoes Stuart Howe's suggestion that the technical qualities of the product gave it a leg up:

> We held onto it for a few days longer than other breweries typically might with cask ale, seven to ten days, so when it went into pubs, it was ready to go. There was less sediment so, crucially, the yield was better. They'd always get another pint or two out of a tub.

But suggests, contradicting Howe's underdog narrative, that the capital Kehoane and Baker put behind the product helped enormously:

> When someone ordered a tub of Doom Bar, they got the works. No expense was spared on point-of-sale material. No flimsy, flappy cardboard pump-clips -- proper enamelled ones, and glasses, beer mats, bar runners... I knew once I'd got a pub to take it once, it would stick, and I could move on.

This 'stickiness' was a recurring theme: Doom Bar was a reliable product (critics might say bland) that won customers' loyalty, and that of publicans in turn. That meant a small sales team could dominate an entire region, getting the beer into every freehouse in, say, Taunton, and then moving on.

There is an ironic kicker in Jason Merry's story as he acknowledges, without bitterness, that Doom Bar has become a challenge in his new role: "Now I'm with Otter I spend a lot of time trying to undo my own work. Doom Bar is everywhere and, like I said, it's hard to dislodge it. People are very loyal to that brand."

We asked our followers on Twitter for their thoughts on Doom Bar and got some interesting responses. Given the obvious self-selection – people who follow us are, by definition, to a greater or lesser degree, 'beer geeks' – it wasn't surprised that many were critical:

'It's the only [boring brown bitter] I won't drink anymore, even as a distress purchase. I had a pint of Hop House lager when last faced with DB as the only ale on.'

'It's the Devil's vomit.'

'Never drink it, never have, never will... [because it's] ubiquitous, aggressively marketed, in every pub you go into…'

'I used to quite like it - when I only got to drink it when I went to Cornwall. Seemed fairly characterful and tasty. Not cutting edge, but respectable. And then... Molson Coors. I don't believe it's the same beer now, bland even when well kept, and it seems to encapsulate all that's wrong with globalisation. Will only drink it as an absolute last resort - or last but one, if GK IPA is the alternative.'

But other comments were perhaps surprisingly positive, such as this from Michael, who Tweets @bringonthebeer:

The biggest shame for me over the whole issue was that an ale which was an occasional treat (yes, I like how it tastes – subjectivity rules!) has now become as ubiquitous a background feature as any other mass market beer, through no fault of its own… Doom Bar is a middling inoffensive beer in itself and it's a better fall back option in mass market pubs than Ruddles or Abbott or, ye gods John Smith's or Worthington. I do have qualms about a certain % of my £ propping up 'big beer' but I try to remember that there's a small Cornish brewery underneath all the hype and hostility.

Steve (@untilnextyear) pointed out Doom Bar's success in broadening the appeal of cask ale:

I remember 10+ years ago it being the saviour of a pub I went to frequently that previously didn't serve real ale and had said it had no demand for it. Suddenly, there was a different crowd and happy real ale drinkers who had in the past steered clear.

    Journalist Tom Davidson used to like Doom Bar, but doesn't anymore, and puts forward an interesting argument for why that might be: "The ale… is often stocked at pubs which don't specialise in beer but want something to offer the beer-drinking punter… Sadly for a beer I once cherished, I've gone off Doom Bar so entirely due to poor pints I make almost every effort to avoid it."

On balance, then, it seems Doom Bar was successful because it required less care from publicans, and less waiting, with each cask yielding a little more beer; because its owners invested in marketing, especially at point of sale, conveyed a sense of quality and reliability to consumers; because it reminded people of holidays, and an aspirational lifestyle of sand, surfboards and picnics; and because it became a name brand, like Guinness, to which publicans and drinkers are extremely loyal.

    In our experience, Doom Bar doesn't taste any worse now than it did a decade ago. If anything, we've found ourselves enjoying it a little more – does it seem a touch drier and lighter these days, perhaps? So we don't buy into the narrative that Molson Coors ruined a once decent beer; rather, we think they were drawn to a beer that was already successful because it was precision engineered for the mainstream.

Guinness jumps the shark

First published at allaboutbeer.com in 2016.

Guinness is a mighty global brand but there are signs that it is struggling to maintain its position as The Stout. In Britain in particular its popularity has been sliding for almost a decade: between 2008 and 2014 sales dropped by approximately 50 million litres per year, from more than 250m to around 200m.

Quite apart from cold numbers there is the woollier but very much related question of status. We know from anecdotal evidence that among British beer geeks the standard Guinness stouts are not regarded with much fondness at all – a situation all the more surprising when its recent history is considered.

In the mid-20th century, it is no exaggeration to say that Guinness was regarded as about the hippest beer around -- a brew for connoisseurs, and a beer of almost mystical complexity and brilliance. That view was expressed eloquently by the humourist Paul Jennings in a 1959 article in The Times of London in which he referred to a long-running advertising campaign featuring pints of Guinness with smiling faces in their foam:

> This smile is the nearest they have got to expressing the true mana of Guinness — that great Irish mystery and paradox, the light froth from the unimaginable dark heart of the liquid, the light from darkness, like the laughter and wit that well up from the Irish soul itself... I, like any other non-Irish consumer of Guinness, drink it because it is there... [in] the sense in which Mallory said that Everest was there. I might drink beer automatically, but Guinness is a thing, it has to be reckoned with.

Back then, enthusiasts shared details of the oddities of its manufacture such as the addition of soured beer to give the finished product its tang, and discussed how temperamental it could be if stored and served at the wrong temperature, or for too long, or not long enough.

As far as British drinkers were concerned there was a strict hierarchy: draught Guinness brewed in Dublin was swooned over.

Bottled Guinness brewed in Dublin was a close second. The products of Guinness's London brewery, Park Royal, which opened in 1936, were poor relations, but still quite acceptable.

Bottled Guinness was a staple in most British pubs, and cities with substantial Irish populations also had draught Guinness if one knew where to look. From the 1930s the truly discerning would trek to London's East End to drink draught Guinness (probably London brewed) at the White Hart on Mile End Road, AKA Murphy's, or in central London could visit Mooney's on The Strand and Ward's Irish House at Piccadilly Circus.

In the 1950s, recognising that draught Guinness had a cult following, management took steps to increase the supply, establishing a small team to work on the challenge of serving it in a way that preserved its mystique – and especially the creamy head – without requiring publicans to be expert Guinness tamers. By 1958 they had perfected a system known as Easy Serve which used a mix of nitrogen and carbon dioxide to create a soft, stable head without fizz.

The popularity of this new form of draught Guinness among UK drinkers took the brewery's management by surprise. As Brendan Nolan, a Guinness advertising man, once observed, drinkers viewed it as, 'At last, the real thing,' and its fame spread by word of mouth. This was frustrating for some at the London brewery who knew that the draught version was pasteurised, unlike the bottles.

Veteran beer writer Roger Protz recorded in his memoir A Life on the Hop, published in 2009, a peer's observation that if all kegged (i.e. pasteurised, filtered, artificially carbonated) beers had been as good as draught Guinness then the Campaign for Real Ale (CAMRA) would never have got off the ground. This is a remarkable testament to just how good it must have been at that time, when 'keg' was otherwise utterly reviled.

Throughout the 1960s and into the 70s Guinness fought hard to own the UK stout market and established British brands such as Mackeson, a sweet stout produced by Whitbread, lost ground to the beefier, drier Irish incomer. In 1969 Bass Charrington and Watney's, two of the huge conglomerates that dominated British brewing at the time, contrived a rival brew called Colonel Murphy's, but they gave up after six months and surrendered, agreeing (after years of pressure from Park Royal) to sell draught Guinness in their own vast estates of pubs. Soon, Guinness seemed to be in every pub, in every home, and on every TV – VHS to Mackeson's Betamax.

Already brewed and drunk around the world in various forms, with the roll out of Irish theme pubs from the early 1990s, draught Guinness was soon to be found in everywhere from Mongolia to Manitoba, emerging from increasingly elaborate chromed fonts, dripping with condensation, each pint cosmetically identical to the next. Literally iconic.

But, somewhere along the line, the beer itself seems to have lost the very soul that helped it rise to such dominance. Beers that are around for a long time often come to be perceived as Not What They Used to Be (see also Pilsner Urquell, for example). Sometimes that is down to jaded palates, or is the result of a counter-cultural bias against big brands and big business. Both of those might apply to Guinness but there is also objective evidence of a drop in quality, or at least of essential changes to the product.

Guinness has tended to be secretive about process, recipes and ingredients but we do know, for example, that the temperature of draught Guinness dropped significantly from about 1988 onward, falling from a typical 12 degrees Celsius to a target of 7 degrees. This is one thing that caused those drinkers of traditional cask-conditioned ale who had regarded draught Guinness as the one tolerable keg beer to turn against it.

Still, the bottled version remained unpasteurised and bottle-conditioned, and its reputation among the cognoscenti soared. But, as the 1990s approached, the firm was convinced the creamy head was the key to the beer's appeal and so began to put all its effort into marketing canned beer with a surge-inducing 'widget'. The bottle was no longer the prestige take home product. By 1989 the only place bottle-conditioned Guinness could be found in England and Wales was in pubs and it was phased out entirely from 1994.

These measures, though they increased sales among mainstream drinkers, might almost have been designed to alienate enthusiasts and writers who had previously championed Guinness, such as Roger Protz who today says, 'I was devastated when Guinness turned Original from a bottle-conditioned stout into a run-of-the-mill filtered beer.'

Bill Yenne's 2007 authorised history of the brewery, Guinness: the 250-year Search for the Perfect Pint, has Guinness master brewer Fergal Murray confirming that roast barley extract added to the boil has indeed replaced roasted barley proper in the mash tun. David Hughes, who worked for Guinness in London from 1972, includes in his 2006 book *A Bottle of Guinness, Please* many details of how Guinness has been made through the years. He records that hop extracts were introduced to the process for London-brewed Guinness from 1983. He also mentions that high-gravity brewing – brewing at high strength and then, in layman's terms, watering down – was introduced in 1990.

Beyond what's on record, there are also rumours that wood-ageing of the soured blending beer has given way to an addition of food-grade lactic acid. We put this to Diageo's press office which was unable to confirm or deny but arranged for us to speak to a brewer, albeit with the caveat that they didn't expect anyone at the brewery would be willing or able to give away such information either.

When master brewer Steve Kilcullen called he was charming but defensive. With some prodding he admitted that hop extracts were used but said, 'I have to say I don't think there's any difference in flavour.' When asked about lactic acid, he became almost frosty, choosing his words with the care of a Soviet diplomat: 'There's a number of elements we don't talk about, as I'm sure you'll understand.' One change he was happy to discuss was the reduction in dissolved oxygen in the beer over the last 20 years: 'Dissolved oxygen is a total no-no, it imparts off flavours. If you drank a beer with dissolved oxygen in high concentration you'd say, it's off, it's not right.'

The problem is, as independent breweries become ever more transparent, this tight-lipped protection of trade secrets and 'mystery', as its staff members seem to have been drilled to mention at every turn, gives the unfortunate impression that perhaps Guinness is not as proud of its processes and ingredients as it likes to insist.

While each of the changes listed above might, in isolation, be possible to dismiss as making a negligible difference to flavour, together they must surely have an effect. Is Guinness a different beer now than 60 years ago? Definitely. Is it worse? It is certainly hard to imagine it inspiring any writer today to swoon as Paul Jennings did in 1958.

It is probably no coincidence that the great drop in UK sales happens to coincide with when the rise of American-style craft beer in the UK, and the approximate doubling in the number of independent breweries. Where Guinness was once the choice of the free-thinking iconoclast, that role is now more ably played by a strong IPA, quirky saison or, yes, an alternative stout from the brewery on the corner. In Britain and Ireland today the absence of Guinness is often an important way in which a bar or pub signals its status as a Serious Beer

Place. Martin Hayes is the head of the Craft Beer Company which runs a string of beer-focused pubs and bars across London, none of which serve Guinness. 'Our perspective is that it's available across the board,' he says, carefully. 'Our focus is on smaller producers. It's not a comment on Guinness per se.'

The Porterhouse, with branches in Dublin and London, is famous for its own range of stouts. They pay homage to Guinness with their creamy nitro heads but, at the same time, amplify the flavour. Meantime, founded in London by Alastair Hook in 2000, has had a strong bottle-conditioned porter, in 750ml champagne-style bottles, as one of its flagship beers since 2005, and also has a London Stout. When in 2011 Camden Brewery released a nitrogenated draught stout, Camden Ink, its name and graphic design inspired by tattoo culture, it promptly displaced Guinness from many of the more fashionable bar counters across London.

The last year or two has seen a further flurry of new stouts launched by regional brewers keen to convince committed Guinness drinkers to switch to something reassuringly similar, but different. Cornish brewery St Austell, founded in 1851, recently launched Mena Dhu, a stout which, on draught, looks just like Guinness but has a deeper, smokier, sweeter flavour. The bottled version, with live yeast, lacks the creamy head but evokes the supposedly ambrosial packaged Guinness of 30 years ago. (The recipe is completely original.)

For its part, Guinness is trying to boost its credibility by launching a range of craft beers – well, sort-of. Two historically inspired bottled stouts – West Indies Export and Dublin Porter – are good but probably not exciting enough to win over cider drinkers, lager lovers or BrewDog fans. A lacklustre golden ale that is actually brown, and experiments with IPA and lager, don't seem to be hitting the spot either. A handful of more adventurous beers, such as a toasted oatmeal brown ale with vanilla, are coming out of the Open Gate microbrewery at St James's Gate, open to the public at weekends.

Our suggestion is simple, if not original: they should take standard Guinness and pep it up, just a touch. Make it a notch stronger, a little more bitter, and ship at least one version with live yeast. When we've floated this idea in the past, however, we've been told by those in the know that it is a pipe dream: Guinness is now too big to change course, and the brewery is too sterile and streamlined to allow for packaging with live yeast.

In the meantime, other brewers ought to look at Guinness and learn: if your core product has cult status, be certain before you decide to let it slip away, because when it's gone, it's gone.

Pale and hoppy

First published at allaboutbeer.com in 2015.

So yellow it looks almost green, like elderflower cordial or the white wine of the Rhine, and from it rises a vapour -- pagan tendrils curling into the nose and throat, possessing the palate even before a sip has been taken, and triggering memories of nettles, cut grass, pine forests, and the waft of weed on a city street in summer. All this against the shadows and shining wood of a well-worn pub in a northern town where the sun hasn't shone since the other side of Christmas. All this at £2.80 a pint, and at five pints per session, with no hint of a hangover though the green and the gold lingers, fastens its fingers, and pulls you back.

Some of the best beers being made in Britain today belong to a style that has no name. They are the colour of pilsner, usually made with only pale malt, but they are not mere 'golden ales' – 'golden' is not, after all, a flavour. They have extravagant, upfront New World hopping suggesting tropical fruits and aromatic flowers but they are not US-style India Pale Ales because their alcoholic strength is likely to be somewhere between 3-5% ABV. Though this might sound like a description of US session IPA, beers of this type have been around in the UK for more than 20 years. If they are given a name at all, as in Mark Dredge's 2013 book *Craft Beer World*, it is usually a variation on the simply descriptive 'pale'n'hoppy'.

In the mid-20th century there were several British beers noted for their pale colour, Boddington's Bitter from Manchester being the most notable. That particular beer was also intensely hopped although the hops were English and were used to generate a bitterness that 'clawed at the back of your throat' rather than delicate aroma. As the 1970s and 80s wore on, strong dark beers such as Theakstons's Old Peculier and Fuller's ESB became cult favourites among beer geeks, while pale yellow lagers became fashionable with mainstream drinkers. Boddington's Bitter darkened in colour and gradually lost its bitter edge.

As a result, when, in the late 1980s, the first golden ales emerged, they seemed positively and refreshingly innovative. Exmoor Gold from the Somerset-Devon border can claim to be the first of this new breed but it was really Hop Back Summer Lightning, first brewed in 1989, that triggered a trend. Conceived by former big-brewery man

John Gilbert as a cask-conditioned lager, it instead became an ale that merely *looked* like lager, which he hoped would lure drinkers back from then highly fashionable brands such as Stella Artois. It won a string of awards and, before long, any brewery hoping to appeal to connoisseurs had to have a golden ale in its range.

That cosmetic trend coincided with another new development: the arrival in Britain of American and New Zealand hop varieties, along with US beers such as Sierra Nevada Pale Ale and Anchor Liberty, which showed those hops off at their best.

Sean Franklin first experimented with American Cascade hops as far back as the early 1980s. Having worked and been trained in the wine industry he was an expert in the characteristics of different grape varieties and believed similar subtlety could also be drawn out of hops. His first brewery didn't work out, however, and he ended up driving a taxi for five years. When he returned to brewing in 1993, he had, in effect, conceived a new type of beer, as he explained in an interview we conducted in 2013:

> I'd had Summer Lightning and that was a great inspiration, a lovely beer. Flavour is about competition, the different components coming up against each other. So, when you use crystal malt and Cascade, you get orange and toffee. When you use Cascade with just pale malt, you don't get orange – just that floral, citrusy character. The plainer the background, the better. It allows the essential character of the hops to show much more clearly.

The flagship beer of his new brewery, Rooster's, was Yankee – straw-coloured, hopped with then-obscure Cascade and, though still essentially a golden ale, a touch more aromatic than most UK drinkers were used to at the time. At a mere 4.3%, however, it also fit comfortably into British pub and beer festival culture, which then, even more so than now, required beers to be drinkable by the pint and, ideally, in multiple pints over the course of several hours. Along with a range of stronger beers brewed by Brendan Dobbin in Manchester at around the same time, it turned many British real ale drinkers into confirmed hop fanatics.

A contemporary product developed quite independently was Oakham's Jeffrey Hudson Bitter, or JHB, also first brewed in 1993. Despite its name, which suggests something old-fashioned and varnish-brown, it too was inspired by Summer Lightning and has always been golden with extravagantly fruity late-hopping (a combination of Challenger and Mount Hood) suggestive of elderflower and lemon peel. Hopping levels have been constantly nudged upwards over the last 20 years to accommodate the palates of drinkers spoiled by double IPAs – head brewer John Bryan estimates that there are about two-and-a-half times as many hops now as in 1993 – but it still seems relatively restrained compared to some newer iterations of the style. Oakham's own Citra, for example, was the first UK beer to use that hop variety, in 2010, and is even more flamboyantly pungent than its older sibling.

Nigel Wattam, Oakham's marketing man, says that the majority of Oakham's range is 'very light, or really dark, with not much in-between'. On the appeal of 'pale'n'hoppy' beers more generally he says, 'I think we've converted a lot of lager drinkers because it's the same colour, but it has more flavour.'

There is a similar logic behind Kelham Island's Pale Rider, which was first brewed in 1993 in Sheffield. The brewery was founded by the late Dave Wickett, an influential figure on the British beer scene with a hand in several other breweries, and whose former employees and associates include many of the current generation of UK craft brewers. Writer Melissa Cole credits Pale Rider with arousing her interest in beer and in her book, *Let Me Tell You About Beer*, records that it was initially conceived to appeal to female drinkers, with restrained bitterness and ramped-up aroma. Popular among northern real ale drinkers for a decade, it became nationally famous in 2004 when it was declared Champion Beer of Britain by the Campaign for Real Ale (CAMRA). It is best enjoyed in Sheffield at the brewery tap, the Fat Cat, where its feather-light body and punchy, peachy perfume makes it easy drinking despite its 5.2% ABV. Nonetheless, the brewery has also produced Easy Rider, a similar beer at 4.3%.

Another cult favourite is Hophead from Dark Star, a brewery in Brighton, a fashionable coastal resort an hour's train ride south of London. Mark Tranter, recently voted the best brewer in the UK by the British Guild of Beer Writers for his work at his own brewery, Burning Sky, worked at Dark Star from the 1990s until 2013. He recalls that, at some time after 1996, one of the owners of the Evening Star pub where the brewery was then based went to California and came back with Cascade hop pellets. These, along with other US hops available in small quantities via hop merchants Charles Faram, formed the basis of 'The Hophead Club', conceived by Dark Star founder Rob Jones. At each meeting of the club members would taste a different single-hopped beer. 'Cascade was the customers' and brewers' favourite, so it was not long until that became the staple,' recalls Tranter. When he took on more responsibility in the brewery, Tranter tweaked the recipe, reducing its bitterness, and, in 2001, dropping its strength from 4% ABV to 3.8%. Today, with the brewery under new ownership and with a different team in the brew-house, the beer remains single-minded and popular, giving absolute priority to bright aromas of grapefruit and elderflower.

If the style isn't officially recognised, how can you spot a pale'n'hoppy on the bar when out drinking in the UK? First, turn to smaller microbreweries. The larger, older family breweries have not been hugely successful in this territory, perhaps being too conservative to embrace the fundamental lack of balance that characterises the style. (There are exceptions: Adnams Ghost Ship, for example, has been a notable success both among beer geeks and less studious drinkers.) Secondly, look for a conspicuous mention of a specific hop variety on the hand-pump badge, along with names that include 'Hop', 'Gold' and sometimes (but less often) 'Blonde'. Pointed mentions of citrus are another giveaway. Finally, a very broad generalisation: breweries in the north are particularly adept -- we once heard the style jokingly referred to as 'Pennine Champagne' after the range of hills and mountains that runs from Derbyshire to the Scottish border.

Salopian Oracle (Shropshire, 4%), Burning Sky Plateau (Sussex, 3.5%), Marble Pint (Manchester, 3.9%) and Redemption Trinity (London, 3%) are among the best examples.

Rooster's Yankee, Kelham Island Pale Rider, Oakham JHB and Dark Star Hophead are all available in cans or bottles, though they are best tasted fresh and close to source. From US brewers, the nearest equivalents are among the new breed of session IPAs and pale ales, such as Firestone Walker Easy Jack. These two distinct traditions – UK pale'n'hoppy is traditional session bitter with a glamorous makeover, whereas American brews are big beers reined in – have ended up in a remarkably similar place. For all of those who like to wallow in hops over the course of hours, both are good news.

The mystery of Old Chimneys

First published at allaboutbeer.com in 2016.

There is only one British beer in RateBeer's top 50 chart – Old Chimneys' Good King Henry Special reserve imperial stout – which, as far as some people are concerned, makes it The Best Beer in Britain.

But here's the wrinkle: hardly any British drinkers have heard of it, let alone tasted it. An informal poll conducted via Twitter revealed that, of the 264 people who responded, only about half were aware of the brewery at all and only around 20 per cent had ever tasted *any* of the brewery's beers. (And bear in mind that our Twitter followers are by definition 'beer people'.) Nor has it ever placed in the Campaign for Real Ale's annual champion bottled beer of Britain competition.

So how did Old Chimneys' Good King Henry Special Reserve (GKHSR) gain its lofty reputation? The answer lies in large part with one super-fan, and in the strange dynamics of beer rating communities.

Alan Thomson, Old Chimneys' founder, has just turned 60 and has been working as a brewer for almost 40 years. Having graduated with a degree in bio-chemistry, in 1977 he got a job with Vaux, a large brewery in the north east of England, where he worked until the mid-1990s in, as he puts it, 'the mainstream of brewing'. Then in 1995 he moved to the East Anglian county of Suffolk and set up his own small brewery primarily producing cask-conditioned beer for the local pub market. He is as bewildered by GKHSR's rise to global acclaim as anyone else: 'I wanted to escape from the rat race, not get back into it!'

His head-scratching confusion is only compounded by the circumstances in which this particular beer came to be:

> I first brewed Good King Henry, the normal version, in 2000. It was already a strong beer at 9.6% made with a fairly high proportion of malt extract to get up to that strength. I don't know if I should say this but... The first batch of Special Reserve was the result of a cock-up in 2002. I miscalculated and added too much malt extract.

It then occurred to him that an 11% ABV beer might be just the thing to celebrate the brewery's upcoming tenth anniversary. He threw in some winemakers' oak chips and left it to mature for six months before bottling and then left it alone. When he came to taste it in late 2004 he was delighted to find that it had come good: 'I thought, ooh, hold on, that's absolutely beautiful… I'm on to something here.' He brewed a second batch while the first batch was sold to local drinkers over Christmas 2004.

So far, so ordinary. What happened next, however, is that it began to escape from Suffolk. Some bottles were sold at the 2006 East London beer festival run by the Campaign for Real Ale, with bottled beers sourced by festival organiser Keen Massey. It is an event heavily attended by 'tickers' and RateBeerians, as users of the site are known, and the first handful of RateBeer reviews are all traceable to this event. That's also where RateBeerian Chris Owen bought bottles for his stash only he went a step further: in the summer of 2007 he took them on a trans-Atlantic trip to a RateBeer summer gathering in the US. 'There weren't too many UK Imperial Stouts around in those days,' he says, 'and since it's better to take a "big beer" to that sort of event rather than some bottled bitter or the like which in all probability wouldn't come across too well, I guess it was a bit of a no brainer.'

There, drinkers not only from the US but from all around the world had the opportunity to try a beer that had an added mystique because Alan Thomson made so little effort to market it: 'Apparently the only way to get this beer is to trek to the brewery and basically get it from the hand of the brewer himself', said user 'badgerben' in his 2007 review. This was essentially true. Even today, there is no email address given on the Old Chimneys' website and Thomson did not, at that time, dispatch beer by mail order.

The flurry of high rankings that followed that summer gathering – most awarding 18, 19 or 20 out of 20 and accompanied by profuse thanks to 'Chris_O' – put the beer into the Top 50 chart. That might have been a blip except those events brought it to the attention of Edinburgh beer lover Craig Garvie. He is an enthusiastic character, often to be seen at beer festival in a colourful bowler hat, steampunk shades and with his beard dyed one colourful shade or another. A particular fan of strong stouts he knew he had to get his hands on GKHSR:

> I phoned up the brewery and basically begged him to sell me some. He wasn't doing mail order then but I said I'd take all the risk, pay whatever he wanted. That first order

was for twenty-four bottles, twelve of the Special Reserve, six standard, and six of his other beers.

Craig Garvie was to become one of the key players in the further spread of GKHSR:

Because it was rare to everyone but me, because I had a lot of it, I kind of handed it out to anyone that wanted it. Like, my postman got a bottle, and if someone at work said it was their husband's fiftieth birthday I'd say, 'Do they like beer?' and they'd get one.

He acknowledges, however, that his motives were not purely altruistic: 'I was doing a lot of trading on RateBeer and was suddenly able to trade it for other rare things with people in the US.'

He has been buying GKHSR by the case, sometimes more, sometimes less, every year since, and either trading or giving much of it away. As another RateBeer user, Andrew Drinkwater, says, Garvie is 'effectively their international distribution arm... posting bottles to people who are almost certain to rate it highly'. Though he is not the only person to have shared bottles of GKHSR Garvie remains perhaps its most vocal hypeman on social media, organising social tastings in Scotland and elsewhere and writing many, many reviews on RateBeer of each bottle he has drunk. 'It's definitely the beer I drink most of – maybe eight bottles a year or something like that,' he says – an unusual tally for someone with what he calls a 'RateBeer problem' normally compelled to seek fresh 'rates' over familiar beers.

Does the beer deserve its consistent place in the top 50 beers and its status as RateBeer's top English beer? It is generally felt that RateBeer has a bias towards scarce beers such as Westvleteren XII, and towards imperial stouts in particular. Beer writer Bryan Roth has conducted extensive number-crunching on RateBeer data and in a 2013 post on his blog *This is Why I'm Drunk* observed that: 'More often than not [imperial stouts] are limited release, limited distribution and well hyped. It's a perfect storm.'

Even Craig Garvie, devotee that he is, acknowledges that there are other strong British stouts that are just as good. Nonetheless, he says, if it wasn't a fundamentally good beer, whatever the hype around it, the ratings would eventually drop off. They haven't:

It has been in the top 50 for a long time which is not true of many beers. I can think of a few that were there when I started and have gone. One of the problems of RateBeer is that you do get fads for certain breweries but Old Chimneys' hasn't been like that. It's never been impossible to get hold of and it is a great beer so I don't think it lets people down, it doesn't disappoint.

Others we spoke to said the same thing: its fame might be a quirk of the way RateBeer functions but the praise is not undeserved. We tasted a bottle of the 2013 brew supplied by Craig Garvie from his personal stash. It is a dense, luscious beer with an intense dessert-wine sweetness and an undercurrent of beef and bitterness. There are other beers that taste similar – Prince of Denmark, a 7.5% ABV stout brewed by Harvey's of Lewes for example – but, based on this brief encounter, GKHSR is no fraud.

For his part, Alan Thomson has mixed feelings, saying, in his quiet way:

I find the idea of having a worldwide following a bit odd and I can honestly say it's not what I had planned. Sometimes I do wish it had never happened, when all hell breaks loose every autumn with people trying to get hold of the beer. I get phone calls from everywhere, all round the world, not just America. I ask myself, 'Why am I doing this?'

He is personally more fond of another beer he brews – an 11.4% oak-aged ale called Red Admiral – not least because, unlike GKHSR, it was executed as planned: 'I suppose I've always felt a bit resentful that my best known beer is the result of making the best of a balls-up so, from a professional point of view, Red Admiral is much more satisfying.'

Mixmaster, mix faster

First published in CAMRA's BEER *magazine in 2018.*

Have you ever ordered a half-and-half, a Granny, Ram-n-Spesh or even a Proporval in the pub?

Until quite recently mixing beers was a perfectly normal activity. We know that Londoners in the 18th century drank blends of mature and fresh beer, for example, and by the mid-19th century 'half-and-half' was an everyday phrase defined in James Camden Hotten's *Slang Dictionary* as 'a mixture of ale and porter, much affected by medical students'. He also tells us of 'cooper' which was a blend of porter and stout, reflecting a fine distinction rather lost on us today. By the 1930s 'mild-and-bitter', or 'M&B', was the most common blend – so popular, in fact, that a wartime propaganda film depicted it as the quintessential drink of pubs in the north of England. By the late 1950s the trend was for mixing highly carbonated bottled beers with draught to liven up the latter, or for mixing lager with lime juice. In an uncredited article in *The Times* in 1958 one commentator observed that 'the brewer has to contend with astonishing permutations and combinations of his own [beer]… brewed with extreme trouble to be drunk on its own.'

In the 1970s early beer books such as *Beer and Skittles* by Richard Boston listed a whole range of mixed drinks from the basics to more advanced combinations, although it was obvious by this time that they were developing novelty value. The following list derives primarily from Richard Boston with additions from various other 20th century sources.

- Shandy – lemonade or ginger beer mixed with bitter or mild
- B.B. – burton (AKA 'winter warmer') and bitter
- Half-and-half – bitter and stout, or bitter and mild
- Brown split – bitter and bottled brown ale
- Black velvet – Guinness and champagne, or Guinness and cider
- Lightplater – draught bitter with bottled light ale
- Granny – old (ale) and mild

- Mother-in-law – a sexist joke very much of its time – "old and bitter"
- Boilermaker – brown ale and mild
- Blacksmith – stout and barley wine
- 'Happy Days' – wee heavy and bitter
- Dragon's blood – barley wine and rum
- Dog's nose – bitter and gin
- Milk and Mackeson – 'better than it sounds' Richard Boston says.

Then, somehow, this kind of thing seemed to go out of fashion. Draught mild, along with bottled light and brown ales, became rarer, for one thing. At the same time monolithic brands grew increasingly potent so that customers came more and more to order 'A pint of Brand X' rather than by style. And pubs became more business-like, not only more reluctant to pander to the foibles of regulars – or, indeed, to have regulars – but also less likely to have staff sufficiently well-trained and confident to pull pints of half-n-half in the age of Trading Standards.

In the past decade or so we have had mixed success (no pun intended) ordering this kind of thing. Sometimes we've asked in Young's pubs for 'A half pint of Special in a pint glass and a bottle of Ram Rod, please,' only to get a withering look and, 'Ram-n-Spesh, you mean?' On other occasions we've been looked at as if completely unhinged when asking for a half-and-half of Fuller's London Pride and London Porter, or when topping up a half-finished pint of some less exciting beer with Guinness.

Which brings us to one good reason for mixing beers: done right it can rescue a mediocre pint. Of course in an ideal world every pub would have great beer in great condition but sometimes, in the real world, compromises have to be made, which is when those bottles of Mann's Brown Ale in the fridge or the half of draught stout come in handy, adding another layer of depth to bland bitters or masking and diluting off flavours. Mann's is a fairly one-dimensional beer but added to another one-dimensional beer can do wonderful things. Bottled light ale is rarely seen these days but bottled bitters or even bottled or draught lager can work just as well, lifting a tired pint without overwhelming its flavour.

Sometimes, though, mixing beers can be more positively motivated – actively creative rather than merely pragmatic. We've all had beers we think would be perfect if they were a little more or less sweet/bitter, hoppy/malty, flowery/restrained, boozy/sessionable and so on. We know of one veteran beer enthusiast who mixes alcohol-free beer with potent bottled ales to bring them down to cask strength. Gary Gillman, a part-time scholar of beer history based in Toronto, Canada, has written about his mixing habits, often with the aim of recreating specific beers from the past that are no longer available. "I like to do porter and a barrel-aged beer to emulate an 1700s-1800s porter," he told us in an email, "Rodenbach and Fuller's porter, say. Or Orval with IPA or pale ale to impart a touch of 19th century Brett."

This last is one of our favourite tricks, too. Orval, a Belgian Trappist beer, derives its unique character in large part from the non-standard yeast strain *Brettanomyces,* or 'the British fungus', which adds a funky, quirky dustiness that's hard to describe. It would have been a key component of many of our native beers before they were cleaned up in the later industrial age. With that in mind we've had great success blending Orval with beers such as St Austell Proper Job, at the ration of one part Orval to two parts of the Cornish IPA, which we called 'Proporval'. Another successful mix was Orval and Thornbridge Halcyon (Orvalcyon) and it also worked brilliantly with Adnams' Tally Ho old ale. It even worked wonders with the famously bitter German lager Jever. We like doing this so much we've started to wish draught Orval existed so that we could order beers with a 'top' of it in the pub.

Going even further into the leftfield, but echoing the tradition of dog's nose and dragon's blood, adding a tot of red wine or sherry to dark beers or strong ales can go some way to simulating the acidity and oxidation of 'vatting' or cellaring, and mixing acidic scrumpy cider with pale ale can provide a creditable alternative to Belgian gueuze if you like your beer on the wild side.

Some people react with horror to this kind of thing, considering it positively sacrilegious, especially when revered beers such as Orval are involved. Others are offended by the idea of overriding the intentions of the brewer. But, really, this is part of the fun, and part of the point: it is irreverent and puts the drinker in control, giving them a chance to create a unique beer without actually getting their wellies anywhere near a mash tun.

Of course, if truth be told, while mixing beers to achieve a specific effect can be great fun it rarely produces anything greater than the sum of its parts, turning up more clashes and cancellations than true harmonies. Perhaps that commentator in *The Times* sixty years ago perhaps had it right when they suggested a reason for the tendency to mix beers, blaming it on "the intriguing snobbery of pub drinking – the desire if you are a leader in a pub community to cut a dash and be different".

The pubs of Boggleton

First published on our blog in 2017.

> "The development of Boggleton, a small English town which I have traced at set periods in the next pages, is symptomatic of all England. We can learn the character of a country from the scars and wrinkles on its face." – John Betjeman

With apologies to Sir John what follows is our attempt to condense the overall plot arc of the English pub in the last two centuries. It was originally written as a long read to go alongside the launch of our second book which tells the story of the development of the pub in the 20th century.

1837

Boggleton, being a relatively sober town much dominated by church folk, had only twelve pubs, to serve a population of 3,000 people. They were not called pubs at the time, however. One, The Dolphin, was most certainly a great Inn, situated on the main street, busy with coaches and the horses that drew them. It had beds, served meals (grudgingly, it must be said) and all sorts of drinks from ale to wine. The building rambled, was riddled with mice, and was marked by a gilded sign hanging over the street depicting something like a mer-tiger. The Red Lion on the market square was smaller, sagging and smoky, intricately half-timbered. It too was an inn, at least on paper, but people rarely stayed or ate there. Sometimes it was referred to as a tavern, but it was not quite that either — there was nothing of the city about it, and it had no wine of distinction. It was most often called a 'public house' and was busiest on market days when farmers from the surrounding villages came into town, stuffed into shirts and waistcoats, sweating and merry.

The rest were beerhouses, or beershops – small establishments more-or-less resembling the cottages that surrounded them. They were licensed to sell only beer and were brought into being by the passing of the 1830 Beerhouse Act. None had prominent or elaborate heraldic signs and many were simply known by the names of the people who ran them. Thompson's Beerhouse was typical: a single room – formerly the parlour of old Thompson's own home – with bare plaster on the walls, scrubbed floorboards, a bench against one wall, and a wooden cask of home-brewed beer on a rough-hewn table in the corner. The beerhouses could be wild places and soaked up working men's wages which worried the pious people of the town, but all they could do was complain, and watch like hawks.

1867

When the railway came in the 1850s, New Boggleton was created. There came row after row of houses for railwaymen and for workers at the new factories, as well as suburbs and villas for the well-to-do. And for 100,000 people, twelve pubs were hardly enough.

Despite the efforts of the Boggleton Temperance Society, founded in 1855, the beerhouses had grown in number and some, the most successful, had increased in size, too, until they rivalled The Red Lion. Thompson's had become The White Hart and scarcely a trace of the original dwelling from which it had sprung remained.

Nor could the Temperance Society prevent the magistrates from granting licences for new beerhouses on street corners among the terraces, until it was said that from any point in town you could always see two pubs. The Venezuela on Oxford Road, serving the piston works, was purpose built by the firm that constructed the surrounding houses in 1860. It was small but nonetheless had two rooms, one a touch more respectable and suitable for foremen and clerks.

Amid the new shops and offices on the busy town centre streets there also appeared a handful of fully-licensed public-houses in a more ornate style gesturing at, but stopping short of, big city glamour. The exterior of The Adamsbec Arms was typical: built by one of the eight local breweries, it was blazoned with painted signs, a large lamp brought up from London hung over the door, and there were classical and gothic details thrown together like fruit in a salad. High windows, sparsely engraved and inlaid with small but colourful stained panels, made warm jewels of the light inside. The pub, named after the wealthy family whose stately home once stood near the town, had pretensions, offering chop lunches, and furnished snugs in which businessmen might conspire. For all that, the main bar was still a bare room where people spat, swore and ate street-sellers' pies of indeterminate filling.

Road traffic had dwindled and most travellers now stayed at the new Railway Hotel opposite the station, leaving the poor old Dolphin stranded at the tumbledown, half-abandoned village centre. One of its wings was entirely closed off and near collapse — a sad relic of the pre-industrial age.

1907

Eight breweries became six, each with its own estate of fully-licensed pubs (as they had at last come to be known) acquired out of pragmatism as the number of outlets for their beer began to shrink after a long boom. Some pubs that had seemed smart 30 years before were now decrepit and dirty, like The Venezuela. The brewery that owned it had no incentive to keep it up. If a tenant could be found, and the customers kept coming, that was fine. If the council and magistrates pressed them to surrender the licence of this and one or two other pubs in return for the right to build a big new one, where more beer could be sold by fewer staff, all the better.

The third generation of the piston making family – one brother a Liberal politician, the other running the firm – stopped short of being teetotallers but did subscribe to modern ideas about drink and public houses. Consequently, they sponsored a grand new public house on the edge of the factory estate, to be run by a professional manager from London employed on a fixed salary by a trust. It was their idea that, with such a place on their doorstep, the workers might drink less and eat better food, perhaps while reading an improving newspaper. Some did, but others grumbled that The Earl Grey was like 'a ruddy morgue' – too big, too clean, with altogether too much sarsaparilla where there ought to be mild ale. If it failed as a pub, The Earl Grey was at least well-built, decorated in the arts and crafts style, and was the making of the young architect who took on the job and wrote it up for the journal of his institute.

1937

Six breweries became two through mergers and expansion. The survivors were both substantial concerns whose managing directors were public school men and members of the Brewers' Society, more at home in London than Boggleton, truth be told. Greenleaf's beer was cheap and, it was said, 'Not fit to wash the dog', while Ironside specialised in refined draught bitter and bottled pale ale for the national market.

Greenleaf's estate of pubs was rather sorry comprising most of the remaining slum beerhouses (though no-one called them that anymore) and one larger pub just off the town centre which, though intended to be the flagship house, always looked as if it needed spraying with insecticide. They refurbished when the money could be got together but otherwise were quite happy to wait for the pubs to be demolished for road widening or slum clearance and claim compensation.

Ironside, on the other hand, had an in-house architects' department led by the man who had built The Earl Grey before the war. It was responsible for several impressive new public houses in Boggleton. The Heart of Oak, built to serve Adamsbec, the Homes for Heroes council estate near the old Abbey, came first, with bowling green and baronial affectations. Though only a decade old it was often mistaken for a medieval inn. On summer nights, the sounds of a band could be heard drifting over the lawn as couples in Sunday best swooned on the terrace in the moonlight.

Then, at the head of the widened London road, there came The New Red Lion – new indeed, its outlandish curves covered with white plaster, resembling a cinema or cruise ship more than a pub. In lieu of a painted sign it had a sculpture of a lion that might have passed for something raided from a tomb in the Valley of the Kings, but was actually the work of a London man who also designed sports cars and, it was said, had two wives. At weekends, the car park filled with motors which disgorged laughing young people into the lounge where they drank cocktails, best bitter and lager. The people in the public bar were just the same Boggleton folk, though, in flat caps and work boots, tiptoeing about to avoid smudging the specially designed geometrically patterned linoleum.

In the meantime, The Dolphin, that ancient coaching inn, lost a wing and all its stables (a branch of Boots was built on the site) but gained a car park. It was given incongruous half-timbering, too – nailed on, in line with fashion, and public expectation of a Quaint Old Inn.

1957

After the war, Ironside swallowed up Greenleaf, and Boggleton found itself down to a single vast, towering brewery – one of the town's largest employers. The Greenleaf pubs were either sold off or, when permission could be gained from the Ministry, refurbished in a cut-price version of the modern style. Once building restrictions were lifted and the rationing of supplies came to an end, Major Ironside, so often seen shooting about town in a sports car with his military moustache fluttering in the breeze, cut the ribbon on five new pubs in a six-month period.

The Sir Edmund Hillary, The Spitfire, The Atomic Arms, The Pistonmakers and The Longwood were like quintuplets – the same size and basic shape, made from the same materials (brick, wood, glass, asbestos, fibreglass, and so on), and with signs painted by the same artist over the course of one fortnight. Like the new housing estates on which they stood, they were the product of much study and theory, but lacked romance. The city folk who moved to ever-expanding Boggleton to take houses on those estates liked the new pubs well enough but were often to be heard reminiscing in bitter-sweet terms about the Victorian ones they had left behind.

The Heart of Oak on the inter-war housing estate had gone bad. Major Ironside regarded it as a burden – too big, too elaborately decorated, too old-fashioned, and too out of the way to be turned into a restaurant. An attempt to bring it up to date by knocking down interior walls and closing the billiard room did little to help. The council bought the bowling green and on it erected a health centre.

The New Red Lion, on the other hand, had found a place for itself as a place where boys on motorbikes congregated. They drank more coffee than beer, and occasionally raced or brawled, but it was better than demolition, just.

The Dolphin had shrunk further and become a tea shop – hardly The Dolphin at all, except that the sign remained. The Old Red Lion, however, was much as it had ever been only now university people with architectural gazetteers came to look at it and take photographs: 'A remarkable survival! Fine vernacular style.'

1987

Ironside having sold out in the 1960s almost all of Boggleton's pubs now belonged to one of the big London breweries who had outfitted them with up-to-date matching plastic signs in the corporate style.

There were exceptions. In the old town centre, now crowded with antique shops, The Dolphin became a pub once again under a sign that said: 'THE OLDEST PUB IN BOGGLETON'.

The owners of The Red Lion disagreed, of course, and had signs of their own: 'A PUB FOR AT LEAST 400 YEARS – 10 REAL ALES'. There, a refit carried out in the 1970s had added more wooden beams, brand new authentic fireplaces, and at least a ton of horse brasses. The line of hand-pumps ensured a constant turnover of out-of-town pilgrims as well as a regular clientele of social workers, college lecturers, and journalists from the local newspaper.

A few doors down was The Angel Inn, converted from a run of three ancient cottages knocked together, and with yet another sign: 'ON THIS SITE SINCE THE 17th CENTURY'. A subtle fib, of course, but the sloping floors, bulging walls and creaking timbers sold the con – several guidebooks insisted it was an ancient pub and The Angel's owners did not correct them. The small brewery installed in the basement turned out a house brew, Angel's Tears Strong Ale, 'brewed to an old recipe'.

Out on the post-war housing estates the 'modern' pubs suffered a variety of fates: The Sir Edmund Hillary was renamed The Charles Dickens and given plastic bow windows; The Spitfire burned down and was not replaced; The Atomic Arms and The Pistonmakers were popular, both being far from town, but grew tattier and less appealing to outsiders with every passing year; while The Longwood became a kind of nightclub with blacked out windows and bouncers. None of them looked modern anymore, just plain, and unlike their Victorian predecessors they gained no character with age.

The Art Deco New Red Lion was gone, demolished to make way for a bypass. The Heart of Oak on the Adamsbec estate hung on, at least ostensibly, though its multiple bars and function rooms were all closed, trade being continued in one small, sorry front bar. The kitchens and living quarters upstairs were flooded and home to flocks of pigeons. A tree grew from the roof.

In the terraces of New Boggleton, now itself more than a hundred years old, many of the corner pubs had gone, but a few could still be found, kept alive by their darts teams and Saturday night pub crawlers who would make their way into the centre on foot and stop for one or two at each pub they passed.

The Venezuela, in London brewery livery, looked smarter than in many years. A person with a notebook and camera came one day and marvelled at the wonderfully preserved snug, the ornate windows of c.1898, the surviving but unused gas lamps, the pre-WWII bell pushes, and every other feature of which successive generations of publicans had been faintly ashamed. It won an award simply for existing. When the brewery tried to knock down a wall, there was a protest, with songs and banners. The locals watched with amusement as anorak-wearers crept in through the door and ordered pints of mild, otherwise drunk only by Old Harry who lost a leg at El Alamein.

2007

Inclusion on the Campaign for Real Ale's list of heritage interiors couldn't save The Venezuela. The pub company that acquired it from the London brewery after the Beer Orders were passed in 1989 didn't know what to do with it and waited until no-one was looking before tearing out the fixtures and fittings in a 'contemporary makeover' that made it feel cold and dead, like bleached coral. It was permanently either UNDER NEW MANAGEMENT or A GREAT OPPORTUNITY TO RUN A PUB. Its pulse slowed almost to a stop.

All the estate pubs were gone –burned down or turned into convenience stores – except The Heart of Oak, closed for a year, now, with steel shutters on its windows, but still standing and theoretically ready for duty. The locals watched it anxiously — would it too go up in flames one day?

The Dolphin was bought by a television chef and became a gastropub – the kind of place where staff said, 'Yes, of course you can just have a drink' without conviction, ushering such thirsty unfortunates into a corner out of view of the dining room. A little more prim than two hundred years before, perhaps, but not inapt for an establishment where respectable travellers had stopped on their way from town to another.

The Angel, after a decade as Ma Flaherty's, had just reverted to its old name, but with a new surf-and-turf Cajun barbecue concept menu. The Adamsbec, lately known as Stinky O'Hara's, became The

Cork & Lobster wine bar. The Red Lion, firmly protected by the heritage establishment, had been saved the indignity of being renamed, but the London brewery (which had long stopped brewing) made it the restaurant of a new budget hotel next door, with full continental breakfast buffet and two Olde Red Lion burgers for £9.

The biggest change of came with the conversion of the old Quaker Meeting House into a brand new pub, The Josiah Jenkins, by a national chain. It gained a never-ending new conservatory with space for fifty tables and informative posters recounting the history of the town. Josiah Jenkins himself looked down from the wall with distinct disapproval as meal deals and pitchers of lager were ferried about beneath him. Local antiquarians were divided – it was an act of vandalism, said some, while others suggested that the alternative – collapse or demolition – was worse. The pub was lively, at any rate, and brought the breath of life to the old town.

2017

When the city people realised Boggleton was only an hour's commute on the fast train, or a short drive down the motorway, they began to arrive in numbers. They colonised the villas and the larger terraced houses where factory managers and clerks had once lived. Tin pots of herbs appeared on windowsills and refurbished Victorian front doors were painted in Greek Thyme or Atlantic Mist.

For The Venezuela, this was good news. The pub company that had all but forsaken it leased it for what they thought was a punishing fee to a young entrepreneur. It was renamed for the first time in its life: 'The Ven'. The frontage was painted black, the name picked out in wide-spaced sans serif text. Picnic tables appeared on the pavement and signs offered Sunday roasts, burgers and buttermilk fried chicken. The new furnishings looked remarkably like those that that had been cast into a skip a decade before – mismatched chairs, church pews, and unadorned wooden tables. Young parents came with strollers and dog owners with poodles. A few old Boggletonians who had hung on in the area took it more or less in their stride, ignoring the jazz soundtrack, working on their pints in the company of the ghosts of their grandparents.

The Heart of Oak was in the process of coming back to some kind of life in the hands of a community group. The ballroom, they said, would make an ideal arts cinema, once the rotten floor was fixed, and there was interest in turning the lounge into a yoga studio. The smaller public bar, the old reading room, would make a good coffee bar and community library. And there would be beer, of course – hopefully made on site, using ingredients grown by the cooperative allotment project, assuming the grants came in as planned.

On the Longwood Estate, where the post-war pub of the same name had long ago collapsed as a result of fire and flood, an unlikely event occurred: in a parade of shops, between a butcher and a shop selling fishing tackle, there appeared a brand new pub. The Lanky Plank had enough room for ten customers at most and sold only real ale. The landlady, who had sunk the entirety of a redundancy cheque into the project, was scarcely out of the local paper in the first year and won every CAMRA award on offer. Most of the locals were bemused but there were a few loyal drinkers whose custom was bolstered by a constant stream of anxious visitors clutching copies of the Good Beer Guide. It felt, oddly, more like Thompson's beerhouse of 1837 than any other pub in town.

The German Invasion

First published in CAMRA's BEER *magazine in 2018.*

For British drinkers in the 1970s German beer culture held a certain allure. For some it was about the quality and purity of the beer. For others, it was a perception that beer halls and the Munich Oktoberfest were great, debauched, joyful booze-ups of a sort unavailable in Britain. The media helped with first newsreels and then TV news unable to resist the spectacle of swaying, red-faced crowds of Bavarians. Perhaps the cold war played a part, too: young men returning from military service brought with them tales of lager-fuelled merriment all across West Germany.

It was in this context that a German-inspired beer festival took place at Alexandra Palace in North London in October 1972. Organised by a private firm, it attracted coachloads of thirsty Britons in search of stein-clashing fun from places such as Blackpool and Birmingham. It was a disaster, as it happens, with 45 minute queues for beer, but it played an important part in the founding of CAMRA for it was here that the new and surging Campaign carried out a first and last joint protest with the declining Society for the Preservation of Beers from the Wood, which it usurped. German style festivals with Bavarian bands and all the trimmings actually carried on throughout the 1970s in places like Norwich and Solihull, but seem to have been written out of history, or at least forgotten.

Permanent Bierkellers began to appear in British towns and cities from the late 1960s. Rigby's in Liverpool gained a Bierkeller bar in 1968 run by a bona fide German, Werner 'German John' Burchardt – a prisoner of war who didn't go home. Most of these 1960s Bierkellers weren't pubs but a kind of cabaret-nightclub-restaurant hybrid described in the trade press as 'showbars'. They were characterised by live music and crowd interaction, their décor and entertainment pointedly kitsch. By 1971 Peter Hepple writing in showbiz trade magazine the *Stage* was able to observe that "you are likely to find a German bier keller in any part of Greater London", from the Schloss Keller on the Strand to the Löwenbräu Keller in Croydon.

Leeds had the Hofbrauhaus in the Merrion Centre from 1972, serving Hofbrau lager imported in tankers from Munich along with

Schnapps and Bockwurst. In a 2011 article for the *Yorkshire Evening Post* John Frank, who designed the interior, recalled being sent to Munich and Düsseldorf on a research trip: "It was important to recreate the atmosphere and in my opinion ours were more German than the German ones". Drinkers at the Hofbrauhaus describe funny-tasting German bread and rounds of 'Ein Prosit' led by the band every ten minutes or so. There were also branches of the Hofbrauhaus chain in Sheffield and Hull.

Across the Pennines in Manchester there were several, most notably the Löwenbräu Keller at number 1 Piccadilly described in a 1975 guide to the city's pubs:

> Unlike other beer kellers in the city, the large basement area is a fairly reasonable recreation of a Bavarian beer hall... Seating is on long wooden benches arranged round the small sprung dance floor and bandstand, and the low ceiling is gradually being covered with candle writing... To get into a real Bavarian mood when you're there, buy one of the mock Bavarian hats.

Lager brands, then on the rise, supported these Bierkellers by sponsoring promotional events. Barbara Allen of Richmond was crowned Miss Löwenbräu in Manchester in September 1972, winning a trip for two to the Munich Oktoberfest, along with a prize-bundle of swimwear and (it was the 1970s after all) cigarettes.

Seaside resorts were especially ripe for Kellermania. A trailblazer was the Austrian biergarten which opened in Lytham St Annes from the summer season of 1966, with continental lager served in 'Steins'. In the years that followed Blackpool gained the Talbot Bierkeller, opened by Bass Charrington in around 1970; a Hofbrauhaus; and the Jager Keller. The latter was established by the Forte hotel group opposite Blackpool's Central Pier in the summer of 1971 and occupied a basement bar with room for 400 people. Its music was supplied by, among others, Harrison Mann's Oompah Sound. Elsewhere on the coast Southend in Essex got a Bierkeller in 1972; Pwllheli, Gwynedd, in 1974 (with 'Baron Wolfgang' in charge of the house band); and Peel on the Isle of Man in 1977. Even Butlins joined the fun: by 1979 it was boasting 25 Bierkellers across its suite of seaside holiday camps.

As the decade wore on, however, the oompah bands and German theme lost their novelty. The bars became seedier with the relatively innocent sexiness of dirndl-clad waitresses giving way to strip-shows, and bockwurst to bangers and mash. Their fate was tied to that of lager which in the 1960s was a classy continental drink for sophisticated types but by the dawn of the 1980s had come to be associated with football hooligans and crude masculinity. One person we spoke to recoiled at the thought of a Blackpool Bierkeller they visited in the late 1970s: 'It was a dump!' Eventually many Bierkellers simply became generic nightclubs or concert venues, like the Bristol Bierkeller which came to be associated with the punk movement and later indie music. (Its closure was announced at the beginning of 2018 to the dismay of music fans.)

And yet, 40 odd years on, Bierkellers never completely went away, and the idea of the Bierkeller retains a fascination for British drinkers looking for a laugh. London has several, such as Katzenjammers at Borough, the Munich Cricket Club in Westminster, or the two Bavarian Beerhouses in the City of London, and though most beer geeks wouldn't touch them with a Stocknagel they are inevitably heaving with young office workers and groups up from the Home Counties for a night out.

Meanwhile, the Blackpool Bavarian Bierkeller – the same establishment founded in 1971, as far as we are able to ascertain – has a promotional video which repeatedly mentions SWAYING as a key part of the fun. Until someone works out how to bring that kind of primal, communal warmth back to the English pub – ever more polite and respectable with every passing year – the faux-German beer hall will continue to appeal.

Welcome to Adnamsland

First published on our blog in 2014.

There is no train to Southwold and the nearest station is at Halesworth, a small inland market town of weathered red-brick. Before catching our connecting bus, we spent an hour wandering in the unseasonably warm late September sunlight, past the old maltings by the railway line, and along the high street – or, rather, the Thoroughfare. It was busy, in a sedate way, populated with butchers, bakers and other family businesses. There were also occasional reminders that this is part of the world is rich in history, such as the grotesque lions, fox, monkey and other animals carved in naive medieval style over the entrance to an otherwise nondescript café.

We enjoyed our first pints of Adnams's beer on home turf, more-or-less, at the White Hart. Startlingly different to how it had tasted so many times in lacklustre London pubs, we found Southwold Bitter crisply hoppy, with an almost desiccating bitterness – brown, yes, but certainly not boring. We could not help but wonder with some excitement how much better it might taste in Southwold, under the watchful eye of the brewery.

Southwold isn't merely by the sea – it's at sea, as if designed to make naval captains on half pay feel at home while they await a new commission. Gunhill, at the top of town, has a row of cannons pointing out into Sole Bay, and there are white-painted semaphore posts at various points along the seafront. Most obviously, there is the lighthouse. It is no wave-battered Wolf Rock, being, rather, a block in from the promenade and cosily surrounded by terraced houses. By day, it looks merely picturesque. At night, however, as its beams rotate silently across the sky, projecting far out to sea, it becomes imposing, reassuring, and rather magical.

Photographers seem drawn to another local institution – the pastel-painted beach huts which line the sea wall. They're certainly photogenic but also hint at something unnerving about Southwold – it is a town mugging for Instagram, permanently made-up and presenting its prettiest profile.

The town centre has more than its fair share of businesses selling an aspirational vision of the country-coastal lifestyle – designer hunting jackets, red trousers, polka-spotted Wellington boots, and striped sailor shirts that wouldn't last ten minutes in a gale eight at German Bight.

We heard hardly any Suffolk accents. The ripest belonged to a farmer selling apples on the market square, although he was so square-jawed and stereotypically rugged that we weren't entirely convinced it wasn't Rupert Everett preparing for an acting role.

While we were buying apples, a London cab sailed by, but it wasn't black – it was purple, and covered in slogans in yellow type – the campaign vehicle for the right-wing populist political party UKIP, no less. We later saw it parked in a driveway on the edge of town.

What saves Southwold from feeling completely twee is the presence of a thumping great working brewery. People in boiler suits shared the streets with well-to-do second-homers up from London; the smell of mashing malt and steeping hops was always on the air; and whenever the scene began to resemble too closely an episode of the *Vicar of Dibley*, a fork-lift truck would come skidding out of the brewery gates, heading for one of the many ancillary workshops or warehouses.

For a small town (its population is officially only 800) Southwold has plenty of pubs, most, if not all, owned by Adnams.

The Lord Nelson is the most immediately eye-catching. Only a few steps from the sea, its hanging sign constantly creaks in the breeze, and frosted windows break the warm light inside into gleaming, flickering spots. We visited on Friday night and found it busy but not quite crowded. There was a group of young people drinking the seasonal dark Old Ale from dimpled mugs and a tableful of white-haired locals on lager, bitter, whisky and wine. The walls are covered in nautical memorabilia and legal documents relating to the pub's ownership in years gone by. It is the kind of Olde Inn tourists look for but is by no means insincere.

The Red Lion is similarly cosy, but the service was more business-like on our visit, with two professional barmen despatching drinks with efficiency, and as much banter as necessary, but not a word more. A man at the bar who had over-indulged on Broadside was lecturing them about something or other, obnoxiously and only semi-coherently, but they took it in turns to listen to and humour him.

The Sole Bay Inn is a corner pub in what looks like an early Victorian building within sight of the brewery gates. Recently made over in bright-and-breezy beachside style, it felt modern and fresh when busy, but rather sterile when quiet. We saw it in the latter mood on a week night as we sipped Adnams's own whisky and sloe gin while the manager polished the bar, determined to stay open until the scheduled closing hour, despite the end-of-season atmosphere. When the pub was busy, a large part of the crowd seemed to be brewery staff, which must say something.

The Harbour Inn, on the way out of town towards Walberswick, sits on the edge of the River Blyth and, as publicity for the pub wryly observes, 'sometimes in it'. It has lots of levels and small rooms and the one in which we found ourselves had a hatch opening on to the floor-level of the upstairs bar through which pints were passed by crouching staff. All the electrical points were mounted around the ceiling, out of reach of the average flood, and the flooring and furniture were designed to withstand an influx of muddy water.

But Adnams also has the drink-at-home market sewn up with two outlets in town – a small corner shop near the Red Lion, and a vast modern showroom where beer plays a supporting role to wine, spirits (Adnams produces its own vodka, gin and whisky), retro-vintage advertising and high-end kitchenware.

We spent much of each day tramping from one village to another, or around suburbs that had once been villages, researching family history, searching for names on headstones and war memorials, and following the folk footpaths Jess's ancestors might have used, from churchyard to pub. As we wandered, we realised something: though almost every village we passed through had a whitewashed Adnams pubs at its heart, the brewery does not entirely dominate this part of Suffolk.

Dunwich is famous primarily because the oldest part of it was swallowed up by the sea. It used to have a superior harbour until the sands shifted several hundred years ago, and Southwold gained the upper hand. There is a lingering pride in Dunwich's historical status – in the vast number of herring it used to pay in taxes each year, for example – and perhaps also, even today, some bitterness. The Ship Inn, a safe distance from the fragile coastline, is all dark wood and corners. It serves Adnams, but also beers from Norfolk. Its large, sloping garden is home to several decrepit fruit trees, and we found the grass thick with rotting apples and pears. A tweedy, well-to-do elderly couple stalked through collecting the fallen fruit in carrier bags, exclaiming cheerfully, 'We feed them to our pig!'

In Kessingland, we found more apples, cluttering up bus stops, rolling in gutters, and for sale in plastic bags on trestle tables on driveways and lawns. Another town which is no longer as important as once it was, it lacks Southwold's prim cuteness, being more the kind of place where pensioners in anoraks huddle under shelters eating sandwiches from Tupperware boxes, and where working people actually live. There is no freshly-painted Adnams house, either. One pub is boarded up, while another looked rather down-at-heel and was closed, and so we killed 30 minutes in Livingstone's, a 'fun' pub on the site of the local wildlife park, 'Africa Alive!' Cavernous and dimly lit, it throbbed with dance music playing for the benefit of the bar staff and two young men at the pool table. There was Adnams's ale but it was served alongside beer from a local microbrewery.

    At Carlton Colville, now on the edge of Lowestoft, but once a village in its own right, we enjoyed pints of Elgood's from Cambridgeshire at the Bell Inn, and helped the publican round-up a gang of dogs which had escaped from the garden and were causing chaos on the main road into town. As we waited for a bus, we noticed that the hedgerow opposite was overrun with wild hops.

    In Lowestoft proper, we knew we weren't in Adnamsland anymore. The town expanded dramatically as a fishing port in the 19th century and again in the 1960s with North Sea oil exploitation, but has since declined considerably along with those industries. Its high street is now too long for the number of businesses in operation and what should be a quaint old town feels run-down and, frankly, rough. Adnams, with its *Country Living* brand, doesn't seem to 'do' decline, and is barely present.

    What is the secret to Adnams's success, and why is it not held in the same contempt as its near neighbour, Greene King?

    For one thing, Adnams's beer is, on the whole, good. Though none of the pints of bitter we drank in Southwold were as transcendent as our first in Halesworth, they were always satisfying and interesting, with a suggestion of salty shrubbiness which evoked the marshy landscape. Old Ale, really a sort of 'best mild', was resolutely old-school – all caramel and brewing sugars. But, as well as satisfying the needs of traditional ale drinkers, Adnams has also dipped its toes into the (not literally) murky waters of 'craft beer'. The extravagantly perfumed, citrusy Ghost Ship is Adnams's take on 'pale-n-hoppy' cask-conditioned golden ale, and sits alongside new keg beers such as Dry Hopped Lager and Innovation IPA – the latter a more successful experiment than the former, but both better on draught than from bottles.

Adnams has also avoided gaining a reputation for ruthless business practices: if it has been in the habit of taking over other breweries and their brands, either it happened a long time ago, or we haven't being paying attention.

While we were in town, we learned that the firm has expanded into Holkham in North Norfolk – geographically distant, but culturally similar – which confirmed our feeling that its ambition has been directed not into indiscriminate expansion, but into becoming part of a genteel middle class lifestyle: the brewing equivalent of John Lewis.

The Good, the Bad and the Murky

First published on our blog in 2015.

At the end, you'll find a brief postscript which updates some of the details for 2019 and notes which of our predictions and hints were wrong, right, or somewhere in between.

We submitted the text of our book, *Brew Britannia: the strange rebirth of British beer*, in October 2013 and it was published in June the following year. Because the 'strange rebirth' it described was still underway, it wasn't possible to provide a satisfying full stop to our attempt to tell the story of how British beer got from Big Six monopoly of the early 1970s to the vibrant scene we currently enjoy. The purpose of this update is to summarise developments in the past 18 months, to explain how (if at all) they fit into the ongoing narrative, and perhaps also to see if a punchline might be in sight.

In doing so, we have considered the ongoing creep of 'craft beer' into the mainstream – or is it the mainstream annexing and absorbing 'craft'? We have also identified points of stress and increasing tension in an industry in which there is a decreasing amount of elbow room.

Like the last couple of chapters of *Brew Britannia*, this is commentary rather than history. It is in many ways a greater challenge to squeeze the truth out of people who are running active businesses than it was to get 40-year-old gossip out of CAMRA veterans of pensionable age. Nonetheless, as with the book, we have tried where possible to track stories back to their sources, to pin down dates on the timeline, and to avoid making assumptions – 'Sez who?' has been our constant challenge to each other. In a handful of instances, however, the only answer has been, 'Sez us'.

A London Particular

In *Brew Britannia* we wrote about Moor Beer Co. whose unique selling point is that its beers are not fined (that is, cleared of suspended yeast using 'finings') and thus may be served in any state from clear to cloudy depending on the preferences and skill of each publican. As we observed in the book, that alarms many drinkers who believe firmly that beer should always be perfectly clear – a proxy for underlying quality – and the debate has continued to rumble on, giving birth to a buzz-phrase in the process: 'London murky'.

In September 2013, Glasgow-based blogger and CAMRA activist Robbie Pickering wrote that, 'Five Points Pale Ale is in the "London Murky" style pioneered by The Kernel.' In an email, he explained what prompted him to come up with that turn of phrase:

> In 2011 or so, there were three things that distinguished The Kernel's beers: their flavour, their downright cloudy appearance and the inexplicably thick layer of sediment in the bottom of every bottle. It seemed to justify giving a name to this sort of beer which was different to anything else in the UK market at the time.

There was something catchy about the phrase 'London Murky' and, before long, it began to crop up frequently in the conversation around British beer. Though Pickering did not intend it as pejorative, those irritated by the idea of craft beer as a movement, and prone to complaining about fanboys, hipsters, hype and hazy beer, found it easy to weaponise. Tony Naylor, one of the few people regularly writing about beer in the mainstream press, had this to say in a *Guardian* article entitled 'Unfiltered beer: would you drink a cloudy pint?' published in May 2014:

> I'm torn. I can't deny the aesthetic appeal of the perfect clear pint. But I also realise that is a rather daft, inherited prejudice. Moreover, this criticism of 'London murky' (the argument is that upstart hipster brewers are using the excuse of making raw, natural, big-impact beers as a cover to chuck out haphazard, unbalanced rubbish) seems to spring from a general cynicism about the febrile creativity of the craft beer scene, rather than objective fact.

Elsewhere, however, there are signs that it might yet become a vague localised style like Irish stout or Yorkshire bitter. In May 2015, The Pelt Trader, a City of London bar run by the Bloomsbury Leisure Group (Holborn Whippet, Euston Tap), was featuring this description of a beer on its website:

The Kernel 4cs IPA 7.1% £3.00/half – Punchy Bermondsey IPA in the 'London Murky' mould.

Beer writer and blogger Bryan Betts has even attempted to define the parameters of this possible new style describing 'cloudy golden ales with some underlying sweetness, tropical fruit notes, and lots of hoppy bitterness'. In the same piece he also sounds a note of caution, suggesting that some London brewers are 'deliberately over-murkying things, which is just silly'. (And note the use of murky as a verb – this beer is not merely passively unfined.)

We would not be surprised to see this new London style, which some love and others hate, recognised formally in brewing competitions in years to come. When we can buy a bottle of London murky brewed in Berlin, Barcelona or San Diego, then we'll know for sure it has become 'a thing', as London porter did centuries before.

I Can I Can't?

When we were writing *Brew Britannia* canned beer remained largely the preserve of bigger breweries. Bass and London Pride could be found in cans in supermarkets, priced more cheaply than in bottles, but the canned beers that tended to come to mind were things like Carlsberg Export, Stella Artois and Fosters, or maybe Gold Label Barley Wine and Mackeson stout. Real ale drinkers by definition like their beer on draught, in a glass, and, depending on their age, might equate canned beer with either Ind Coope Long Life or with UK-brewed global lager brands. Meanwhile, most craft beer aficionados were hung up on elegant glassware, corked bottles and draught keg.

Once again, we must look to BrewDog as the source of a change in the those perceptions and preferences. Seeking ideas from the US scene, as they have always tended to do, James Watt and Martin Dickie took inspiration from an American brewery, Colorado's Oskar Blues, which started canning its beer in 2002. In 2010, BrewDog began to discuss with their fans on the brewery blog the idea of canning their own beers. The reaction was fascinating with comments falling into two broad camps. First, there were those appalled by the idea, like 'JH':

No way to the can!! The design is good granted but your beers are way too high quality to be put in a can – cans are for mass produced shite like Foster's. How on earth are we meant to enjoy an imperial stout out of a can?! This wouldn't be innovating-it would be trying to drive more sales and margin out of your product but at the expense of your product. You are pioneers in bringing the UK scene up to scratch with the US scene but this would be a kick in the teeth to those aspirations. Don't become Foster's!

Others, however, were tentatively interested, either because they had been impressed by canned beer from the US, or because they could see other advantages as summarised by 'Tom':

More environmentally friendly, easier to store & ship, you can take cans to many beaches and campgrounds where bottles are prohibited, AND it's better for the beer too – less light & air makes for a much fresher brew!

After several more such blog posts and discussions, by February 2011, the first cans of Punk IPA were rolling off a line at Daniel Thwaites's brewery in Blackburn. Having listened to feedback from customers on preliminary designs, they were small 330ml containers of the kind more usually used for soft drinks which helped to set them apart from the 500ml or 440ml cans used by mass-market brands. That summer, many discovered the appeal of a fast-chilling, more portable vessel and cans found their fans, though the bulk of Punk IPA and BrewDog's other beers continued to be sold in bottles.

From 2011 to 2014, beer geeks got used to the idea of a beer they liked in a format for which they had previously reserved derision, more US imports in cans began to appear on the UK market and, soon, cans became a kind of fetish, each new canned product being greeted with fizzing excitement on social media. Camden Brewing acquired a canning line in 2013 and suddenly Camden Hells, a good but unexciting beer, gained a new glamour in gleaming post-box red 330ml containers.

The UK brewery which is perhaps most closely associated with canned craft beer, however, is another London firm – Beavertown. It began life in 2011 in the kitchen of a pub-cum-barbecue restaurant in Hackney, East London. In 2013, its founder, Logan Plant, son of Led

Zeppelin's Robert Plant, moved to larger standalone premises and then, in May 2014, to an even bigger industrial unit at Tottenham Hale, out near the top end of the Victoria Line. With the move came the installation of a new toy – a canning line from the same Canadian firm, Cask Brewing Systems, that had supplied Camden. Nick Dwyer is part of Beavertown's management team, though he joined the company as an illustrator, which is telling in its own right – it is a highly image-conscious business. We spoke to him in May this year and asked, first, why Beavertown began canning:

> We were bottle-conditioning our beer, hand-filling bottles, and found that it tasted a certain way at packaging but, down the line, the taste was changing. The seal was bad on the bottles, and light-strike was affecting them within minutes of leaving the brewery.

He confirmed that the idea came from America – 'Logan spends a lot of time in the US and had been hanging out at Oskar Blues' – but also via BrewDog, with whom Beavertown have close ties. Even in 2014, the reaction was not universally positive:

> We did have people say, 'I'll never buy your beers again!', and asking, 'Cans? Why?' But all it took, really, was a couple of leaflets explaining the benefits and people became more positive, and before long it was, 'What are you putting into cans next, guys?'

As far as Mr Dwyer is concerned quality and shelf-life were the primary drivers but he acknowledged the aesthetic appeal of the can, too:

> Cans are a great canvas, although they can be hard work. You've only got six colours to play with, and the underlying metallic colour of the can, and you can't really do special finishes. We did ask for a varnish to make them more matte, more tactile. The designs aren't anything special – you wouldn't want them as prints in their own right – but if you don't know the beer, they'll grab you.

Beavertown's colourful cans, splashed with Dwyer's quirky sci-fi artwork, speak of youthfulness and a hip sensibility which is very distinctly not that of your real ale drinking uncle. When we visited the brewery last summer as part of our book promotion tour, no-one was interested in buying bottles from the on-site shop and bar – all they wanted to know was which cans were in stock, and which beers were being canned next. At around £2 each, the cans were good value and, crucially, easy to carry on buses and the tube.

Not everyone on the industry side is convinced by 'craft canning', however. Rob Lovatt, head brewer at Thornbridge, wrote a blog post explaining exactly why the UK craft beer pioneers had no plans to jump on this new bandwagon:

> Although the can format is being sold as the best way to eliminate oxygen from the beer after packaging, it is during the packaging process itself that the greatest danger lies. I am unconvinced that the canners towards the lower end of the market are capable of sealing the can without potentially picking up detrimental levels of dissolved oxygen.

When we spoke to Roger Ryman, head brewer at St Austell in Cornwall, he echoed these sentiments, and expressed scepticism that the kind of canning lines being installed in smaller breweries are really up to the job. (Though St Austell does have its Korev lager packaged in 330ml cans under contract at a larger brewery.)

Nonetheless, in the last year, hardly a week has gone by without one brewery or another announcing that they have acquired the capacity to can their beer, or are at least making plans to do so. Companies operating mobile canning lines have even popped up, setting up on site at breweries around the country to package limited runs of beer in unprinted cans to which labels are later applied. These ad-hoc products look rough and ready and, in our experience taste rather the same way. But apparently, while can fever continues, that almost doesn't matter: they are still cute-looking, convenient, cold after 15 minutes in the fridge, and, perhaps most importantly, are simply something different in a culture which craves novelty.

Crowds & Community

BrewDog's Equity for Punks (EFP) crowdfunding scheme closed in January 2014 while *Brew Britannia* was on its way to print. It raised more than £4 million and reached its funding target a month early. Grumbling from habitual critics of BrewDog, however, was a taste of things to come.

Beyond the world of beer, so-called 'crowdfunding fatigue' has been growing for some time and really seemed to set in during 2014. It is a response partly to the overwhelming growth in the number of such campaigns – in 2011, 11,130 projects were successfully funded through the Kickstarter platform; in 2014, it was 22,252, even in the face of increased competition from a flood of new services working the same territory. But it is also an inevitable response to attempts by the already wealthy to exploit this new source of finance for their projects. *Scrubs* actor Zach Braff's attempt to fund a film through Kickstarter caused a major stink – why didn't he pay for it himself?

It is in that context that there was a strong negative reaction to a project launched by Stone Brewing in 2014. Greg Koch, founder of the San Diego brewery, has long taken a mentoring role with BrewDog's James Watt and Martin Dickie who are open in the inspiration they take from him and his brewery's beers. In August that year, Koch launched an IndieGoGo crowdfunding campaign to help raise money for a bold European expansion plan. There was an immediate backlash, as summarised by Canadian beer writer Jordan St. John:

> When a really large brewery creates a Kickstarter it's absolutely inexcusable. Stone's current Indiegogo campaign is shockingly exploitative and cynical. Worse than that, it is actively evil.

Stone raised the $2.5 million they wanted but Koch, whose public persona usually tends towards the brash and sarcastic, felt obliged to issue an uncharacteristically meek video statement in which, though he stopped short of apologising, he expressed his sadness that the scheme had upset people, and attempted to reframe it as a 'beer pre-sales event'.

What all this meant was that when, in February 2015, Camden Brewery launched a crowdfunding scheme of their own under the name 'Hells Raiser', it was not greeted warmly by worn-out commentators or some hardened beer geeks. Camden's public image did not help. Though it is, for the moment, much smaller than either BrewDog or Stone, Camden is a slick outfit with high-gloss branding and a pointedly commercial mainstream lager, albeit a good one, as its flagship product. None of its beers, even Pale Ale, are cask-conditioned thus alienating a substantial body of more traditional drinkers who equate 'real ale' with good beer. A proportion of Camden Hells has at times been brewed in Germany and Belgium, despite the implications of its name, and this fact was, if not concealed from consumers, then at least obscured, which irritated those (including us) who value transparency. Camden has also been involved in two trademark disputes, of which more later, and, in both cases, though Camden did nothing wrong, per se, they emerged faintly tarnished as corporate-minded bullies pushing around underdogs. There were, however, also criticisms of Camden's scheme based on the numbers they presented, as explained to us by financial journalist and former beer blogger John West:

> Camden Town Brewery's crowdfunding effort looks to raise £1.5m in return for a 2% stake. On this basis, they are valuing the group at £75m... That is an eyebrow-raising valuation.

He crunched some numbers and was unable to come up with a valuation anything like Camden's. He also pointed out that the value of a key investors' perk in the form of discounts on Camden products was not as exciting as it might seem at first:

> Ponying up £100 will give you a lifetime 5 per cent discount; £1,000 a 10 per cent discount. As with BrewDog's Equity for Punks Mk.1 in 2009 (which offered a 20 per cent lifetime discount to participants), mileage will vary on the usefulness of this reward: discounting the Camden investment to zero by way of illustration, to break even on the reward alone would mean spending £2,000 on Camden Town Brewery beer online or in their tap and pubs (of which there are currently just three venues, all in London).

Despite all that, Camden not only reached their target but smashed it, raising 188 per cent of their initial goal.

BrewDog launched Phase IV of Equity for Punks in May 2015, seeking to raise £25m in 12 months; within a month, it had already reached £5m. People outside the commenterati are, we might conclude, less cynical and fatigued, and perhaps also just less coldly logical: they know they might not make a profit or even get their money back (BrewDog are obliged to warn them of that fact at every turn) but the game itself is fun. As well as being an extremely attractive source of finance, crowd-funding schemes are also yet another way for breweries to offer 'fan service', and to engage with their consumers.

On the Turn

During 2014-15 there were a handful of public spats between breweries over trademarks, most notably Camden vs. Redwell, Camden vs. Weird Beard, Brewster's vs. Anarchy (formerly BrewStar) and Everard's vs. Elixir.

The first on that list arose when Camden mounted a legal challenge against Redwell, a small brewery in Norwich, on the grounds that, by calling one of their beers Hells, like Camden's best-known product, they were attempting to mislead consumers ('passing off'). As part of their response Redwell, who had previously defeated a similar trademark claim from energy drink brand Red Bull, launched a crowd-funding campaign aiming to raise £30,000 to cover legal fees. Despite its relatively modest target and an underdog story, it closed in March 2015 having raised less than £2,000.

Some disputes, though they have also gone public, remained civil, such as Chapel Down vs. Magic Rock, which was resolved by Magic Rock agreeing to change the name of one of their beers – Curious pale ale became Ringmaster because Chapel Down's Curious Brew had a stronger claim to the name. Brewers have told us, however, that these are just the tip of the iceberg: Oliver Fozard of Rooster's reports 'a few', while Magic Rock's Richard Burhouse says that his brewery has had four such disputes, all solved behind closed doors, though he suspects there have been hundreds across the industry. There are only likely to be more such conflicts, some no doubt nasty, as the market becomes more crowded, and as better established breweries grow and have more at stake.

Meanwhile, we have begun to receive emails and private messages via Twitter that suggest more widespread tensions, unfortunately usually on the condition that we won't share details or name names. For example, we have been told of small breweries struggling to compete with, first, even smaller ones willing to sell their beer cheap, if they get paid at all, for the sake of exposure; and, secondly, with an emerging class of well-established firms who can afford to shift beer in bulk, and have the cash-flow to wait for payments. At the same time, the owner of one tiny brewery has told us that he has been all but bullied by existing local concerns who feel they have first dibs on the handful of free-houses and farmers' markets in town.

Of course beer is a business like any other – Richard Burhouse says it is 'naive that people think breweries wouldn't want to protect their brands' – but for consumers who have bought into the admittedly facile mantra that 'beer people are good people', and an ideal of community co-operation between 'little guys', it is rather saddening. When a national or multi-national company brings in the lawyers and 'bullies' a small brewery, there is a reliable goodies vs. baddies narrative, but that is not always the case when one part of the supposed community butts up against another.

Another blow to the idea of the inherent goodness of The Beer Folk came with the news in November 2014 that the founder of Hackney's London Fields Brewery, Jules de Vere Whiteway-Wilkinson, had been given more time by courts to repay a £3.2 million debt to Her Majesty's Revenue & Customs (HMRC) resulting from a 2004 conviction for dealing and smuggling cocaine and other drugs. (Joel Golby of *Vice* magazine called him 'the hipster Tony Montana'.) Though his past had not exactly been hidden it came as a surprise to many. When he was arrested on a separate charge of tax evasion in December the same year, and the brewery was raided by police, there was a palpable sense of disappointment. London Fields looked doomed but, in fact, has struggled on, its owner having convinced the courts that the best way to ensure he is able to pay his debts is by continuing to sell beer. In March 2015, it was revealed that brewing staff had been made redundant as production of beer was moved to Tom Wood Beers in Lincolnshire – a PR problem for a brewery with 'London' in its name, regardless of practicalities.

Vertical integration

In the 20th century, the largest British brewers did everything: they had breweries, bottling plants, fleets of lorries, teams of salesmen, PR departments, cooperages, carpentry shops, brass bands, typing pools and, of course, vast estates of pubs. The kind of micro-brewery that emerged in the 1970s has tended to reject all of that, remaining instead small, lean and agile, largely out of financial necessity. But, like gravity, the urge to 'bring it in house' seems to be an irresistible force and, even as *Brew Britannia* was at the printers, we observed an interesting development: more and more hip bars were setting up breweries, while at the same time breweries were building bars.

The Sheffield Tap's brewery was up and running when we interviewed Stuart Ross there in 2013. Mark Dorber, formerly of the White Horse in West London and now running two pubs in East Anglia, as well as the Beer Academy training programme, commenced brewing at the Swan in Stratford St Mary in 2014. Small Bar in Bristol acquired a small brewing kit in the summer of the same year, and Leeds's North Bar (*Brew Britannia*, chapter twelve) announced the launch of their brewing company in May 2015. There are more, and more on the way.

At the same time, UK breweries have begun to realise the benefits of selling draught beer direct to the public. Traditionally in the UK brewery taps, if they existed at all, were in pubs near the brewery gates rather than on site or, in the case of larger breweries, were on site but reserved for staff and corporate events. In the US, however, where many craft breweries grew out of brewpub setups, the tap room has long been a quintessential part of the experience. For British brewers inspired by the American scene the idea of delivering beer straight into the waiting hands of drinkers, as fresh as can be and without interference, in stylish industrial-minimalist surroundings – bars made from old pallets, concrete flooring and so on – was irresistible.

The Kernel brewery launched in Bermondsey, South London, in 2010 and began opening its doors to drinkers on Saturdays from 2011 – 'basically two tables with rickety benches right outside the tiny brewery' as recalled by London-based beer blogger 'Jezza' who now co-manages the website *BeerGuideLondon.com*:

> [It was a] hugely enjoyable opportunity to drink the freshest possible beer at source, in amongst the brewing

equipment with a chance to chat to the owners, brewers and staff.

Two more breweries, Partizan and Brew by Numbers, run by disciples of The Kernel's founder Evin O'Riordain, opened nearby in the following year so that, by 2013, a low-key, ultra-hip bar crawl had been established. That July, food and drink blogger Matt Hickman wrote a post on his website, *MattTheList.com*, suggesting a route taking in the three tap rooms and, with Distillery Row in Portland, Oregon, partly in mind, referred to it in a throwaway comment as the 'Bermondsey beer mile'. He explained how that particular term came to stick:

> It came up in conversation many times with friends who live in Bermondsey, in a very harmless way really (hence why it's quite understated in the blog). It is my invention as far as I know ... Lots of people were already writing about it, calling it similar things – Beermondsey made a few appearances – and somebody else would surely have got to Bermondsey Beer Mile soon after us.

In the months that followed, more breweries arrived in the area – FourPure (2013), Anspach & Hobday (2014), Southwark Brewing (2014) and U-Brew (2015) – along with an upmarket bar-off-licence called the Bottle Shop, and the Bermondsey Beer Mile became longer and even more enticing. Matt Hickman recalled, however, that efforts to market the Beer Mile, driven primarily by Jack Hobday of Anspach & Hobday, caused some friction between the brewers:

> A Twitter feed was set up just to retweet tap lists and opening times, and to gather photos and friendly tweets as people enjoyed their Saturday afternoons. A website was considered but after chatting to other brewers, not everyone was keen for understandable reasons and we ended up not taking it any further. I think had it not been called Bermondsey Beer Mile (which has the ring of a boozy stag-do unfortunately) and just been a nice info account, it might still be there.

Regardless, like The Rake back in 2008, Bermondsey attracted journalists and bloggers who liked the catchy name and the sense of a 'happening'. As a result, it was soon overrun with visitors who had read about it in the *Evening Standard* or *Time Out*, in search of something new and interesting to do with their precious leisure time. Here's how *Ratebeer* forum user 'imdownthepub' described it in April 2015:

> The first time, a year ago, was with the Ratebeer crew and I remember it having families and couples popping into the Breweries, all civilised and very pleasant. Now I'm not sure I had rose coloured spectacles on for the first trip, but this second trip seemed very different. There were huge groups of lads getting pretty drunk, stag parties and a very confused Hen Party, rather over dressed for the occasion… Huge queues for single loos, people urinating in the factory unit areas, The Kernel closing early due to the issues, no family groups that we could see just a few couples clinging together.

So we should perhaps not expect too many more such crawls to be established in other cities, though it seems now almost obligatory for start-up breweries to include space for a bar in their plans – showrooms for their style as much as commercial ventures. We asked Richard Burhouse of Magic Rock what lay behind the decision to open a tap room at his brewery in Huddersfield, after some false starts:

> Essentially so the brewery has a 'heart', somewhere we can serve the beers as fresh and well looked after as possible. Doing it this way is convenient as the tap can help contribute to the lease of the whole brewery site. Plus people are very interested in visiting breweries, and having the tap at the brewery means they can do a tour while they're here. It just makes a lot more sense to me than running a bar off site. Although that might follow at some point.

In November 2014, thanks to campaigning from a dedicated group of publicans, CAMRA, and others, the possibility of more small-brewery owned pubs perhaps came a little closer within reach. It was then that the Government introduced a compulsory 'market rent only'

(MRO) option for pub licensees, loosening the grip of 'pubcos' on Britain's pubs. Pubcos (pub companies) are the large and largely unpopular businesses which acquired surplus pubs from the Big Six breweries in the 1990s when the so-called Beer Orders took effect. Their business model relies on luring publicans with the promise of low property rent which is then made up by requiring them to purchase beer and other stock through a central supply network, from a limited range, at inflated prices. MRO now gives those publicans the opportunity to say, when their rent is reviewed, that actually, they'd rather pay full-whack for rent on the pub and then buy whatever stock they like, from whomever.

That joins another piece of potentially significant legislation on the books -- the power to designate pubs as 'assets of community value' (ACV) as introduced in the 2011 Localism Act. Where pub companies had previously been in the habit of selling off supposedly unprofitable pubs for repurposing as shops or for demolition, the ACV power, as long as someone is motivated to evoke it, now gives them motivation to sell such 'community locals' on to businesses, campaign groups or individuals who might be able to make something of them. ACV has already, according to a Government statement at the end of 2014, already saved some 100 pubs.

None of this is likely, frankly, to lead to a flood of paradisiacal free-houses bursting with micro-brewery beer – pub companies have already begun moves to sidestep the challenge by converting some of their premises to managed chain pubs rather than tenanted houses, and many publicans are understandably most excited by the freedom to buy not better or more interesting beer, but cheaper. Nonetheless, it may well give room for manoeuvre to enterprising individuals, existing pub chains and, of course, breweries. Thornbridge, for example, already run many pubs in the Sheffield area, most of them through an arrangement with pub company Enterprise. With money rolling in from profitable brewing operations and the MRO enshrined in law, breweries keen to take on pubs ought now to find it easier to do so, and it is just possible that estates of tied houses, Big Six style, could make a comeback.

If so, however, they might well find themselves in competition with a new, smaller, more agile competitor.

Almost too wee

A couple of people have asked why we didn't write about micropubs in *Brew Britannia*. The honest answer is that we'd hardly registered their existence. When we started writing our book, there were around 15 micropubs in the UK and by the time we submitted our draft, there were 40 or so. But, 18 months on, there are 116 with more on the way, and the founder of the original micropub, Martyn Hillier, believes this is only the beginning:

> The FT asked me last year – how many will there be in five years' time? I think there'll be 10,000 if they keep opening at their current rate but I couldn't bring myself to say it – I thought they'd laugh -- so I said 5,000.

If micropubs were a chain then Martyn Hillier would be the CEO. As it is, he runs his own tiny pub in Herne Bay, Kent, while acting as the figurehead for something that, for once, truly does deserve to be described as a movement. Born in Ruislip in North West London in 1959, he grew up there and in Kent, moving back to the city when he was 21. As a young man in the 1970s, he gave up on his preferred draught mild because it was so often of poor quality and became instead a lager drinker. Then, in the 1980s, he discovered David Bruce's Firkin brewpubs which led him to become a fervent believer in real ale. (Though, as it happens, CAMRA did not consider the Firkin beer to be 'real' under the strict terms of their technical definition, as explained in chapter seven of *Brew Britannia*.) A few years later, Hillier moved back to Kent and opened an off-licence in Canterbury selling cask ale to take away and bottled Belgian beer, alongside the usual wines and spirits. After many successful years, that was put out of business by the opening of a big-brewery-owned off-licence nearby in 1997, and so Hillier moved again, to Herne Bay. There, he took on a former butcher's shop and converted it into another off-licence. In 2003, he had a bad-tempered conversation with a local licensing officer, which concluded with a suggestion from the policeman:

> He said, 'You know they're changing the licensing laws, don't you? You could open a pub.' I thought, 'A pub!? Me?' Pubs were all lager drinkers and smokers and trouble.

But I thought, 'Hang on – this would be my pub, so no smoking, no lager.'

Until 2003, would-be new licensees were required to demonstrate the *need* for a new pub or bar in a given area, which it was all too easy for breweries, pub companies and other competitors to challenge. Gaining a new licence was expensive and fraught. With the introduction of the Licensing Act 2003, all they had to do was convince magistrates that there would be no increase in crime or public nuisance, and no risk to public safety or children – a far easier and, crucially, much cheaper process. By the time it came into effect in 2005, Hillier was ready to go and immediately turned his off-licence into a tiny pub under the name The Butcher's Arms. It has space for a handful of customers and only the smallest of bars as a mount for beer pumps rather than as a barrier between Hillier and his customers.

> Within three years, it was CAMRA Kent pub of the year. In 2009, I supplied beer to the regional CAMRA AGM, and then got invited to deliver a presentation to the national AGM in Eastbourne... So I stood up in front of 400 people and told them to open their own. Most of them didn't get it – when I said micropub, they thought I meant microbrewery, and that I was getting my words muddled... Peter [Morgan] from Hartlepool got it straight away, though – he understood it. He opened [the Rat Race] within six months, and then Just Beer in Newark opened soon after.

The appeal of the micropub to would-be publicans is easy to understand, as especially as explained by the evangelical Mr Hillier:

> Micropubs make money. Some of them have turnover of £250k a year... I stay below the VAT threshold and I don't have any staff. Shops are ten-a-penny thanks to supermarkets and what else do they do other than turn them into charity shops, pound shops, bookies? I don't pay business rates – I'm at less than £6000 rateable value... Running a micropub is perfect for a 55-year-old who's just taken early retirement. I take the piss – if the pub is empty at 9, I close up, because it's my pub. (It's usually busy,

though.) It's the 10th anniversary on 24 November and it's flown by because it's not like work.

With a certain type of drinker, too, they are undoubtedly popular. Sussex-based beer blogger Glenn Johnson is a huge fan of micropubs and explained why in an email:

> The appeal of micropubs to me is their simplicity. Beer plays a massive part as they all sell an ever-changing beer range from independent micros which is what I want from a pub. Many towns are now dominated by Wetherspoons when it comes to a decent beer range but micropubs offer a better beer range without the distractions, in an intimate friendly environment. They are all run by beer enthusiasts from what I have seen so you won't be fobbed off with anything that isn't in great condition and the beer novice will be guided to a beer they might like depending upon what they normally drink. This personal service also has great appeal. They are probably aimed at real ale drinkers in their 40s + who feel alienated by modern town centre pubs.

But how important are micropubs in the story of beer and breweries? By definition (that is, the official definition provided by the Micropub Association) they serve only real ale and their focus (to generalise very broadly) is on session-strength bitters and golden ales, usually with a local connection. For breweries too small to deal with Tesco or Enterprise Inns, but not trendy enough to generate huge amounts of excitement among geeks – that is, the kind of brewery that makes up the vast majority of the much-trumpeted c.1,300 – they might well be a boon. Martyn Hillier is certainly convinced that they are good for small breweries which, instead of selling via SIBA, pub companies or distributors, can deal directly with publicans, thus maximising the profit on each cask of beer sold.

We gave quite a bit of space in *Brew Britannia* to the emergence of 'craft beer bars' – a type of drinking establishment that was and is pointedly not a pub – but they remain fairly scarce, even with BrewDog's rapid expansion across the country, and are primarily found in larger cities. Might it be that the micropub is part of the same phenomenon but expressed differently to suit the needs of smaller towns with older populations? That is, an alternative to corporate blandness and central control which could not have existed before the Beer Orders of 1989 under the iron grip of the Big Six brewers, or (in most cases) before changes the 2003 Licensing Act made it easier to turn a retail unit into a drinking establishment.

At any rate, there can scarcely be any town in Britain that does not have empty shops and that cannot muster 20 dedicated real ale drinkers, so we'll be surprised if there aren't 500 micropubs by 2017.

Sorry, Ronnie!

One of the most significant developments of the past 18 months has been the launch by the J.D. Wetherspoon (JDW) chain of a dedicated craft beer menu with its own BrewDog-style logo and punning sub-brand, 'Craftwork'.

There are more than 800 Wetherspoon pubs around the UK occupying prime spots on high streets. The first opened in 1979 when Norwich-born, New Zealand-raised entrepreneur took on a pub in Muswell Hill, North London, and renamed it after one of his school teachers. To a certain extent a product of the CAMRA-led 'real ale revolution' of the 1970s, for a long time, JDW pubs were popular because they had beers other than the usual suspects – 'We were offering a range that others couldn't – like the craft beer bars do today, I suppose,' Tim Martin told us in an interview in February 2015. Nor did it hurt that those beers were sold at below the usual price, in clean, comfortable, traditionally pub-like surroundings, even though the units they occupied were often former shops or showrooms. In the 1990s, the chain went national and became more ambitious, taking over old cinemas and other large premises, while retaining a steely focus on low prices.

These days, the pubs divide opinion. They can lack character and, in an age when traditional pubs are under threat, sometimes seem to represent a Wal-Mart tendency, out-pricing competitors. Those who love them, however, dismiss critics as snobs and point to Martin's continued commitment to offering a keenly-priced and varied range of real ale – even quite average branches offer six or so at any one time – as an example others should follow.

Even those who turn their noses up, however, had their attention grabbed by new arrivals from New York City which hit the shelves of JDW pubs in March 2014: three different and exclusive canned beers from Brooklyn's hip Sixpoint Brewery. Since 2013, JDW had been carrying Brooklyn Lager, Goose Island IPA and BrewDog Punk IPA but those beers had lost their glamour through ubiquity (all three are readily available in supermarkets) and, in the case of Goose Island, big-brewery takeover. But Sixpoint was different: these beers were not brewed under contract in the UK, or under a sly sub-brand owned by a multi-national brewing company, and so by most standards, and certainly under the definition established by the US Brewers' Association, they are bona fide 'craft brewers'. Nor were they otherwise available in the UK. As if that were not lure enough for Britain's beer geeks, JDW sold the cans in the first instance at two for £5 – cheaper than most bog standard lagers in the average UK pub. (And as of June 2015, they are available in our local branch for £1.99 a can.)

Some beer geeks refused to play along, insisting that they would continue to support independent local businesses rather than a colossal chain. Others, however, bought cans unopened and took them home to drink, or began to use JDW to bring down the overall cost of a night out by 'pre-loading' on bargain craft beer before heading to a more expensive specialist bar. Some were simply pleased to know that they could rely on JDW for an interesting beer during their Saturday afternoon shopping trips.

JDW must, to some extent, have been happy with this first phase as the range was expanded six months later, in October 2014, when the Sixpoint cans were joined by kegged beers from BrewDog (This Is Lager) and US brewery Devils Backbone (though the beer is actually made at Banks's in Wolverhampton), as well as bottles from Rogue (Oregon) and Lagunitas (California). Types of beer that were once to be found only at North Bar in Leeds or the Rake in Borough Market are now available, at pocket money prices, a few steps from WH Smith and Boots the Chemist, everywhere from Penzance to Inverness – a remarkable change in the landscape of British beer.

Have Wetherspoon customers taken to the new offer – are people actually *buying* these beers? Perhaps unsurprisingly, JDW are not willing to share commercially sensitive sales information and gave us only a bland PR statement in response to that question. Members of staff we have asked in various JDW pubs in different parts of the country have, however, given similar answers: they sell well enough to be worth the bother. One barperson said, 'We get through 'em, but it's usually the same few people who come in and drink a few in one sitting – they tried them and got a taste for them and now that's what they drink.' Meanwhile, commentators have observed deep discounting in some pubs, which they have interpreted as a sign that the experiment is failing. In an email, however, one experienced industry journalist questioned that assumption:

> My perception, and this is entirely anecdotal, is that the JDW craft experiment has been a bit patchy. They have definitely been using discounts and deals to shift the Six Point cans, the BrewDog bottles and some others, but the thing to bear in mind is that JDW, ironically given [Tim Martin's] views on supermarkets, operates a lot like Tesco in that they have a built in promotions strategy so there will always be certain products from every range offered on discount or buy-one-get-one-free style deals. The craft beer is no exception, so it might be that the bargain bin offers and discounts that I've seen, and clearly others have reported to you, are planned rather than panic.

Ultimately, the best indicator of the success of the Wetherspoon craft beer package will be whether it is still there when it the chain's menus are refreshed in autumn 2015. If the craft beer range is not selling, we can be sure that Tim Martin won't hesitate to ditch it.

Breaking away from the peloton

The announcement in May 2015 of the launch of a new body called United Craft Brewers (UCB) may or may not be big news – not enough time has passed, nor enough detail been specified, for us to say at this stage. Its founding members, however, are an interesting bunch. Along with beer distributors and importers James Clay they are:

- Beavertown (London)
- BrewDog (Aberdeenshire)
- Camden Town (London)
- Magic Rock (Huddersfield, W. Yorkshire)

Whether those are the best breweries in Britain today is open to debate but they are certainly some of the most talked about who, between them, occupy a huge amount of space in the conversation around 'craft beer' in the UK.

Inspired by the highly successful US Brewers' Association (BA), UCB aims to produce its own definition of the contentious term 'craft brewer' in consultation with members with the intention of preventing companies such as, for example, Greene King from successfully marketing themselves as such. With the marketing nous of the names above, and the media clout of BrewDog in particular, we would be surprised if they are not to some degree successful in that endeavour. Here's the BA's definition, which will likely form the basis of UCB's:

Small
Annual production of 6 million barrels of beer or less (approximately 3 percent of U.S. annual sales). Beer production is attributed to the rules of alternating proprietorships.

Independent
Less than 25 per cent of the craft brewery is owned or controlled (or equivalent economic interest) by an alcoholic beverage industry member that is not itself a craft brewer.

Traditional
A brewer that has a majority of its total beverage alcohol volume in beers whose flavor derives from traditional or innovative brewing ingredients and their fermentation. Flavored malt beverages (FMBs) are not considered beers.

(Those numbers will, of course, require adjustment for the UK market – all but a handful of the big multi-nationals operating in Britain would meet those criteria.)

With the Campaign for Real Ale representing cask ale producers to a limited extent, and SIBA representing better-established independent brewers (i.e. microbreweries founded from the 1970s-2000s), there may well be increased tension between these factions…

Or perhaps, if overlap between membership is limited, helpful collaboration?

Regardless of its success, the confidence of the founders of UCB in founding an entirely new organisation is perhaps a sign that Britain has an emerging class of young brewers who are the most likely to follow the path set by Sierra Nevada in the US, which is now so big that it operates across multiple sites in the US and has a vast fleet of trucks to service them.

Perestroika and glasnost

There are signs, at last, that the Campaign for Real Ale is taking active steps to find a way to live with 'craft beer', though the organisation's leadership daren't state it quite so boldly for fearing of prompting hard-liners to mobilise the tanks.

In March 2014, Mike Benner stepped down as Chief Executive of CMRA and took a job at SIBA. In September, he was replaced by Tim Page who, after 27 years in the army, worked in government and the charity sector. The Chief Executive is to Colin Valentine, the current chair of CAMRA, as a permanent secretary is to the secretary of state in a government ministry – that is, ostensibly a servant of the elected representative but, in fact, powerful in his own right. In April 2015, at CAMRA's annual general meeting (AGM) in Nottingham Page gave an agonisingly careful speech in which he repeatedly emphasised his love of real ale and his belief in its quality, while also attempting to send subtle signals about the need for change:

> My key role, as I see it, is to challenge the organisation. At the moment I still consider myself a bit of an outsider – I'm still learning. And because I've got no past history in the campaign I can come in and ask, quite legitimately, some questions – you've been inside the organisation maybe you've just thought, well, there's no point in asking it. Well, I'm asking those questions and perhaps in doing that, I might act as a catalyst for change, where change is appropriate – change for the better, not just change for change's sake.

Later in the same presentation, he suggested that CAMRA ought to be 'inclusive rather than exclusive, tolerant rather than intolerant'. This may have been an oblique acknowledgement of CAMRA's ongoing struggle to address the issue of sexism in its ranks – in October 2014 a leaflet distributed to universities with the aim of recruiting young members featured a young man flirting with burlesque dancers, and sexist cartoons and articles continue to crop up in branch magazines. In the run-up to the AGM, Robbie 'London murky' Pickering attempted to propose a motion addressing this problem which was not put forward on the grounds that the bulk of what he suggested was already policy; that policy was reaffirmed at the AGM and there is evidence of steps being taken to tackle instances of sexism in branch magazines in its wake.

Talk of tolerance and inclusivity served double-duty, however, as a reference to the politics of beer dispense and culture, and Page went on to observe that, like him, many who later fall in love with cask-conditioned beer do not start out that way. Though he didn't say as much outright the implication was that those who are excited by kegged craft beer are primed for conversion to the cause, and should not be seen as the enemy. We spoke to Tim Page and, though his every word was chosen with care, he did make more explicit his own attitudes to 'craft beer':

> There's a distinction between acceptance and recognition – we can acknowledge that there are other types of beer out there while still promoting real ale as the 'premier cru'... I think the dispute with CAMRA [in 2011] was canny PR on the part of BrewDog but I also believe there is a false distinction, and my own kids are evidence of that. They'll drink something like Adnams in one round and then, in the next, some craft beer at £6 a bottle, which they also enjoy, because it's very clever and tasty.

He was also at pains to emphasise, however, that his views are not fundamentally important:

> I've been out and about meeting and greeting branch members and some have been wary, while others have said, 'Oh, great – you're just the man we need.' And I have to say, well, wait a second – I'm not here to force change

the membership doesn't want. I'm confident that common sense will prevail and that the will of the majority of members will win out. Will there be some who don't like change, however careful? Of course.

Veteran beer writer Tim Webb, co-author of *The World Atlas of Beer* among many other volumes, has been a member of CAMRA since 1974. In recent years, however, he has become an eloquent critic of the Campaign's failure to react to the emergence of good beer that does not conform to its definition of 'real ale'. For example, in a letter to CAMRA's newspaper, *What's Brewing*, that appeared in February 2014 he wrote:

> The challenge for the Campaign is how to adapt to the much-improved world of beer it helped create. Lukewarm acceptance of, or being not against the greatest improvements to beer tastes in a century, is not a good enough stance. To younger eyes it makes CAMRA look like a much-loved grandparent who wants to keep driving even though they can't make out the road ahead.

He expanded on his views in an email in June 2015:

> I am frequently shocked by the lack of knowledge a large number of older Campaigners have about beer, a fact reflected in the dotty definition of 'real ale' that has been perfected in recent years. Obsessed with the presence of yeast and the absence of extraneous carbon dioxide it has nothing to say about ingredients, brewing methods or even the type and quantity of conditioning, Two generations of beer drinkers now seriously believe that a fast forward version of light ale, often barely conditioned at all, is the finest achievement of 300 years of British brewing, while at the same time most of the rest of the world enjoys discovering infinite variations on the beer styles that put British brewing on top of the world for two centuries.
> It's ignorant and what is worse a sizeable proportion of these cognoscenti don't want to learn.

In recent months, though, Tim Webb has grown more optimistic. Tim Page has convinced him that he means business and, in practical terms, in the kind of gesture that would have excited Cold War Kremlinologists, in the spring of 2015, Webb was invited to join CAMRA's influential Technical Committee. This announcement about a motion passed at the AGM sent a similar signal:

> CAMRA's technical group previously confirmed that beer served from Key Kegs can qualify as real ale (providing there is yeast in the keg which allows secondary fermentation and it is served without gas coming into contact with the beer) – however this motion called for the introduction of a pro-active labelling system to help promote and highlight real ales being served via key-kegs.

Unlike traditional casks, key-kegs prevent oxygen coming into contact with the beer inside. Unlike the standard design of keg, however, nor do they allow it to come into direct contact with carbon dioxide (which gives standard keg its fizz), instead using gas to press down on the *outside* of an inner sac which contains the liquid. That liquid might have been carbonated with an injection of gas but, in many cases, any fizz it has was acquired as through the action of yeast as it fermented and conditioned in large tanks at the brewery. Their existence has highlighted a division between, on the one hand, those who believe 'real ale' requires live yeast and the absence of carbon dioxide and, on the other, those who apparently believe it requires the beer to come into contact with oxygen.

The announcement sought to placate members who might be anxious that the way was being opened for CAMRA to embrace Watney's Red Barrel by reassuring them that this was nothing new while, at the same time, sending a signal to 'progressive members' that the juggernaut was grinding slowly forward. And that's how we expect CAMRA to play this in the years to come – slow change without big announcements – merely the occasional sounding of a dog whistle through selected channels. That way, they will hope to avoid scaring away conservative members many of whom (not all) also happen to be older and therefore, for various reasons, make up the bulk of the *active* membership. But even if the process of change does prove turbulent, as Tim Page put it:

There's never been a better time to undertake this process of navel gazing. We've got more members than ever – 173.5k – and we're in good health financially, with trading and so on. So now, while we're riding high, is the right time to make changes… if they are needed.

Poochie Is One Outrageous Dude!

Larger, better-established breweries have continued to make attempts to engage with the craft beer craze with mixed results, often inviting derision in the process. In the first instance, they have continued to launch sub-brands and spin-offs.

In the spring of 2014 Marston's of Burton-upon-Trent – which owns several other breweries including Ringwood, Banks's and Jennings – launched a range under the Revisionist name with its own distinct branding and website. It included a black IPA, steam beer, German-style wheat beer, Belgian-style saison and several other such stylistic oddities. These beers were made available in kegs through the Marston's pub estate and elsewhere and in bottles as an exclusive own-brand line for Tesco supermarkets. The Marston's name appeared prominently on the labels and there was no attempt to pass the range off as the products of a smaller independent brewery.

In the autumn of the same year, though it already had a range of bottled and kegged beers being pitched as 'craft', Greene King of Bury St. Edmunds launched a range under a new name, Metropolitan, also distributed exclusively through Tesco. Few breweries agitate beer geeks like Greene King and this prompted grumbles, notably from beer writer Will Hawkes, who described it on Twitter as 'Greene King pretending to be a small brewery'. Others argued that these projects and others like them were good news – hadn't we all been demanding strong IPA and saison in supermarkets for years? And now we had it, we still weren't happy.

In January 2015, a piece of creative mischief by Jon Rowett cast a light on how awkward it can be when lumbering beasts attempt to imitate more agile independents. Trolling in the old-fashioned sense, he posted what purported to be an email from the Greene King marketing department announcing a product launch to an unofficial Facebook forum for CAMRA members and sat back to watch the reaction:

Following a bumper year in 2014, which saw over 22% real sales growth in our craft range (Old Golden Hen, Hoppy Hen, and Greene King IPA Gold) this February we are launching a fresh new beer: Greene King IPA X-Treme.

Initially available at select Greene King pubs in London and the South East, Greene King IPA X-Treme is a hopped-up, punked-out IPA for the Download Generation. Weighing in at 4.5% ABV and dry-hopped with Northdown, Centennial and Fuggles hops to a blistering 35 BUs, this new addition is guaranteed to create a stir amongst craft beer aficionados and die-hard real ale fans alike. This IPA has been hand-crafted by our craziest beer anarchists in Bury St Edmunds and we're rather proud of it!

It was perhaps a touch too believable in a world where Charles Wells, brewers of the staid Bombardier Bitter, works with US brewery Dogfish Head to produce DNA New World IPA. Before long, social media was alight with outrage and mockery: 'Frankly it made me want to be sick on my own face' said one Twitter user; 'that's like giving David Cameron a Mohican' said another. (Some of the commenters knew it was a hoax but were simply joining in the trolling.) Greene King issued a denial through the trade press and the excitement passed. It was only a bit of fun but, like all the best jokes, it was amusing because it had the ring of truth about it: it was just the kind of thing everyone expected Greene King might do.

Greene King is big but it is not multi-national, and huge multi-nationals tend to take a more direct approach: they increasingly buy into 'craft' simply by buying craft breweries. In recent years, brewing companies such as AB-InBev have been on a shopping spree acquiring established American craft breweries such as Chicago's Goose Island. When they took over the Seattle-based Elysian Brewing in January 2015, we wondered on our blog when they might turn their attentions to the UK and, when they did, which breweries might be in their sights. Beer writer Melissa Cole repeated her prediction that South London's Meantime, founded by Alastair Hook, was a likely target in the wake of the appointment in 2011 of a new CEO who had previously worked at SAB-Miller. There was little surprise, therefore, when in May 2015 it was announced that SAB-Miller had indeed bought Meantime.

What were SAB hoping to achieve? Meantime's brand remains strong and its position in the London market – a staple of restaurants, style bars and 1990s-style gastropubs – was no doubt appealing. From Meantime's point of view, there was cash in hand for the founders and investors (most of whom are Alastair Hook's friends and family), the promise of investment in the brewery, and access to SAB-Miller's sales and distribution network. Meantime's credibility among true believers has been somewhat diminished, though it had already been on the wane for some years beforehand; and SAB-Miller has perhaps gained a little second-hand 'cool'. It makes complete sense commercially but it is hard not to feel a little sad at Meantime's loss of independence and, perhaps more importantly, anxious for what the future might hold. In June 2015, reporting for the *Business Insider* website, business journalist Oscar Williams-Grut said that Camden Brewery had fended off a takeover attempt from an unnamed multi-national during their crowd-funding campaign. (The offer was of $116 million dollars, said Williams-Grut, so perhaps that £75m valuation wasn't so eyebrow-raising after all.) Camden refused to respond to his queries. We can expect much more of this in the next year or two.

Co-opting craft beer through sly imitation or buy-outs is not the only way for established firms to breach the gulf: friendly cooperation makes for much better PR. Early in 2015, Adnams of Southwold collaborated with one of the stars of the craft beer scene, Magic Rock of Huddersfield. Whatever antagonism beer geeks may feel or perceive between these two camps is not necessarily reflected in the feelings of the brewers themselves. Fergus Fitzgerald, head brewer at Adnams, and Stuart Ross of Magic Rock are of similar ages and are both easy-going. When they worked together to brew a cask-conditioned saison called The Herbalist early, it gave Adnams a bit of glamour but without winding up those on the lookout for evidence of big beer muscling in on craft turf. Friendly cooperation is ultimately more appealing to many consumers than 'them and us' rhetoric.

Approaching total beer

There is a sense in the air that a golden age has passed – that the days of giddy excitement are over, when almost anyone could snap up a vacant industrial unit, brew something half-way interesting, and then wait for the cash and adulation to roll in. There is less room for the homespun and the naive in 2015 than there was in 2013 – people are still happy to pay a premium for the strange, the rare or the local, but they want to get their money's worth. In the words of Andy Parker, the award-winning home-brewer behind the embryonic Hampshire-based brewery Elusive, 'Who would start a brewery in London selling hoppy pale ales today?'

> I wouldn't want to rely on it. There are many established breweries who are likely to have a more refined product and much more capacity than the new kid on the block.

Indeed, the boom in London brewery numbers appears to have peaked in 2014 after a frantic few years which saw the total surge from less than 10 to more than 70. (See Des de Moor's recently published second edition of *London's Best Beer* for more detailed information.) With the arrival of the much-lauded Cloudwater among others, 2014-16 appears be Manchester's moment. Perhaps Birmingham will be next? Depending on which list you consult, Britain's second biggest city has only five or six active breweries, none of them of the post-BrewDog school, which suggests there might still be at least some territory waiting to be seized.

So, micro-brewing, craft beer, or whatever you want to call it, is leaving its 'growth spurt' phase, but there's no need for gloominess: the fact remains that the modern British beer drinker is spoiled compared to those who blazed the trail in the 1970s. Tensions or not, there are more breweries and more beers than there have been for decades, and more stylistic diversity than there has *ever* been in the UK with everything from German-style Gose to old-fashioned Burton ale currently in production. (And contrary to hysteria from some quarters, this broadening of variety has not put traditional bitter in danger of extinction, though mild might be said to have fallen between the cracks.)

Looking at the IPAs in Wetherspoon and saison in Tesco, perhaps the legacy of 50 years of alternative beer culture is that the standard – the quality and variety of beer on offer in non-specialist outlets, no hunting required – has been tugged a little nearer the ideal.

Notes from 2019

Shortly after this piece was published Camden Brewery was taken over by multinational firm AB-InBev and the United Craft Brewers fizzled out. Beavertown was absorbed by Heineken in 2018. This year, Magic Rock was itself taken over, by Lion Nathan, meaning that only one of the original UCB breweries,, BrewDog, is still independent.

The march of the micropubs continues but Martyn Hillier has reined in his expectations: his prediction is now for 500 micropubs rather than 5,000. As of April 2019, the Micropub Association lists 350.

CAMRA's Revitalisation project rumbled on for several years reaching a head in April 2018 with a vote at the AGM on accepting or rejecting a set of recommendations which amounted to a comprehensive modernisation of the organisation. The members, predictably, voted for a fudge, accepting most measure but rejecting one symbolically important suggestion: that CAMRA should 'act as the voice and represent the interests of all pub goers and beer, cider and perry drinkers'. In May 2018, Tim Page resigned.

Contrary to our cautious conclusion London has continued to gain breweries and now has more than 100, although takeovers and closures seem to be accelerating. Nationwide the sense of gloom within the industry and among observers persists, and some breweries have certainly shut down. The rate of growth in brewery numbers does, finally, seem to be slowing.

Don't worry, be (mostly) happy

First published on our blog in 2018.

For the last year or so we've been slowly chewing over a single big question: how healthy is British beer culture?

You might remember, if you're a long-time reader, that we first wrote about the idea of healthy beer culture in 2013, but that was a set of bullet points. This post expands on those ideas with another five years'-worth of evidence, experience and thinking.

We should confess that our starting point is one of mild frustration at the pervasive idea that British beer – and beer culture more generally – is ailing. We see various worries expressed on social media, and in blog posts and articles, each one discrete and personal, but adding up to a mass of anxiety. If you're in this bubble it can feel like the end times.

To provide fuel for this specific blog post we asked our Twitter followers to tell us what, if anything, made them worried for the future of British beer. Some statements echoed things we've seen said many times before, while others flagged issues we had not considered. Quite a few effectively cancelled each other out, highlighting the absurdity of thinking about British beer as a monolith. There is no single idea of what healthy looks like, and no victory that won't feel like a defeat to somebody else.

In this post we want to focus on some of the most commonly expressed fears, question whether they have a basis in reality, and consider the likely impact of those that do.

Let's begin with a staple of beer commentary for the past 25 years or so: the perils of the pursuit of novelty.

Always New, Always Shiny

We tend to celebrate stylistic diversity. It seemed exciting to us that even in a small, distant town like Penzance, where we lived until last summer, it was increasingly easy to find draught beers at a range of ABV, across a spectrum of colour, expressing different degrees and varieties of hop, malt and yeast flavour.

A contrary view might be, though, that the more beer styles there are, the fewer truly great examples there will be in each category. What if more choice across 150 styles just means less choice for fans of any particular one?

Then there is the question of keeping those styles in appropriate balance. How can we be sure, for example, that the increasing popularity of golden ales won't crush traditional bitter into the ground?

There's certainly no denying that beer styles do disappear, coming into and going out of fashion over the course of years or decades. The demise of mild, the biggest selling style before the 1960s and now hard to find on draught outside certain hold-out regions, is one notable example.

But rest assured that bitter, which usurped mild and was itself usurped by lager, is not, for now, scarce.

Every Fuller's pub sells London Pride, and most Sam Smith pubs have Old Brewery, to name two examples. In Bristol, throbbing with craft beer vibrations, there is nonetheless plenty of Bass, Greene King IPA, Doom Bar, Courage Best, Bath Ales Gem and Butcombe. And here are the ten best-selling cask ales in Britain as of August 2017 according to CGA:

- Doom Bar, £137m per year
- Greene King IPA, £89m
- London Pride, £69m
- Abbot Ale, £36m
- Deuchars IPA, £35m
- Pedigree, £28m
- Wainwright, £24m
- Landlord, £25m
- Tribute, £22m
- Old Speckled Hen, £21m

Of those, only two approach golden ale territory (Deuchars, Wainwright); two (Landlord and its tribute, Tribute) are more amber than brown; and Abbot is notably strong. But none on the list are especially floral or citrusy, and all are essentially variations on bitter or pale ale at between 3.7% and 5% ABV.

In our view, if you live in England and can't go out and find a pint of bitter with relative ease, or even a choice of bitters, then you're being fussy about pubs, fussy about beer, or perhaps just plain awkward.

On the flipside, we're also baffled by the suggestion that hazy IPAs have somehow come to dominate. It's interesting that Adnams has brewed one as an experiment, and we were amused to see that beer blogger Alec Latham encountered a cask version of the style at a regional beer festival, but, equally, we can go weeks without seeing one on sale.

This really is a case of where the so-called 'bubble' might be distorting perceptions. NEIPA is highly visible on social media, and very present in a particular subset of specialist bars. Even so, we've yet to find a situation in which, even if one or more NEIPAs were on offer, there weren't also plenty of other options available. BrewDog Bristol might have three NEIPAs on at once, but will also have four different lager sub-styles, stout, and a choice of amber ales.

Regardless of their reach, we're yet to be convinced NEIPAs are more than a passing obsession, like black IPA before them, or that they have untapped mainstream appeal. We haven't seen much evidence of them flooding supermarkets, or turned up in Wetherspoon pubs – both key barometers of broader acceptance, which is certainly a necessary step before anything like dominance.

Session IPA, on the other hand, we do foresee muscling in on bitter's turf. Essentially one-dimensional, they are easy drinking if you have some tolerance for bitterness, and the typical ABV puts them right at home alongside big brand lagers and cask bitter. One staff member at a traditional family brewery told us that management there is all-but obsessed with session IPA, and there's evidence of this tendency appearing in tied pubs up and down the country.

Another observation we've heard many times over the years, from many different brewers, is that customers and pubs won't buy the same beers twice, which makes it difficult to establish a core range and a steady trade.

From the perspective of brewers and retailers the pursuit of novelty is a concrete, practical problem, as it has been since the genesis 'guest ale' culture in the 1990s, and the extreme manifestation in scooping and ticking. How can a brewer operate if their customers demand a new beer every time? Some cheat, brewing essentially the same beers with different names, or blending two beers to create a third, or chucking caramel into a pale beer to create something that at least looks new. Others drive themselves half-mad attempting to innovate, brewing with ever-weirder ingredients, or strange techniques.

Of course it's natural – healthy, even, if we can use that word yet again – to be interested in new things. To want to try them, at least, and if you're lucky to enjoy unfamiliar sensations and flavours. This is how the next porter, mild, bitter or golden ale is discovered.

But we also think there's something else going on. When a customer says they want something different or new, and when a publican relays that request to a brewer, we're certain that at least some of the time what they're really saying, in a gentle way, is that they haven't yet found a beer they really love, which is a step up from mere enjoyment.

The stereotype of the endlessly flitting beer geek might have some basis in reality but, speaking for ourselves, when we find a beer we like in a pub, in great condition, we tend to stick with it for the session, or even over a few sessions, until the cask is dead. Timothy Taylor doesn't struggle to shift Landlord, even at a premium price, and Beavertown can't brew enough Neck Oil to meet demand.

Or, bluntly: if a brewery's core range beers don't seem to be earning repeat orders it might be because, even if they're excellent in every way, they need a little more work to attain that magic quality that inspires loyalty, or at least the desire for a second pint of the same.

Too many breweries – the end is nigh!

When we wrote *Brew Britannia* there was white-hot excitement in the air. Breweries were opening everywhere, every ten minutes, in places nobody ever expected to see such a thing. They were brewing everything from black IPA to saison, using every variety of hop on the market, while some experimented at the far edges of convention with hazy, sour, wild, weird beers. Pubs were boosting the diversity of their offers and craft beer bars were appearing not only in more and more cities but even small towns, such as Newton Abbot in Devon. It felt like a golden age.

Even then, though, there were people fretting about how long it could last. This 2013 blog post from Dave Bailey (a committed and open-hearted industry commentator as well as an interesting brewer) made the case:

> The total volume of beer being consumed in the country has been declining for some time. Despite this there has been a steady increase in the capacity of micro-brewing. Yes, this is partly driven by an ever increasing demand from drinkers, which in turn, it could be argued, has been inspired by the increasing choice that has occurred… Locally to me there continues to be a disturbing increase in the number of breweries. I'm not even going to quote a number, as to be honest, I'm not sure it is possible to count… Here you see I'm starting to be negative, having started this post on a fairly positive slant. I find it disturbing because I do not believe it is commercially sustainable. Really, I simply don't believe it is.

Many of those who responded in the comments agreed with that analysis: 'The "bubble" is certain to burst soon and unfortunately, may take some talented brewers with it, leaving some mediocrity behind.'

But these doomsayers were wrong, or at least made their call too soon. When that post appeared the Campaign for Real Ale's count of UK breweries stood at around 1,100. Almost five years on that number stands at more than 1,700. In other words, if there is a bubble, it wasn't ready to burst in 2013.

Five years ago, it turns out, there was unsuspected room for growth in places such as London, which went from having a mere handful of breweries to the latest count of 112, and Bristol, which had around seven breweries within its city boundaries in 2013 but now has a fluctuating fifteen or so.

It seemed back then that the limited number of free taps open to the market across the British pub industry was fatally low and that too many breweries were already competing for them, driving down prices and quality. But many of us underestimated the potential for the rise of the micropub and the brewery taproom (of which more later), and perhaps also the potential for craft beer to pop up in surprising places – chain hotels, for example, or noodle bars.

And, on balance, we can't find any particular reason to think the clap of doom any more likely in 2018 than 2013, other than that if you say "It's going to rain" every single day you will eventually be right.

After all, entire cities remain relatively short on breweries-per-head, such as Birmingham (thirteen breweries for 1m people) and Cardiff (five for 450k), and also have vacancies for the kind of unconventional free-of-tie venues that might support them.

That's not to say that individual brewers haven't had, and aren't continuing to have, a challenging time.

In March 2018 Dave Bailey announced that his own brewery, Hardknott, was to cease production on its own plant though the brand is to live on in some form. He is less optimistic than us, writing: 'It continues to frustrate me that many commentators in the industry are heralding how massive the craft beer thing is, and yet stupefied by what appears to me to be an inevitable likelihood of massive attrition of many small brewers as they realise that making money at this daft job is the preserve of very few.'

During 2017 we did our best to keep a log of every brewery closure in the UK – to really focus on the reality of the situation – and there were a few notable casualties. Cottage Brewing in Somerset and Tom Wood's in Lincolnshire, for example, both went into administration, while Ballard's shut up shop after almost 40 years trading.

If we were to draw a conclusion from those and similar announcements it would be that there is a particular squeeze on conservative, locally-focused brewers founded in the wake of the real ale boom of the 1970s. These are breweries whose beer has neither the national cult reputation of, say, Timothy Taylor, nor the novelty of the current generation of craft brewers.

Breweries will continue to come and go. Some will find their niche, make their name; others will struggle, and eventually succumb. From where they are sitting this might not feel like evidence of a healthy culture but from a consumer perspective, we're afraid to say, it probably is.

Quality is poor

The word 'quality' comes up time and again in the conversation. What is the good of all these breweries, and all this choice, if the beer you spend rather too much on is mediocre, or even bad? If the quality isn't there.

Before we got into this one, however, we wanted to probe what people mean by 'quality', our impression being that like 'craft' it is a vague term used by different people to suggest different things. To this end we ran a simple poll on Twitter and these were the results:

It's evident that to most respondents 'quality' is about technical prowess. It suggests that a beer is well-engineered – that a brewery QA tester or competition judge would find no concrete flaws. It isn't sour, hazy, buttery, and so on. (Unless of course it is meant to be, and advertised as such.)

As a subset of that, others tend to use it to refer to how the beer is delivered at point-of-sale, especially in relation to cask ale and the old-fashioned cellar skills needed to present it at its best. (A well-made beer can be ruined by careless handling; and a mediocre one, it seems, elevated through the skill of a good publican.)

For another, smaller group, quality refers to some aspect of the beer beyond the technical: is it exciting, original, innovative, interesting, perhaps a bit 'fancy'? These people, we would guess, also enjoy consistent beer without obvious flaws, but would rather drink a less than technically perfect NEIPA for example than, say, a very precisely brewed but restrained 3.7% English bitter, or a basic lager.

We know from our own experience that finding a good pint of cask ale can be difficult, even in breweries' own prestige pubs where it ought to be a given, and that too many bottles and cans can be substandard.

But is there really any reason to think that, on the whole, the quality of beer – in either the technical sense or in terms of sheer character – is any worse now than 30 or 40 years ago? In 1985, for example, Roger Protz wrote in his regular column for *What's Brewing*, the Campaign for Real Ale newspaper, of what he called 'Our Ailing Ale', reporting on a conversation with CAMRA co-founder Graham Lees:

> 'What's happened to ale in this country, Protz?' he demanded. 'It tastes like warm tea.'… During the course of the next few days… Graham returned again and again to what he saw as the sad decline of the quality of our much of our cask beer. I did not disagree with him, for I too have become increasingly concerned by beer that is as

undemanding on the palate as it is demanding on the wallet... [Many] have lost their zip and character. Boddingtons, Brakspear, Gales and even – and I say this with terrible reluctance – Adnams, seem to be pale shadows of their former selves... Even when the beer is without blemish, it is too often served so badly that you might as well sit at home and put up with 'stewed cardboard' home brew.

It's a fact of life that things were always better a decade or two ago, and people will be saying the same a decade or two in the future, too.

We do suspect that some cellaring skill has been lost. This is a point Steve Dunkley, brewer at Beer Nouveau in Manchester, and a former cellarman, makes frequently, as in this extract from a post on his blog:

I started in the trade when I was 18, and I learned from someone who'd been doing cellar work for years. The pub I was working at also sent me on a course to get qualified in it, and I learned a lot. Not just the guidelines of how to stillage a beer, but also what's actually going on inside the cask, and how it's affecting the beer. I also learned how to strip and rebuild most dispense equipment, and the importance of cleanliness on it. Back then there were only about 300 breweries, and the bar I worked in tried to get as many different beers as possible each year, I remember breaking the 600 mark one year! Without knowing about beer itself, there was no way that we'd have been able to keep beer in good condition. Just because it's bright doesn't mean it's right, and a chill haze doesn't mean it's drain pour. Even back in the 90s. Understanding that leads to good beer going over the bar, and we built up a reputation for it... I think these days we're in desperate need of cellar staff. Quality is such an important issue in a flooded market, and brewers can easily point the finger at the end of the chain.

With the death of the brewery-pub tie there are also fewer opportunities for publicans to really get to know a handful of standard beers very well, which issue is only compounded by the tendency to novelty (see part one, above) and wider ranges of beer in individual pubs and bars. This is a particular bugbear of *Good Beer Guide* pub-crawler Martin Taylor:

> One of the themes of my blog… is that the explosion of choice is rarely beneficial to quality… The argument for heading for pubs with many pumps seems to be that anyone who cares about cask would have at least half a dozen on, to which CAMRA members cask drinkers will gravitate, leaving the local bar with Doom Bar and GK IPA(provided on sufferance) to serve soup to Carling drinkers… And reading CAMRA magazines it's hard not to be persuaded that more is better, with Pub News focusing on quantity and rarity, and quality barely mentioned.

He is right, we think, and our feeling is that choice across town – different ales from different breweries in different pubs – is preferable to a whole world of options in a single pub.
Overall, though, we suspect there is a lot more that is very good in 2018 than there was in 1978. It's just that it's harder to find among all the noise and excitement; and we have all become so much more demanding and experienced as consumers.
Very much signs of a healthy culture.

Beer excludes

Another issue that came up more than once in response to our Twitter query, and at intervals in the wider discussion, is the fear that beer was becoming elitist and exclusive.
And when it comes to the sharp end of High Craft Beer – limited releases, festivals, events, subscription services, and the very most specialist bars – this is certainly true.
Yes, the most expensive beer is relatively more affordable than wine of equivalent cachet, and, yes, almost all sectors have a high-end out of reach to all but the wealthiest or most dedicated followers. It is also possible to access craft beer on a budget with sufficient know-how.

But the fact remains that people on limited incomes are excluded from the full range of the experience, and that will only become more of a problem if those who seek to bump the price of beer upwards are successful.

(Some businesses are tired of scrabbling for profit and see getting customers to pay more as an obvious fix; others regard this as a necessary step towards improving pay and conditions in the brewing and hospitality industries; and yet a third group looks at it as a step towards rebuilding beer's self-esteem, by reinventing it as a 'premium product'.)

This is a rare instance of where those who talk about beer might be able to do some good, however, by highlighting an important fact: craft beer (definition 2) is only a small part of beer culture, and perhaps not the best part.

In the past we've referred to Schrödinger's Craft Beer, poking fun at the view that craft beer is simultaneously:

A niche interest engaging only a handful of people and venues, undeserving of all the attention it gets; and

A looming existential threat to traditional British beer and pubs which must be stopped!

But we've looked into the box and… It's number one. Craft beer is significant, and still has room to grow, but it is not the be-all-and-end-all. Not many people drink craft beer, and even fewer people drink only craft beer. We certainly don't, interested as we are in the phenomenon, and even the Craftest of the Craft talk breathlessly about, say, Fuller's ESB, or even bottled Budweiser.

We revisited a previous post on this subject and, on further reflection, would now express the practical solution like this: don't propagate the idea that price or exclusivity are synonymous with quality, and make an effort to celebrate the affordable.

Beyond price there's also the exclusion due to gender, sexuality, ethnicity, age… In short, like it or not, beer remains the realm of the middle-aged white man, into which others are expected to integrate rather than being accommodated. And so they don't bother.

Sexist branding is just one aspect of that – one which continues to throw up constant disappointments, often from unexpected quarters, as people struggle (we think sincerely in many cases) to get their heads around the fact that what was unremarkable in 1998 makes them look bad in 2018, or that 'banter' doesn't translate to those who don't know you and aren't in on your jokes.

But progress is being made.

The turning round of Castle Rock's Elsie Mo was one big step. A prominent target for criticism, the World-War-II themed pump-clip was redesigned as a tribute to women who served in the war rather than a lazy call-back to pin-up porn of the past. Robinson's, though, seemed unrepentant, and defiant, making a public stance against "political correctness". Except that this week they too came round to the idea, announcing (albeit clumsily) plans to rebrand their popular golden ale:

The current label was designed in homage to the classic 1940's Memphis belle style pin up 'nose art' of WW2 aircrafts which was so iconic of the era. However, it is no secret that, in the wake of the #MeToo movement and the backlash against sexual harassment and abuse, Dizzy Blonde has been the focal point of the sexism debate in the beer industry. Despite the fact that Dizzy Blonde is a much-loved brand by many, we don't have our heads in the sand. It is time to acknowledge that the presentation is not universally accepted by a society that strives for, and celebrates, equality.

Those who want to see change should take heart from this. If it doesn't speak to a fundamental shift in values it at least reveals the calculations businesses are making, weighing the short term risk of annoying a small group of anti-PC types against the longer-term benefits of attaining broad appeal, and of staying in step with their industry peers.

The kind of smaller brewery whose marketing machines amounts to the head brewer at the kitchen table with a laptop on Sunday night might take longer to change, or perhaps not. We know of at least one publican – by no means grandstandingly 'woke' – who has privately told breweries with sexist branding that if they won't change their designs, their pub won't sell it, because it embarrasses them to have it on display, and to have make excuses for it, in 2018.

Here, the culture is experiencing growing pains, but will be fitter and stronger at the end of the process.

Pubs are endangered

The closure of pubs, and struggle of those that survive, is a huge worry for many people, and is something we addressed in the epilogue of *20th Century Pub*:

> We feel unfashionably optimistic for the pub. It's survived this long, after all, despite bombs and the Band of Hope, and pubs remain the jewels of our high streets and villages, giving character and life to our towns and estates.

Optimism is a strong word and, of course, we serve it up with a cartload of caveats: perhaps there will be fewer pubs; some particular beloved pubs might be among the casualties; and perhaps the survivors will need to change in ways that make some pub-lovers uncomfortable. But we are certain there will still be pubs, they will still serve beer, and they will continue to be part of the culture in this country.

And, in fact, we expect to see new pubs continue to open. Now, they might not be the kind of pub on which enthusiasts are fixated – vaguely Victorian, just on the border of grubby, with snugs and snob screens – but they will be pubs, like it or not.

We've written at length about micropubs, not least devoting an entire chapter of *20th Century Pub* to the trend, and so won't go over it all again. By way of an update, though, the founder of the micropub movement, Martyn Hillier, has apparently reined in his ambitions, lowering his prediction for the eventual number of micropubs from 5,000 to 500. This feels about right, allowing for the fact that they can go as easily as they arrive, given that they rely on the energy of individuals, and often on the availability of a particular property on especially generous terms.

There are good and bad micropubs, just like any other kind of pub. The best, among which we'd count our local, The Drapers Arms, feel more like 'proper pubs' than many operating in conventional settings. Without pub companies or breweries pressing down on them their owners are able to offer more interesting beer, at competitive prices, and express their own personalities more freely. (For better or worse.) In that context, surrounded by a buzzing crowd, you soon forget that you're sat in a retail unit. They really do have that 'beerhouse' feel.

Then there are brewery taprooms. We have to be frank here: they are not generally to our taste, feeling too sparse, too austerely industrial, to ever replace the warmth of a decent pub. But they are another valid response to the restrictions of pub ownership, and provide yet another option for drinkers who don't feel at home in traditional boozers for whatever reason.

There are also brewpubs – an idea once thought dead in the water, but now multiplying at a surprising rate. There is Wetherspoon (still growing, albeit at a slower pace) and its imitators, the 'pubness' of which can be debated endlessly. And of course, craft beer bars, though outside the biggest cities, it's harder than ever to tell where they end and micropubs begin.

A type of pub we're particularly interested in is the new-build out-of-town brewery family dining house. They're the kind of place beer geeks, even those only mildly afflicted, tend to avoid wherever possible. They rarely have exciting beer being primarily focused on food, and often the only way to reach them is by car. They tend to sit on retail parks or on the outskirts of town surrounded by acres of parking space, perhaps attached to a budget hotel, or serving an estate of brand new private houses. Marginal though they might seem they are by no means insignificant.

'We've opened approximately 80 new builds in the past six years', said Greene King's press office in an email, while Marston's told us: 'Our new build strategy over the last five years has delivered over 20 new pubs each year across the whole of the UK'. So from just these two firms that is around 200 new pubs in the last six years.

They seem popular, too, despite their apparent remoteness. Those we've visited, regardless of when we've visited, seem to be permanently busy, whether it's with football fans in search of big TVs, families out for a Sunday roast, or pensioners having tea and cake on a weekday afternoon.

But are they good pubs? As buildings, they tend to be plain or, worse, tacky in the Prince Charles neo-historical style. They generally lack character, despite the local interest information boards and pointedly local names.

But – but! – the best of them gain a huge amount from really being used, by people out in numbers, having fun at volume.

If the buildings are given chance to wear and weather, and if a little more personality is ever permitted to leak through the branded surface, there's no reason these couldn't become as beloved and characterful as any 150-year-old pub.

If there is a threat to the continued existence of the idea of pub it might be the habit of drinking at home. According to stats from the BBPA, in 1980 on-trade sales represented 87.7 per cent of the market; by 2001 that had fallen to 65.7 per cent; and in 2016 it was a mere 48.4 per cent. So, in plain terms, we've gone from nearly all beer being consumed in pubs to less than half.

This tendency is understandable with a decade long freeze on UK wages, changing models of employment which offer less security, and an overheated housing market. We couldn't afford to drink in the pub every night, even if our bodies could stand it, and bottled or canned beer at half the price of the pub is simply too tempting to resist.

But, again, we can't be too gloomy about this: why is there any on-trade at all if the price of booze is the only important factor? Of course it isn't. People need to meet other people, and they need to spend time somewhere that isn't home or work. Give them better beer, and more fun places to drink it and, and they will find the money to pay for a good night out.

Pubs are an important part of a healthy beer culture – more so in the UK than in some other parts of the world – but if drinking at home gets people engaged with beer, and pubs can find a way to offer the best beer experiences, then it's all part of the balance.

Cask is endangered

In a blog post he wrote in the wake of the Revitalisation vote at the Campaign for Real Ale AGM Pete Brown used the knowledge of the cask beer market gained during his run as editor of the *Cask Report* to point out some hard facts:

> Cask ale's health has recently gone into severe decline. Over the twelve months to February 2018, and in the twelve months before that, cask volume declined by over 4 per cent each year – that means almost ten per cent of the entire cask market has vanished in the last 24 months... Now, the plight of cask is actively being covered up. From 2007 to 2015, I wrote eight editions of the Cask Report. Every single one of them contained a figure for cask ale's

value and volume performance versus the previous twelve months. The two editions of the report that have come out since I resigned from doing it have not contained this figure – because it's so bad. The most recent edition of the Report stated that cask had declined by 5 per cent over the last five years, which was in line with the overall beer market. The reason they gave a five-year figure is to disguise the fact that almost all that decline has come in the last two years.

Hard numbers aside, the apparent lack of interest in cask ale among a newer generation of breweries, or at least their lack of desire to slog away at it when it makes them so little money, also tells a story. BrewDog, Camden, Cloudwater and others who have given up producing cask ale might make up only a small part of the total market but they occupy a great deal of the conversation, especially among younger drinkers. Cask, unfortunately, has a PR problem, while keg beer's publicist deserves a pay rise.

If there are real threats to cask ale, many of those threats are the same as they've been for a long time. First, the tendency to the generic driven by monopoly, globalisation and vertical integration. And, secondly, problems with cask itself: the relative complexity of manufacture, distribution and handling; and a lingering image problem.

We don't believe cask is doomed, but we think it might be time to accept its fate as a niche product, in fewer places but handled better. It survived the storm of the 1960s and 70s, in large part thanks to the Campaign for Real Ale, and has come out of the other side as a product with a certain value, if not universal appeal.

It is fondly, even sentimentally regarded. It is a symbol of British (or at least English) national identity, and as a key component in the personal identities of hundreds of thousands of people: I, Ale Drinker.

In the trade, the presence of cask ale is increasingly an indicator of the character of the venue, signifying Proper Pub status – a cuddly kind of conservatism – casting a warm glow over every other aspect of the business.

For producers it is still a relatively cheap and easy way to enter the market, one step up in seriousness from hand-bottling, but requiring less of a financial commitment than kegging, and the market for cask ale remains relatively more open (if more competitive) than that for kegged products.

There are risks, of course. A niche sounds good but could easily translate to a ghetto. It would be bad news if cask could only be found in one type of pub, in certain parts of the country, tangled up in the tripwires of the supposed culture war.

But, so far, we don't see much evidence of this in the places we know such as Bristol where the best cask beer crops up in all kinds of pubs – modern and conservative, hip and square, hippy and heavy metal.

There is now more good keg beer than there was 30 years ago but it isn't a magic solution to the problem of beer quality – bad beer from a keg doesn't taste any better than bad beer from a cask, and keg requires expertise in handling, too. We can, however, foresee a situation in which pubs which currently have a sad, solitary handpump, hardly used, replace it with an unpasteurised, unfiltered keg beer that requires a little less attention, and stays good for a fortnight rather than a few days.

If that happens, cask's share of the market might fall further yet. Certainly the idea that it will ever again be the default in the UK seems faintly ridiculous. Nonetheless it's hard to imagine it disappearing in our lifetimes.

If you want to do something to help cask ale's public image, find opportunities to express the sheer joy that the best of it brings. That can so easily be lost in the gloom that unfortunately hangs about the story.

Tensions and balance

We're more convinced than ever that the key to a healthy beer culture is tension as much as, if not more than, cooperation and collaboration.

People seem to need to something to react against if they are to fully express their own identity, and to make their beer or pub uniquely itself.

Tension drives change, as in the case of the uneasy, sometimes boring, often fraught evolution of the Campaign for Real Ale.

Competing forces pulling at full tilt in opposite directions energise the centre, making bitter that little bit better, and craft beer more accessible, both in terms of flavour and profile.

The push and pull prevents pure capitalism having free rein – monopoly, generic beer, zero choice – while also keeping feet on the ground, restraining prices and pushing brewers to cater to popular tastes even if they don't pander to them.

Perhaps the secret to worrying less is accepting that this turbulence is inevitable and unending. There will never be a time when the dust has settled – when there is no change and nothing to worry about.

The alternative isn't peace, it is stagnation.

And worrying isn't necessarily bad. It's an expression of engagement, a way of caring. Fretting, and expressing that anxiety in the form of a challenge, is part of the system of checks and balances that keeps things bubbling along, and makes beer so fascinating.

Pub Life

That flight of steps down to the bar is a cruel trick to play on an old man who's had a few drinks.

One... two... three... he swings his leg for a moment before concluding that there is no fourth step, and then falls forward, planting himself at a steep angle against the counter.

He gurns at the woman behind the bar and lifts a finger.

'Are you sure, Patrick? Shall I call you a taxi instead?'

He blinks asymmetrically. 'W... What time is it?'

'Eight thirty.'

'One more... usual.'

'I'll call you a cab for nine, then, and you can have one more pint.'

He contorts to dip his hand into the pocket of his sagging jacket, and brings it up like a fairground claw crane, scattering coins across the varnished wood. 'Zat enough?'

She scoots five pound coins towards him one after the other. 'That's for your taxi,' she says, 'and this will pay for the pint.'

Time passes. He drinks some of his beer, and spills the rest. Every now and then, he jerks upright as if startled by something no-one else can see.

As 9pm approaches, he begins to calculate his chances of another drink. 'I wouldn't mind... How much is a bottle of wine to take home?'

Laughing, but firm: 'You don't need a bottle of wine. You need a good strong cup of tea.'

He gurns again. 'What I need... is a good woman.'

Side-stepping, she replies: 'Well, you won't find one of those in this pub!'

'Whisky?' he says, with a hopeful lilt. He pushes some of the coins across the bar.

'That's your taxi money, Pat.'

'Na na na na na na na,' he says, shaking his head, 'Just take it.'

Somehow, he gets his whisky, and downs it as the door opens to let in a cold, watery wind. 'Taxi for Pat?'

The barmaid comes out from behind the bar, puts an arm round Patrick's waist and guides him across the floor.

A smile breaks across his face.
Before she knows it, they are dancing.
Patrick leads, and his feet are as nimble as those of a 20-year-old.
Then the taxi driver cuts in and waltzes Patrick out into the night.
The pub feels cold, quiet and empty.

* * *

A man of indeterminate age, somewhere between 30 and 50, strides up to the bar: 'Shit, man, have I had a rough day.'
The baby-faced, slightly sleepy barman blinks and smiles.
'Yeah? Sorry to hear that, man. What can I get you?'
The customer mounts a high stool and starts to unload his tobacco pouch, ancient mobile phone and various other knick-knacks, constructing a nest.
'Half a San Mig.'
The barman pours the lager and places it on the bar.
'That'll be–'
'Tell you what, I've had such a shit day… Sod it – give me a Sambuca, too.'
The barman turns to look at the spirits shelf. The customer drinks half of his half of lager. The young man turns back. His eyes dart to the half empty glass.
'Er… Black or white?'
'White.'
The barman pours the Sambuca into a thimble-like shot glass.
'That'll be–'
'What it is, my wife – are you married yourself? – my wife, she was meant to meet me this morning but her train got delayed…'
He suddenly drinks most of the Sambuca, chasing it with another gulp of lager.
'…so I've been hanging around Temple Meads…'
'Er, sorry, man, but, er, I'm going to need you to pay for those drinks.'
'Oh, yeah, yeah, yeah, of course, man, no problem, yeah, yeah, yeah.'
He finishes the Sambuca.

'My wife will be here in like two minutes and she's got the cash.'

The barman begins to vibrate anxiously.

'I really need you to pay for those drinks—'

'Yeah, yeah, yeah, no worries, man, no worries – I'll just give her a call.'

The customer very obviously pretends to make a call on what, at second glance, might actually be a toy mobile phone. And are his shoes… Are they held together with Sellotape?

He stands up, pockets his tobacco almost as if by sleight of hand, and retreats to a corner, and then further into the corner, and then clear through the corner, out of a side door we hadn't noticed.

The barman deflates as he puts what is left of the glass of lager on the back shelf.

'I'm so stupid,' he says partly to himself, partly to us, but mostly to his own sneakers.

He makes sure to take the money before handing over our pints.

* * *

A small pub with dark walls, swirling with psychedelic rock, and swirling also with sweet cherry-scented vapour.

Four men are gathered around the bar, three of them playing 'Cards Against Humanity'.

They all have the build of nightclub bouncers but one is dressed in heavy metal denim; another like the croupier on a Mississippi gambling boat; the third in tatty biking leathers; and the fourth, disappointingly, in jeans and trainers. The first three have different varieties of ostentatious facial hair; their less showy friend is clean-shaven.

No, his flair is not sartorial; rather, he is generating his own fog with an illuminated sci-fi e-cigarette. Clouds and clouds of it. He is too drunk or too disinterested to join the game, or perhaps just concentrating too hard on his art.

Croupier reads from his card: '"What do old people smell like?"'

Bike Leathers slaps his thigh: 'Oh, I've got the winner right here, my friend… "Sneezing and farting at the same time"!'

Everyone cracks with laughter, except the Vaper. Though the Vaper isn't playing, he is thinking hard about the question, eyes narrowed and pink, fixed on a faraway place, or perhaps a distant time.

Heavy Metal begins his turn: 'Right – "What do old people smell like?" The answer is obviously, "My balls in—"'

'Decay!' declares the Vaper suddenly, and loudly, killing the chatter in the bar. 'Decay, isn't it? That's what they smell of. Decay. Impending death. Like…' He generates a serving of particularly gothic graveyard mist. 'Like their bodies are breaking down even though they're still… Their eyes are still…'

Silence falls. Vapour churns.

'Another round of these IPAs, lads?' slurs Croupier, slapping his cards down on the table. 'Or is it time to move on to that imperial stout?'

Everyone cheers, except the Vaper.

Vaper just vapes, intensely.

* * *

At 5:45 the crowd is getting restless – where is the pork pie? Where are the cubes of cheese? The nibbles and snacks?

Of course they're a courtesy, not a right, so nobody can complain, even if they do it jokingly. But, still, when you've come to expect it and it isn't there, you get restless, and start thinking about buying a bag of crisps or, worse, going home for tea.

There is a stir. The herald first, mustard and serviettes, then the thing itself, golden and stout, cut into eighths on a plate.

It has to go down in front of somebody and the somebodies it goes down in front of feign disinterest. A regular heckles, "Alright for some." Temptation is too much: after about five seconds, someone shrugs and, takes a slice, might as well, then a second to pass to a friend.

The pie is already looking ravaged, crust crumbling and jelly spilling.

Panic sets in and chairs scrape, everyone rushing but trying to look as if they're not.

Taking three slices, one regular offers a narration to explain his motives: "Best get in before it's all gone, one for each of us."

The entire pie has disappeared before the first bowl of cheese has appeared.

The pub itself seems to sigh with contentment. No need to rush away, stay for another, maybe two. Sunday night saved.

* * *

Two barmen in matching polo shirts, one small, one tall, stand behind the bar with arms folded engaged in debate with a regular sat at the bar.

The tall barman leads: 'No, you're not getting what I'm saying: I'm asking, does a staircase go up or come down? Which way does it go?'

'Up,' says the baffled regular. 'If it didn't go up, you wouldn't need it to come down. That it comes down is a side effect of it having gone up in the first place.'

'No, it's both. It goes up and comes down. It doesn't matter that it was built specifically to go up. Once you've got an up, the staircase has to go down as well. So it goes both ways.'

The small barman frowns, laughs quietly, and shakes his head.

'What are you on about? What are you actually on about?'

'Alright, scratch that, here's another one: is a zebra black with white stripes, or white with black stripes? Eh? Think about it.'

The regular says, confidently: 'White with black stripes.'

'Yeah, but how do you know for sure?'

'Shave it.'

The small barman claps in delight.

'He's got you there, mate!'

'Alright, what about this one: we're all agreed stairs go up and down–'

Regular: 'No, but carry on.'

'– but what about escalators? Does an escalator go up, or come down?'

'You've hoisted yourself by your own petard here,' says the regular. 'It depends which way it's going, doesn't it? I mean, you literally get one to go up, and another to come down.'

'Ah, see, no, you're wrong, and I'll tell you why: because it has to come down on the underside or it can't go up. It's a loop. So escalators always go up and down, just like staircases. Makes you think, doesn't it?'

* * *

Smokers' corner on the pub terrace, by the back door to the toilets.

She is smoking, sipping from a pint of lager, and looking at her phone. He approaches, nods, places his own pint of lager on another wobbly old table, and lights a cigarette.

She stares intently, clears her throat, and says: 'Not being rude… What's that on your T-shirt?'

He sits upright and stretches the fabric away from his gut to display the graphic.

'That's Princess.'

'She's yours, is she? Aw, she's lovely.'

'Yeah. Love of my life I always say. Expecting kittens, as it goes.'

The woman freezes with her beer half way to her mouth and pantomimes astonishment.

'Really? REALLY? You won't believe this but I've literally been looking to get a new cat. I've always had cats, ever since I was a little girl, but I couldn't have one in my last place. Now I just want loads.'

'Well, Princess is white with black patches and the one we think is the father–' He rolls his eyes. '–is black with white. So the kittens'll be one way or the other.'

'How much, then? If I wanted two, say?'

'Hang on, hold on…' He pulls out his phone, fiddles with the screen, and then holds it for her to see. 'Add me on FB and we'll sort it out later, alright?'

'Sorted.'

They both go back to smoking, in silence, and staring at their phones, those two cat people, basking in the sun.

* * *

An old pub in a quiet part of a busy city, and an elderly regular, watery-eyed and pale as paper, is sunk in his usual seat waiting for something to happen.

He looks at the TV, then at his newspaper, then at his watch. He stares into space, and perhaps into the past. He lines up the spare beer mats, then shuffles them out of line again.

Then, at least, some real excitement: a mixed group of twentysomethings enters, laughing and chattering. They are all tall, stylish, and distinctly Mediterranean.

The Regular's glittering eyes track them across the pub carpet. Two per cent of a smile appears on his thin lips.

The Visitors are quietly excited to be in a Real English Pub, staring at the ceiling, the ornate bar, the prints and mirrors.

They all thrust bank notes at one woman, apparently the best English speaker, and shove her towards the bar as they take over the table next to the Regular.

The Regular, his neck long gone, slowly turns his entire torso so he can watch them. The smile increases by another degree.

'Where you from?' he gargles in their direction.

The Visitors freeze and mutter attempted translations at each other. The second best English speaker, bearded and quiffed, acts as spokesman.

'We come from Greece.'

The Regular nods – of course, he thought as much.

'Well, me – I'm a Weegie.'

Silence. Baffled blinking.

'A Glaswegian.'

Further muttering.

'I'm from Glasgow.'

Bulbs light up.

'Ah! Glasgow! Yes, we know it! Alex Ferguson! Celtic football club!'

A lucky guess, apparently, as the Regular is not offended, but after this breakthrough, conversation stalls.

Lagers and gins are sipped as the Greeks look anxiously at each other – when is it acceptable to start talking among themselves again?

After an uncomfortable while, the Regular shifts some phlegm about, and leans closer.

'So,' he says, 'here's what I'm wondering…'

'Yes?'

'When are the English going to give you back those Elgin Marbles?'

And with that, the conversation really catches light.

*　*　*

Why choose this pub, with its bare boards, real ale, hard white light, and stink of pork scratchings? Why make love here?

They arrive through a side door in a swirl of strawberry-scented vapour, interlinked and unable to stop staring at each other.

He is in slacks, leather jacket, slip-on shoes, and sockless. A chipped tooth gives his smile some extra flavour.

She is all dangling bracelets and earrings, hair teased high and fixed with spray – a proper Going Out get-up.

They loudly order drinks, lager and white wine, and lean upon the bar, still tangled together, her hand up the back of his leather jacket, his in her waistband. They whisper to each other over the mostly empty pickled egg jar on the counter and laugh dirtily.

The bearded man behind the bar looks startled. His wife looks startled. The regulars look startled.

The dog doesn't care.

'Hey, babes... Babes...'

Leather Jacket points at the shelf.

'Do you want to play Connect Four?' he says, somehow suggestively.

She goes to the toilet while he sets up the blue rack and sorts the red and yellow counters. She emerges with pupils dilated, blinking and bright, and speaking twice as fast.

They play as if nobody can see or hear them, as if they're Faye Dunaway and Steve McQueen locking souls over a chessboard. Eventually, she wins, and they clink glasses in mutual appreciation.

Then, the game having got them going, they have to get going, linking together again and heading for the door. They stop on the threshold as cold air floods in around them.

Blowing kisses, he shouts, 'Goodbye! We love you all!'

She yells: 'We'll have the KY jelly out tonight, I tell you that much!'

And then they're gone.

The landlord blinks. His wife blinks. The regulars giggle.

The dog licks at an elusive Mini-Cheddar crumb trapped between the floorboards, pursuing his own love affair.

* * *

Last orders, shredded beer mats and sticky glasses everywhere, the regulars lurching out of their seats with groans and kidney rubbing.

'Right, well then, see you Sunday, Jim.'

The landlord looks up from the sink.

'No you bloody won't.'

'Eh? You off somewhere?'

'We're closed for two weeks. There's signs up everywhere – look! I put it on bloody Facebook too.'

'What? Why?'

'Bloody refurbishment.'

'Oh, gawd help us...'

'Jesus Christ. Hope it's not like last time. Didn't recognise the place. It's taken five years to get comfy again.'

The pub is indeed well worn-in: curtains askew and moth-eaten; tables looking as if they've been stoned and stabbed; and seating burst open, showing its yellow foam guts.

'Ten bloody years, it was,' says Jim.

'Cor, don't time fly.'

'Where are we gonna drink for two weeks?'

'You'll bloody live,' says Jim, but there's a shadow of doubt on his face.

'Furnishings staying, are they? Not going all minimal is it?'

'If any of the mirrors are going spare–'

'Not turning into a wine bar, is it?'

'Hope not but they don't bloody tell me anything.'

'Two weeks! Christ.'

'Well, good luck, Jim. See you on the other side.'

Jim waves, casual and dismissive, but Jim looks worried.

We're bloody worried.

* * *

Occasional words rise over the sound of Spotify shuffling on a laptop above the dog's bed behind the bar.

'The thing is, I always say, I'm not actually very sociable. I don't really like people, when it comes down to it.'

'Bloody hell. Why do you come to the pub then?'

'I can summon the energy to do this once in a while... Once every couple of weeks... I suppose I feel as if I ought to. But I shall be glad to leave and be on my own again.'

'Do you have kids or anything, then?'

'No, no...' A sigh. 'Rather pathetic, isn't it? But the silver lining is, I might have completely fucked up my life, but at least I didn't fuck up anybody else's.'

'Ha, well, yes. Right. Uh... Still, you've got your faith, haven't you? That must give you some comfort.'

'Well, between you and me,' (quite loud at this point), 'I haven't, not really, not anymore. I'm not sure I really believe in God at all. Haven't for years.'

'Oh.'

'Mmm.'

'Mmm. Uh... Well, uh, the bitter's drinking very well tonight, isn't it?'

* * *

A West Country cider pub on a sunny afternoon.

A woman approaches the bar holding her glass in front of her, shaking her head.

'I'm sorry, love, but I think you've give me cider instead of San Mig.'

'I just pulled that, didn't I? It's definitely San Miguel.'

'I don't think it is, my love.'

'No, it definitely is.'

There is a silent stand off until the drinker thrust the glass forward.

'Well, taste it, then.'

The person behind the bar rolls their eyes but takes the glass and sniffs it.

'Oh.'

They take a sip and grimace.

'See, I told you. It is cider, innit?'

'Worse. It is San Mig, it's just gone off. This bloody heat... What else can I get you?'

'What other lagers you got?'

'Only that one, sorry.'

'Right, so what else is there?'

'Uh...'

The barperson looks around.

'Cider?'

* * *

Take a gulp and put the glass down.

Place it on the beer mat, right in the centre, right in the ring of dark ink.

As you talk, as you listen, turn the glass on the mat, twisting it clockwise, then back, as if tuning in the conversation on a shortwave dial.

Take a gulp and put the glass down.

Tilt it so that light plays in the depths of the beer, so the foam clings to the sides and then slides back. Swirl it so the foam grows and flows.

Take a gulp and put the glass down.

Sweep the sides of their condensation with your fingers, tracing the shape, clearing the fog to reveal the gold.

Turn the glass, lights flash, sweep again.

Take a gulp and put the glass down, almost empty, light in the hand, almost dead.

Last gulp, then, 'Same again?'

Defer the pleasure. Dip a fingertip in the cream and lick it. Let the beer sit a bit, then sweep, turn, tilt…

Take a gulp.

Acknowledgements

We're grateful to the various magazine editors who have commissioned, polished and published our writing, notably John Holl at *All About Beer*, Ben Keene at *Beer Advocate*, and Tom Stainer and Tim Hampson at CAMRA.

We'd also like to thank the handful of generous people who have contributed to our Patreon, encouraging us to keep this up, and justifying the time spent researching and writing longer blog posts in the spare hours left by our day jobs.

And, finally, we couldn't have written most of this without the patience of brewers, campaigners and beer writers to whom we asked odd questions by email or in person, or who donated newspapers, magazines and books from their own collections to help us build our library.

Printed in Great Britain
by Amazon